WHY DVD?

Today's cutting-edge movie technology enriches your viewing experience as never before. The visual brilliance and audio clarity of DVDs are light-years beyond what video offers. And then there are the extras. . . . DVD fans know the days of simply *watching* movies are over—now, you can immerse yourself in the worlds of your favorite films with fascinating bonus footage, directors' commentary, hilarious outtakes, behind-the-scenes action, "making of" documentaries, and so much more.

WHY *THE POCKET GUIDE TO COLLECTING MOVIES ON DVD?*

Here is the indispensable companion for every DVD viewer—collectors with hundreds of discs, those making the transition from video to DVD, and anyone who buys or rents DVDs. This is the one-stop reference that helps you build an essential DVD collection. You'll find beloved favorites here, and many classics, too—but *THE POCKET GUIDE TO COLLECTING MOVIES ON DVD* goes beyond ordinary movie guides by rating the films based on the extras that are available only on DVD. Browse it or shop with it, and then sit back, relax, and enjoy the show. . . .

THE POCKET GUIDE TO
COLLECTING MOVIES ON

BUILDING AN ESSENTIAL
MOVIE COLLECTION

STEVEN H. SCHEUER
and
ALIDA BRILL-SCHEUER

POCKET BOOKS
New York   London   Toronto   Sydney   Singapore

An *Original* Publication of POCKET BOOKS

 POCKET BOOKS, a division of Simon & Schuster Inc.
1230 Avenue of the Americas, New York, NY 10020

ISBN: 0-7434-7571-2

First Pocket Books printing October 2003

10 9 8 7 6 5 4 3 2 1

POCKET and colophon are registered trademarks of
Simon & Schuster Inc.

Cover design by Anna Dorfman

Manufactured in the United States of America

For information regarding special discounts for bulk purchases,
please contact Simon & Schuster Special Sales at 1-800-456-6798
or business@simonandschuster.com.

For Cecilia, Ella, Emma and Lucas, with love

Contents

Contents ix

Acknowledgments

We are profoundly grateful to the following people:

Brooke Leverone and Travis Houston, masters of all things technical, who also shared with us the wisdom of their youth;

Our agent, Betty Anne Crawford, who is ever enthusiastic, always patient, insightful, and believed in this project from the beginning;

Michael Shepley, publicist-extraordinaire;

the team at Pocket Books, especially our editor, Mitchell Ivers, and his assistant, Josh Martino.

An Introduction to the Pleasures of Creating a Personal DVD Library

If you're reading this page, you either own a DVD player or are considering purchasing one. The DVD is the most popular and successful electronic invention ever to come our way. It appeals to our appetite for accessible, high-quality home entertainment.

Speaking of appetites, food and movies go together. You can't live without the first. You wouldn't really want to live without the second. A good movie is like a good meal; it stimulates the senses and brings pleasure. Unlike the glorious four-star meal or the "comfort" foods we ingest, movies are calorie-free. With the arrival of DVDs, they are easier to watch at home; the experience cannot be compared to watching a film on broadcast television or playing a video in your VCR. A properly produced disc viewed on your home television (you don't need a fancy new TV) is a completely fresh and exciting experience.

Why? First, if the transfer of the film has been done correctly, the colors, images, perspectives, and sound will be far better than you are used to having at home. Even the most lavishly produced video releases can't hold a candle to this new technology. Second, the disc is capable of holding so many images that the opportunity to view "bonus" or supplemental material associated with the movie is virtually limitless. We suggest another use for our book, which is a variation on the idea of a book club. Invite friends over to watch the extras and commentary tracks of a film you have recently seen. It's great fun to see the "behind the scenes" views of the creation of the film with others. We've enjoyed evenings where our friends have discussed and debated whether or not they think the director's intentions were fulfilled. Of course, watching some of the deleted scene sequences with a group of friends is particularly delicious. Inside this book you will find the key to those extras worth your time. Third, unlike the rewound, sprung, or angry videotape, discs have a much longer life span. (With care in handling, they probably can be handed down to your grandchildren.) Finally, because of this new technology, the distributors increasingly are restoring classic films and making feature documentaries that are available only on disc.

However, not all discs are created equal. That's where we come into the picture; we are your eyes and ears. We have prescreened the selections in this book. There's no point in owning a disc if the quality of the picture isn't any better than it would be on late-night television. If you're longing to see a film that is in lousy shape, rent it, don't buy it.

This book is about building a personal library of DVDs. It's about the art of collecting; collecting anything is an art. A serious collector of rare books might specialize in one particular subject or even one author. But it is likely the collector will want as many different examples and editions of that subject or that author's work as he or she can find or afford. It doesn't need to be an expensive or priceless collection to be an interesting one. One of our friends collects souvenir thermometers—we're not kidding! His collection is amusing and innovative because it is so diverse, from the absolutely tacky to the quite elegant. The organizing principle of any collection should be variety.

We believe the process of collecting DVDs is like ordering dinner for a special occasion or choosing a good diet. You want delicious flavors and superb presentation of the food, especially if you're spending a lot of money for a good meal in a restaurant. If you're cooking a festive meal at home, you want the meal to be memorable and your guests to savor every bite. You also want the meal to have been worth your time and effort. If you're deciding on an appropriate diet plan for yourself, you don't want it to consist of only one food group. Even if you are on a very restricted diet, there are still vast choices and variations available, whether high-protein, low-fat, or vegetarian. Nobody wants to eat the same thing every day at every meal.

Likewise, you'll want to have an array of choices in your home DVD library. If you watch only thrillers, you probably don't need our book. But most of us have taste buds that like to be stimulated in different ways. One day, it's macaroni and cheese or nothing. The next day, you might prefer a light salad, and the next week, you might be planning a complicated five-course meal complemented by appropriate wines.

We think it's the same for your movie diet. That's why our primer on building your DVD library is so eclectic. We want you to sample from the many flavors available.

Even if you are mad for one particular country's cuisine, you probably don't want to eat just that all the time. While our choices are overwhelmingly selected from American movies (we couldn't do justice to all the wonderful foreign films in the space we have), you'll find a seasoning of international films as well.

The feast for your eyes should be just as satisfying as a

feast for your stomach. Some nights, you're tired and not in the mood for a serious meal, in a restaurant, a take-out place, or at home. You want to satisfy your hunger pangs and relax. On other nights you're in a romantic mood, and careful attention to a meal is in order.

What you want to watch on DVD at any particular time is also subject to your mood or the time you have to devote to a movie. That's why our suggestions range from dramatic or challenging films to sheer entertainment. You might be surprised at some of the movies you won't find in the pages of this book. We would like to tell you something about how we made our choices. Of course, all lists of the *best* of anything, whether the best movies, restaurants, wines, chocolates, cities, hotels, camping grounds, beaches, or shopping malls, are products of the people who put the list together. So to some extent, this list is about who we are and what we like. However, we worked very hard to make sure that our suggestions for building your DVD library include many of the films that appear on the lists of other experts and film institutions as well.

Some of the best films ever made are still not on DVD or are still in terrible shape on the transfer. Our guiding principle has been "It's about the movie, stupid." First and foremost, the movie needs to be a better-than-average transfer, *at the very least.* If it's not, you won't find it here. Second, the movie needs to make sense to us in some unique way that suggests it's not only something worth watching but something you'll want to watch more than once. What's worth watching is highly subjective, but we think our reviews give you a very good idea of why we believe a particular selection is just that.

We have attempted, in each and every instance, to write reviews for you that are not only informative and honest but also entertaining. The movies represented here are the result of a collaborative effort. We've debated some of these in a pretty passionate manner. But in the end, we have suggested those movies that both of us think belong in a library and not just on loan. That doesn't mean, of course, that you can't use this guide for rentals. Building a DVD library also can mean keeping a record or log of what you've seen that you like and renting it again and again. It's a question of budget, taste, and style. What we've done is give you the tools to decide whether you want to bother to see a particular film at all or again and again.

We haven't based our selections solely on the supplements provided. We obviously paid a great deal of attention to those discs that offer the best extras. However, in the case of some great classics, the bare-bones disc (the movie alone) is a superb treasure. We also warn you when a "special edition" is actually a promotional gimmick, and we alert you to possible rip-offs.

[A cautionary note concerning the much-publicized "Easter eggs" contained on some DVDs is in order here.] A DVD "Easter egg" is a bonus hidden somewhere inside the wonders of the disc technology. When DVDs were first being released, there was a tremendous amount of hype about these and how you might find them. The hunt for the hidden treasures excited some and upset others. Some believed they would find a golden egg; others thought they were all just a bunch of deviled eggs left over from yesterday's picnic lunch. While there are still good eggs out there, many of the more recent releases have only a couple or none at all. (*Moulin Rouge* is a notable exception.) By and large, the average person didn't find that it was a user-friendly feature, and the joy of owning DVDs is that they are so simple to use.

If, however, you're the type who enjoys the hunt for eggs, you'll undoubtedly find all of them on your own. Too often, we found the search was too frustrating for the level of payoff. Especially annoying is that after a good deal of remote control and menu manipulation, too much of the time, what you end up with are more promotional advertising segments or a series of trailers. Or, it's something so lame that it isn't worth viewing. In the places where we think the eggs are tasty morsels, we tell you what to do. We mention only those that will fill your basket with eggs that are at least dyed an interesting color or, better yet, are pure designer chocolate. We leave collecting plain hard-boiled eggs for discovery by those of you who are the die-hard masters of the remote control.

Capitalism makes our country work; we're surely not against it. But do be awake and aware of the marketing devices that are being used to persuade people to purchase discs quickly and sometimes repeatedly. In the case of the big blockbuster hits, it isn't unusual for the distributors to release numerous versions until they finally get ready to produce the one that is truly special. If you can't wait to see a big hit on DVD, rent it, unless your disc budget is very generous. If you do purchase a first release and then want to upgrade to the newer editions, there's always the local used-DVD seller, eBay, your friends, or the nearest hospital, nursing facility, shelter, or other charity that will accept the old DVD.

We hope you'll find many of your favorite movies are reviewed here and that the information we provide is useful to you. We also fervently hope we've included deserving films you've never heard of because they had such limited theatrical releases. There's plenty of the best of the classics for viewers of all age groups. And we've added a few special treats for children at the end ("Hot Dogs and Ice Cream Cones"). If you're a younger person, you may have missed some of the greatest films because they were released before you were born and weren't widely available on videotape. For other viewers, there is an opportunity to see your favorites in this newly enhanced medium.

When we were writing this book, we made a promise that we didn't break. We felt strongly that if the heart or essence of a film was not represented properly or fairly on its disc edition, it shouldn't make the cut. For example, *Titanic* contains some of the most amazing special effects ever seen on the screen. Yet, as we go to print, there isn't a worthy "collector's edition" of the film. It doesn't belong in your library until there is an edition with a documentary that shows how they made the movie. Or, if a movie is primarily memorable because of its ravishing cinematography, and the quality of the DVD transfer is poor or barely mediocre, we've left it out as well. For example, *The Last Emperor* sadly falls into that category.

Even with these sorts of decisions, along with our own personal quirks, we believe we've given you a reliable place to begin. Movies are the stuff of romance. They provide food for our souls. We think we've offered you a very special visual diet. The rest is up to you. Happy viewing!!

Steven H. Scheuer and Alida Brill-Scheuer

Adam's Rib

CAST: Spencer Tracy, Katharine Hepburn, Judy Holliday, Tom Ewell, Jean Hagen, David Wayne
DIRECTOR: George Cukor
SCREENWRITERS: Ruth Gordon and Garson Kanin
RELEASED: 1949 (101 minutes)
RATED: Not rated

Adam's Rib is about a married couple, both lawyers with a tendency to bring the courtroom home. Amanda Bonner (Katharine Hepburn) is defending a woman who tried to kill her husband. Adam Bonner (Spencer Tracy) is prosecuting her. Judy Holliday plays the would-be murderer, Doris Attinger. There's no violence here, just the fast-paced precision of a Gordon-Kanin script. Holliday successfully walks the tightrope between comedy and farce. Watching her read the manual on how to use the pistol makes you scream with laughter. The film is dated enough that the scenes with Holliday and the gun aren't terribly alarming. Tom Ewell stars as the womanizing husband who is more of a jerk than a monster.

By the time the Tracy-Hepburn acting team got to this one, they knew their dance steps perfectly. It was their fifth film together, and it's probably the best of their many films. It's certainly one of George Cukor's finest comedies. Part of the joy, of course, is to see Tracy and Hepburn together in their prime. All the fireworks belong to the two leading stars.

What made the Tracy-Hepburn movies work so well was their personal story and the underlying romantic chemistry. It's as evident here as in all the other films they made. *Adam's Rib* has an exquisite bite and rhythm that make even some of the exaggerated plot contrivances believable. Cukor's direction was understated; he knew what he was doing and where he was going. The dialogue and the performances appropriately take center stage.

Despite its middle age (fifty-four years), it's still an amusing and rewarding comedy about marriage and gender roles. Gordon and Kanin's screenplay provides sharp-edged commentary on sexual double standards. The two-attorney household depicted in the film was unusual in 1949. Despite the many changes for women in the half-century since the film was released, many of the issues remain timely. Tracy's quip about Yale Law School will have you checking the release date; the film has more than a few contemporary moments to it.

EXTRAS
You'll want this classic on your library shelf because of the film, not the extras. The only bonus is an original trailer that is amusing to see.

The transfer to DVD worked out very well. The images are crisp and sharply defined. The sound is absolutely clear, which is essential in a dialogue-driven vehicle. There are subtitles in French, Spanish, and English and a French audio track.

An Affair of Love

CAST: Nathalie Baye, Sergi Lopez
DIRECTOR: Frederic Fonteyne
SCREENWRITER: Philippe Blasband
RELEASED: 2000 (1999 in France, with the title *Une Liaison Pornographique*) (80 minutes)
RATED: Not rated

Based on the premise that nothing lasts forever (especially love), the screenplay gives us a plot filled with the complexity of human sexual interaction. Perhaps the right words are *sensual* and *erotic*. We know from the first frame this couple didn't last forever because their story is told in flashback sequences. "He" is speaking to someone off camera who is asking questions, and so is "She." We know them only as He and She. Perhaps time has passed. The boyish Sergi Lopez has grown a beard, and the lovely Nathalie Baye has dyed her hair dark. It could be time and age, or it could be the director's way of telling us that they are now different people. What the film does best is to illustrate the transforming power of love, even when one is determined not to fall in love. We have come to understand that the French are far more willing to break our hearts than Hollywood, with its preference for a "happily ever after" ending, yet this film surprises.

Wanting to fulfill a particular sexual fantasy, she advertises for a man willing to participate. He responds, and they meet in a café. There's something inherently erotic about the streets of Paris and its cafés filled with secret meetings of lovers, past and present. She is older than he, which gives the film a fresh sense of adventure.

Eventually, they move beyond her fantasy, whatever it was, and cross over into the truly dangerous land of real sex. The setting for their trysts is a French hotel with too much wallpaper and boudoir poof to be anything but a hotel that caters to sexual interludes. We never learn about the secret fantasy. Even when questioned by the off-camera voice, neither will tell what the fantasy was. Is this refusal continued loyalty to their intimacy despite the end of the relationship?

One day, during their assignation, an old man collapses in the hotel's hallway. They rush out to help him. Reality has intervened; they have accidentally become a couple in the outside world. They learn of the man's miserable marriage, and his wife's plight. He and She have moved to an all-too-familiar intersection in the journey of love. Will they proceed as they were? Will they forge ahead and create that thing called a life together, or will it all come apart? Even though we know the ending, we forget ourselves and go forward with their story, hoping for them to continue.

In a café, she professes her love for him. It comes tumbling out of her in a scene that Baye plays with exuberance but without artifice. They go off to think it over. Despite the fact we know what's coming, the romantics among us nonetheless can't help thinking, "If only she had kept her mouth shut and let him talk."

This isn't a film to second-guess. There won't be a French sequel about how they found each other ten years later. It is what it is. Somehow appropriate to the film's mystery is that the DVD doesn't offer any bells and whistles. The subtitles are well done and easy to read. It's a spare beauty and worthy of your DVD collection. It's also likely that unless you live in a city with lots of art house theaters, you missed this one. Even in major urban markets, it came and went all too quickly.

This quiet film with a message about the possibility and impossibility of love will captivate you anew each time you view it. Not everything in your DVD library need be the Hollywood point-and-click extras-galore variety.

An Affair to Remember

CAST: Cary Grant, Deborah Kerr, Richard Denning, Neva
    Patterson, Cathleen Nesbitt, Robert Q. Lewis, Fortunio
    Bonanova
DIRECTOR: Leo McCarey
SCREENWRITERS: Leo McCarey and Mildred Cram
RELEASED: 1957 (119 minutes)
RATED: Not rated

So here is what the fuss is all about. Cary Grant, the most ridiculously handsome man on the screen, if not on the earth, meets Deborah Kerr shipboard. Needless to say, they are attached to others. The film progresses; you love them. No, you love him; you adore him. Nobody is as wonderful as Cary Grant; maybe even Cary Grant wasn't as wonderful as Cary Grant. Kerr's beautiful enough for him; she's lovely enough for him. That is, if it's not *you* he's going to love.

By the way, did we say this is a woman's movie? Well, it is. Or, as Rosie O'Donnell says in *Sleepless,* men never "get" this movie. Who cares? But if you find one who actually does even tolerate this movie, marry him immediately. You don't need to know anything else about him.

There's hardly a woman alive who doesn't know that they decide to meet in six months at the top of the Empire State Building, and she has a ghastly accident on the way. The movie is actually two movies in one. The first half is a wonderfully witty and urbane romantic comedy. Here both Grant and Kerr sparkle with a kind of Noel Coward chatter and timing. Postship, however, the script deteriorates quickly. Actually, it morphs into McCarey's *Bells of St. Mary's*, if you must know. McCarey's apparently unavoidable need to put his Catholicism in front of the love story turns it into a combination of soap opera and *The Sound of Music*. Yet all is forgiven for the final scene, one of the great romantic endings.

Two fine actors put up with playing the ditched lovers with a certain style and grace. This is particularly true for Neva Patterson, who plays the society heiress Grant dumps. You'll remember her for *The Buddy Holly Story, All the President's Men,* and *David and Lisa,* if not for this. Richard Denning plays the rejected male lover with more elegance and panache than almost anyone else ever has. He went on to be the governor of Hawaii in the television series *Hawaii Five-O*. (Maybe women love this film because Kerr gets to choose between *two* quite lovely men.)

Among the best things about this movie are the Manhattan scenes. All good endings have to happen there, if you're a 1950s kid trapped in Suburbia.

Grant was fifty-three when he made the film, and Kerr was only thirty-six. The May-December quality of the romance was never mentioned, because Grant was always about thirty-five, even when he left us forever.

EXTRAS

For fans of this movie, we suggest a purchase rather than a rental, because the extra feature documentary is so juicy. It's filled with gossip and details about the lives of both Kerr and Grant. Grant brought such an authentic touch to the role of the forlorn lover because he was brokenhearted about his own failed affair with Sophia Loren. (And who wouldn't be upset about that?) Kerr's first marriage was faltering, but nobody knew it. (Kerr is interviewed here, as is her daughter.)

There's an interesting analysis of McCarey and his need to remake this film; the original featured Charles Boyer in the Grant role. It is important to forget (if you can) how nasty McCarey was during the McCarthy period. He was a rabid anti-Communist and harmed a number of fine people in his zealous attempt to find the pinko under every bed.

Perhaps the most interesting commentary revolves around how McCarey, a devout Catholic, managed to make a film about a love affair that can be viewed by all ages. No sex is part of the reason. Yet Grant's character, Nickie Ferrante, is openly a womanizer, and Kerr's Terry McKay is a "kept" woman.

The "Backstory" documentary also offers an interesting look at the new technology of the time, Cinemascope—remember that?

Our favorite tidbit from the special feature involves Cathleen Nesbitt, whose own life was even more interesting than that of the character she played. She's now mostly remembered for her role as the mother of Henry Higgins in *My Fair Lady*.

The Age of Innocence

CAST: Daniel Day-Lewis, Michelle Pfeiffer, Winona Ryder
DIRECTOR: Martin Scorsese
SCREENWRITER: Jay Cocks (adapted from the novel by Edith
    Wharton)
RELEASED: 1993 (139 minutes)
RATED: PG

When Martin Scorsese read Edith Wharton's *Age of Innocence,* he was utterly captivated by the tale. With the able assistance of screenwriter and former film critic Jay Cocks, Scorsese set about the daunting task of re-creating the texture and life of New York's high society in the 1870s. If you think this is a far-fetched project for Scorsese, think again. He's in love with New York, and with the movies, even those he doesn't make. His eerie ability to have virtually total recall of any movie he has viewed helps make *The Age of Innocence* a thrilling period film. Through his brilliant cinematic lens of a brain, he has given us a film that would make Wharton herself gasp with envy.

By the time Wharton put pen to paper to write this novel, there was no longer an "age of innocence," here or abroad. There's not much innocence in the novel's plot. But Wharton knew how to use irony both sparingly and effectively. It's an unwieldy novel to put on film; the use of story narration helps immensely. The narrator is Joanne Woodward, whose soft, lilting voice keeps you totally involved. The story is a mannered and restrained love tragedy. Although this is a world governed by a system of unwritten but absolute rules, sheer treachery is beneath all the formality and politeness. It's not as obvious or in your face as Scorsese's portraits of mobsters, but the punishment for disobedience in this world is just as severe.

Daniel Day-Lewis plays Newland Archer, handsome, socially important, and professionally successful. He has embarked on the life he was born to have. Archer doesn't strike you as a man who is anything more or less than his social register description would indicate. He is betrothed to the equally proper May Welland, played with surprising depth by Winona Ryder, and his life rolls on, from teatime to tuxedo hour—until all hell breaks loose in the person of Countess Ellen Olenska. Michelle Pfeiffer plays Olenska convincingly, using some of the same wiles she used in her role as Madame de Tourvel in *Dangerous Liaisons* but in a far more subtle way. Archer is consumed by the notion of his love for Olenska. She is a woman who thinks for herself and marries outside society's acceptable boundaries. Later, with the same independent spirit, she decides to get rid of the unacceptable spouse.

Suddenly, the curtain parts, and Archer sees another world, one dictated by true feelings and freedom. His passion for Olenska is consuming, but he will not act on it, because he cannot. All he has been raised to believe he is and must be works against this love. Just as he might take action, we watch an entire social structure close around him like the bars of a prison. He ends up in a luxurious but solitary confinement of the heart. In the end, however, it's the women who have trumped him.

The expectation of sexual awakening is always just before your eyes but doesn't happen. It is startling to see how much heat can be generated within so many layers of clothing. In Scorsese's love affair with the Wharton novel, one is treated to realistic settings that truly boggle the mind and the eyes of the viewer, from the art on the walls to the meals served. This film is a visual feast.

What about the last scene? Does Archer make the decision not to test the love so many years later? Or does the countess close the window to that possibility? You decide.

EXTRAS

Well, if the movie is a feast, the extras here are a meager fare of bread and water. Either Scorsese didn't have the time to devote to it, or the distributors didn't want to spend the bucks. In either case, or for a variety of other reasons, it's a pity. What this DVD needs is a behind-the-scenes commentary on how the film was made. What you get is a menu of lots of subtitle options, including Chinese, Korean, Portuguese, and Thai in addition to the now fairly standard French and Spanish; the original theatrical trailer; and unremarkable filmographies and production notes.

Why should you own this? If you are building a library of the films of one of our greatest directors, leave a space for this wonderfully satisfying Scorsese departure into a different time. For period costumes, settings, and unrequited love, it's worth viewing again and again.

Aimee and Jaguar

CAST: Maria Schrader, Juliane Kohler, Johanna Wokalek, Heike Makatsch, Elisabeth Degen, Detlev Buck
DIRECTOR: Max Farberbock
SCREENWRITER: Max Farberbock (adapted from the book by Erica Fischer)
RELEASED: 1999 (125 minutes)
RATED: Not rated

In 1943–44 Berlin, Hitler and his war machine were slowly grinding down. It was a very dangerous time for any Jew to remain in Germany. This is the true story of Felice Schragenheim and Lilly Wust. It is a story about World War II told from the point of view of women in Berlin at that time. Mostly, however, it is a story about the love between a German woman who is married and the mother of four children and a Jewish woman who manages to stay below the identification radar. It would be a hard story to invent; perhaps that is why it is so shattering.

This exceptional film made the international festival circuit as well as the Jewish film festival circuit. Its general release was quite limited. Thanks to Zeitgeist Films, it is now available in a special edition with fascinating extra features.

Felice has every reason to hide from the Gestapo. She is not only Jewish but a lesbian and therefore at risk on two counts. Instead, she openly deceives the Nazi establishment. She works under an assumed name for the editor of a Nazi newspaper, claiming she is married to an SS officer. She is a wild thing, with death nipping at her heels. At first, she thinks of the married Lilly as only a conquest. But soon their lives are intertwined emotionally and practically. They live together in Lilly's apartment. When Lilly's husband returns from the front, somewhat mysteriously, he discovers her new attachment and becomes abusive. Their marriage has been a farce for years, each having affairs. But Lilly's relationship with Felice is of a different depth; the husband is repulsed and threatened.

One night, Felice and Lilly rename each other Jaguar and Aimee, as their love names. They write feverishly passionate letters of undying love to each other while sitting together in the same room. They are happy with each other and with Lilly's children. Later, they will send Lilly's four children to the countryside for safety during the Battle of Berlin. The tempo of this film is unlike the usual WWII films because of its intimate detail.

There aren't words that would give full justice to the poetry of their love. In one scene, Lilly begins to tremble; it is one of the most beautifully shot love scenes in recent cinematic history. *Aimee and Jaguar* is a film about two people who touch each other so deeply that gender and ethnicity become irrelevant. Despite her love for Lilly, Felice does not tell her that she is a Jew until well into their relationship.

Felice arranges passports for her girlfriends, and they began to leave Berlin one by one and in groups. When Felice's passport and papers are ready, she is also to leave with a small group of friends. On the day of her scheduled de-

parture, Felice arrives late, refusing to go with the others.
She chooses to stay in Berlin, insisting she will be safe. She
tells her friends the war is essentially over. It is, of course,
her fatal mistake. She stays because she cannot leave her
Aimee. In a realistically harrowing scene, Felice is arrested
in their home.

At the film's end, an old woman waits at home to be
moved to a retirement community. It is Lilly, who no
longer has any interest in life. Forty years later, she still
grieves for Felice. At the retirement home, she finds Ilse,
their mutual friend and Lilly's former maid. The two
women have a rather strained reunion. (Ilse was Felice's
original lover.) During their conversation, we grasp fully
the intensity of Lilly's love for Felice. It is a love that sus-
tains Lilly through her life, into a very old age.

Director Max Farberbock has given us a look at a side
of the Holocaust we have not seen before. It is a bright light
in the darkest of times. This film builds until the very end,
when its energy is as potent as electricity. It's a tragic and
yet life-affirming story.

EXTRAS
Each feature on the menu demands your attention. There
are two behind-the-scenes documentaries. Maria Schrader,
who plays Felice, and Juliane Kohler, who plays Lilly, were
totally immersed in the story of these two women. Their
determination to portray them with accuracy and intelligence is apparent.

When the film was made, Lilly Wust was in her late
eighties, and the interviews with her are almost unbearable
in their intimacy and candor. Lilly made a scrapbook of her
short time with Felice. It's a poignant part of the feature.
There are also photographs of Felice as a young girl, along
with pictures of her family. Lilly talks about the relation-

ship, as well as her decision to allow Erica Fischer to tell their story. It's the Fischer book upon which the film is based. One of Lilly's children converted to Judaism, a fitting memorial to the love these two women shared.

All About Eve

CAST: Bette Davis, Anne Baxter, George Sanders, Gary Merrill, Marilyn Monroe, Hugh Marlowe, Celeste Holm
DIRECTOR: Joseph L. Mankiewicz
SCREENWRITER: Joseph L. Mankiewicz (adapted from the story "The Wisdom of Eve" by Mary Orr)
RELEASED: 1950 (138 minutes)
RATED: Not rated

Astonishingly, this relic from 1950 still has a fascinating plot. It's a study of New York theater life and the treachery that can be involved if you're a Broadway star or a wannabe Broadway star. The skilled and sharp performances overcome the plot's flaws. Anne Baxter plays Eve, who carefully plots to deceive and ultimately replace Margo Channing (Bette Davis) as the light of Broadway. Before Margo can even figure out what's going on, Eve is her understudy and then her replacement. Eve also attempts to take Margo's boyfriend, but that fails. It's the only part of her scheme that does, however.

Davis gives a bravura, old-fashioned, scenery-chewing performance as the dynamic but aging star. Baxter's phony innocence is a perfect foil for Davis. Celeste Holm plays Karen Richards, the overly naive wife of the playwright of the moment, Lloyd Richards, played by Hugh Marlowe. George Sanders plays Addison DeWitt, an obnoxious, controlling, and acid-spewing theater critic. Sanders is positively wonderful and easily trumps the other male performances. Marilyn Monroe plays what she was at the time: a young starlet, unaffected and vulnerable. One of the high points of the dialogue consists of DeWitt verbally destroying Eve with his knowledge of who she really isn't. For most viewers, the best part of the movie is the very last scene. It calls to mind the biblical phrase about reaping what you sow.

Mankiewicz won two Oscars for *All About Eve*, for direction and for the screenplay. It's an unflattering look at women, but in some sense, it can be seen as gender-neutral. It's just as likely that coldly ambitious men could exhibit the same cutthroat and manipulative tactics to end up with top billing without showing any remorse. There's no mistaking what this is, however; it's 1950s America. This is before the women's movement, when women were routinely called girls, dames, or broads. Everyone was led to believe that women readily clawed one another's eyes out. You need to come to *All About Eve* without thinking about what would happen later for women. It's a classic, and it's Davis at her most highly tuned. It's also the film where she quipped her most famous line. The ride for the viewer isn't at all bumpy, however.

EXTRAS

The earlier DVD releases of the film contained no extras of any merit. The Studio Classics line produced by 20th Century Fox offers much more (it also includes an excellent package for *Gentleman's Agreement* and *How Green Was My Valley*). They don't quite have their act together yet, but it's sure a step in the right direction. Unfortunately, in the case of *All About Eve*, a couple of the listed features are not available on the disc. Nonetheless, there's some great stuff in these supplementary interviews and materials.

If you want a peek at the other titles available in the Studio Classics line, this DVD includes a promotional feature, of course.

"Back Story" is the brightest sparkler in your fireworks set. This feature includes behind-the-scenes details as well as some of the dirt. It's long been rumored that the cast of women on the film didn't like one another, Holm acknowledges the truth of the gossip. She and Davis never spoke to each other off camera. As most people know, *All About Eve* introduced the moviegoing audience to the one and only Marilyn Monroe. Not unlike actress Gloria Swanson and the fictional Norma Desmond, Bette Davis and Margo Channing were also near doubles. By the time of this film, Davis was aging, and her enormously successful career was slowing down—that is, until she landed this role, which became her zenith. Davis was married to Gary Merrill, who plays Bill Sanders, the younger man in the film who marries Margo Channing.

Nominated for fourteen Oscars, it won for Best Picture, Best Director, Best Screenplay, and Best Actor (Sanders). How did Davis lose that Oscar? Baxter had refused to be nominated for Best Supporting Actress, and the competition was so intense and hostile that neither won. Instead, the Academy awarded the Oscar to the underdog, Judy Holliday, for her starring role in *Born Yesterday*.

The DVD includes a movie trailer with Davis and a tiny clip interview, the same for the Baxter trailer.

If you enjoy the old Movietone newsreels from the period, this DVD has them. There's Mankiewicz accepting his award, and there's the opening night of the movie (but it's the same clip you've seen in "Back Story").

Don't bother to view the *"Look* Magazine Award," the quality of the sound is horrid.

If you haven't seen the way the restoration process

works on another movie's DVD restoration feature, this one is a good example. The split-screen technique is very illustrative of the work being done on these valuable golden classics. It's not as dramatic as *Roman Holiday*, however.

Almost Famous: The Bootleg Cut

CAST: Patrick Fugit, Billy Crudup, Frances McDormand, Kate
    Hudson, Jason Lee, Philip Seymour Hoffman, Noah Tylor, John
    Fedevich, Fairuza Balk, Mark Kozelek
DIRECTOR: Cameron Crowe
SCREENWRITER: Cameron Crowe
RELEASED: 2000 (124 minutes for theatrical release, 162 minutes
    for bootleg cut)
RATED: R (theatrical release; bootleg cut not rated)

Cameron Crowe's almost flawless *Almost Famous* is now truly perfect in its latest release, called "The Bootleg Cut." The movie, as released, was a fine product, but the new technology makes it even more remarkable.

Perhaps more than most other recent DVD releases, this one shows how Crowe utilized DVD technology to its full powers. When the original DVD was released, he was busy making *Vanilla Sky*. DreamWorks released the first edition anyway, knowing a better one was on its way. If you couldn't wait, you got cheated, because this edition is something pretty wonderful.

Crowe judiciously waited until his reputation was made with *Jerry Maguire* before he turned to his own beginnings. The result was *Almost Famous*, which is about sex, drugs, and rock and roll during the 1970s. It's the story of William Miller (read: Cameron Crowe) and his amazing journey as a kid who wants to be a rock critic. It trivializes the film to suggest it's only about a time when groupies were everywhere and the bands on the road and in the bus were a common part of our culture. It's as much about a boy's rite of passage as anything. The performances knock you out; the story never fragments. It was a wise decision to cast an unknown young actor, Patrick Fugit, as William. Fugit's previous anonymity makes him completely believable. You're rooting for him from the first frame.

William is an odd kid; he's very smart and small in stature for his age. Frances McDormand plays his mother to the absolute edge of realism and lunacy. She's an academic, a vegetarian, an antidrug zealot, and rock-music-phobe. McDormand is totally out there, hanging off the ledge, but the love she has for her son keeps her character from becoming farcical. You either had a mother like this in the 1970s (if you were lucky), or you were a mother like this in the 1970s (if you survived it).

The kid wants to be a rock music critic, and nothing will deter him. The movie is his journey with a fictional band called Stillwater (a composite of at least four bands of the time). He is encouraged by Lester Bangs, who was a real rock critic of the time. Philip Seymour Hoffman plays Bangs superbly. On sheer guts, William gets an assignment from *Rolling Stone* to write a feature piece on Stillwater's concert tour. They don't know he's only fifteen.

William is guided and befriended by a band groupie who calls herself Penny Lane, played by Kate Hudson. (She's Goldie Hawn's daughter and has a share of her mother's early zany, gritty determination.) Billy Crudup, as Russell Hammond, brings just the right amount of kindness and narcissism to the role of the lead guitarist. Despite Bangs's strong admonition to William that rock stars aren't your friends, William has trouble drawing the line between fan and journalist.

William learns a great deal about life on the road, the ethics of a working journalist, and the rights of women and girls (even ones like Penny, who cares less about her dignity than about her status as a "band aide," not a groupie). In one of the most touching pieces of dialogue, William tells Penny that her great love, Russell, who is married, traded her to another band for fifty dollars and a case of beer. Penny wants to know what kind of beer it was. It's only a moment, and it isn't overplayed, but it represents the complexity and the integrity of this artful film. (If you want a glimpse of Penny as a grown-up, rent *The Banger Sisters* with Susan Sarandon and Goldie Hawn. It's not worth a purchase but is worth a viewing.)

EXTRAS

Disc One is the director's version of the film. It contains the much-touted extra thirty-five minutes of footage. There's even a nugget or two of the real Lester Bangs in a somewhat stitched-together interview. Crowe's commentary is the best of the lot. You get Crowe, his real mother, Alice, as well as production crew members and a childhood pal. His mother should get the Good Sport Award.

We found Crowe's top ten albums from 1973 amusing and instructive but not as much as hearing him discuss his original *Rolling Stone* articles.

Two fairly decent eggs appear on this disc. There's a pretentious scene you can access from Crowe's "Love Comes and Goes" (the usual not-so-secret microphone icon is your entrance pass). Good news! The egg is easy to find, and the scene wasn't in the film. In the setup menu (still on Disc One), you can see Hoffman in the role of Bangs (highlight the hole in the record). It's not as exciting as the aficionados claim it is, but it's interesting primarily for the quick introduction by Crowe.

Disc Two is the theatrical-release version of the movie.

There's also Stillwater's Cleveland concert, if you can't live without it. The true joys are in "Unedited." Also included is a CD with six Stillwater songs (only for truly fanatic fans of the film). There's a Penny Lane egg if you go to "Cast" and click "Fairuza Balk."

Amélie

CAST: Audrey Tautou, Mathieu Kassovitz, Rufus, Yolande Moreau, Artus de Penguern, Urbain Cancellier
DIRECTOR: Jean-Pierre Jeunet
SCREENWRITER: Guillaume Laurant
RELEASED: 2001 (115 minutes)
RATED: R

Amélie is France's contribution to the feel-good genre. The title role is played by the irresistible Audrey Tautou. Amélie has had a pretty weird childhood. Her father is a physician who believes touching should be reserved for medical examinations. Her mama takes a suicidal leap. But even with these bleak beginnings, *Amélie* isn't a dark film. It's part fable and part magic realism.

With considerable help from a somewhat make-believe Paris, Amélie creates a new life and a new identity. She works in a mundane bistro, but something startles her (we won't ruin this surprise), and she is catapulted into her new career. Her sole mission is to make people happy, quietly and even anonymously. She's not a saint, though. There's whimsy and mischief. Give in to Amélie's sense of youthful joy, and she might make you happy, too. But you must suspend disbelief for that to happen.

There are many great moments involving things as diverse as a garden gnome who travels (and sends postcards) and a mysterious man in an automatic photo machine. You'll have fun all along the way. There's enough suspense in Amélie's quest for true love to keep even the more earth-bound involved. There's also enough mild eroticism to keep everybody interested.

EXTRAS

"Jean-Pierre Jeunet Commentary" is thoughtfully available in English, although his accent is very French. You might opt for the French with subtitles. He's adorably French in his intense love of the art of film. Watch it.

"Fantasies of Audrey Tautou" is what we would call the outtakes. It's a little bit of the actors clowning around during shooting. Also enchanting is the feature "Home Movies," with more of Tautou and the crew. In "The Amélie Scrapbook," take a peek at the garden gnome's travels, and laugh all over again at this clever conceit.

In "The Look of Amélie," Jeunet talks through his decisions in an illuminating way. The cinematographer shows his vision; it's as though we have his eyes for a few moments. Of the variety of opportunities to hear Jeunet, from commentary to Q&A sessions, we choose "An Intimate Chat with Jean-Pierre Jeunet" as the winner. You also can hear about the controversy at the Cannes Film Festival.

American Beauty

CAST: Kevin Spacey, Annette Bening, Thora Birch, Wes Bentley, Peter Gallagher, Allison Janney, Chris Cooper, Mena Suvari
DIRECTOR: Sam Mendes
SCREENWRITER: Alan Ball
RELEASED: 1999 (122 minutes)
RATED: R

American Beauty took the country by surprise and cleaned up at the Academy Awards. It won Best Picture; Sam Mendes, the English stage director, won for his film directorial debut; Conrad L. Hall took away the statue for cinematography; and Alan Ball won for screenwriting. The Best Actor Oscar went to Kevin Spacey for his much-praised performance as Lester Burnham.

Lester Burnham: suburbanite, detached, distressed, virtually dead, almost dead, finally dead. This wasn't the first film to show the listless and bored lives of Americans who have too much and ask too little of themselves, but it might be the best. *American Beauty* was such a hit because it looked head-on at self-absorption. It is darkly comic, tragic, and compelling.

Annette Bening plays Lester's wife, Carolyn, who hardly notices whether Lester is breathing or not. She just wants a perfect life, with décor to match. Her emptiness is less affecting than Lester's because her character is drawn more like a cartoon than a person. Carolyn insists on an order and elegance at home that is as pathetic as her failed real estate career. She has managed, however, to work in a carefully orchestrated but meaningless affair with a rival realtor named Buddy (Peter Gallagher).

Nothing changes. Nothing satisfies. Nothing seems to mean anything. Well, Lester does masturbate every morning in the shower, which appears to be the only moment of the day when he verifies he's still alive. We know he won't be for long, because he tells us so: "I'm forty-two years old. In less than a year, I'll be dead." At some point in the movie, you think he will be dead because you might kill him yourself if he doesn't get a life. You might find yourself screaming at all of them, "You're alive, make the most of it!"

Lester and his daughter, Jane (Thora Birch), have moved from the hostility of adolescent-parent-interaction to simply no interaction. Birch is awful and extraordinary all at once. This is a story about being too comfortable or complacent to fix anything in your life.

As Lester moves through the last phase of his life, Spacey's performance is completely riveting. New and wacky neighbors are ominous. Colonel Frank Fitts (Chris Cooper) makes our blood run cold. Wes Bentley, playing son Ricky Fitts, catches you and makes you think about all drifting kids. Allison Janney as the half-comatose wife of the insane Colonel Fitts amuses a bit now. We know she got a better job! (She's the Emmy Award–winning actress who plays the president's press secretary, CJ, on *West Wing*.) It's comforting to see her because we know somebody got out of that setting alive.

Lester doesn't get out of his life alive, but in a few brief months, he captures something of what it might have felt like to be alive all along. He becomes obsessed with his daughter's high school pal Angela (Mena Suvari). She's seductive yet still a girl. Lester isn't oblivious to any of the implications. The point of the film isn't whether he will bed Angela or not but that suddenly, in the most unexpected and inappropriate way, Lester's heart finally kicks in, and something matters to him. Spacey's closing speech grabs you every single time you watch.

EXTRAS

"Look Closer" lasts about twenty minutes and is as much about the film's many awards as it is about how the film was made. Nonetheless, we found it fairly entertaining. It's worth watching for the interviews with the cast and crew.

"Audio Commentary" is the standard full audio overlay with Mendes and Alan Ball but mostly Mendes. If you are a big fan of the film, you might want to choose this first as your way of getting back into the story.

The DVD contains more than one hundred story-boards with commentary by Mendes and Conrad Hall. This is technical and fascinating but probably somewhat tedious for the less than full-blown movie freak. Speaking of which, if you have a DVD-ROM player in your personal computer, pop it in and examine the screenplay itself along with some footage.

American Graffiti

CAST: Richard Dreyfuss, Ron Howard, Harrison Ford, Paul Le Mat, Charlie Martin Smith, Cindy Williams, Candy Clark, Mackenzie Phillips, Wolfman Jack (as himself)
DIRECTOR: George Lucas
SCREENWRITERS: George Lucas and Gloria Katz
RELEASED: 1973 (112 minutes)
RATED: PG

The credits are now a Who's Who of the film industry, but thirty years ago, it was a list of talented kids with their futures ahead of them. George Lucas was still in his twenties with only one picture on his credit list, *THX 1138*, a science-fiction thriller that didn't quite work. In 1973, he turned to the 1960s for a film that swept the country with the slogan "Where were you in '62?"

Three decades later, the deceptively simple plot still satisfies everybody up and down the age ladder. In a generic California town (rather loosely based on Modesto), the kids' hearts beat to the songs of the times. Everybody has the radio on all the time; you hear the nutty, if reassuring, ramblings of real-life disc jockey Wolfman Jack. (He's now departed, but this film has given him an eternity he couldn't have dreamed of having, even during a hopeful howl.)

The action takes place during one night. It's late summer, and these kids are moving into the next phases of their lives. Some of them will go to college and move beyond this moment. Although the lives of those who stay behind undoubtedly will change, too, their perspectives may not. The characters are well drawn, making this more than a nostalgic zip through the tunes of the times. *American Graffiti* moves around the characters and their lives in a nonlinear way. It's a filmic way of storytelling we've become so accustomed to we hardly notice it here. Yet this was a daring new technique when the young (pre–*Star Wars*) Lucas directed it.

Curt and Steve, played by Richard Dreyfuss and Ron Howard, are college bound. Curt, the smartest boy in school, has ambivalent feelings about leaving. Should he go? Will he be able to say goodbye to the comforts inherent in knowing your surroundings and hanging out with your buddies? Dreyfuss brings to this performance the angst of a young man but the wisdom of a far more mature actor. *American Graffiti* is filled with cars and cruisin' and the culture of the automobile. This is a snapshot of American life before the killings of the Kennedys and King. The movie is about a place that existed before the reality of *Born on the Fourth of July,* but it could have taken place in the same town.

The kids hang out at Mel's drive-in; it's where the action is, the place to be seen in and around. There are many unpredictable turns in the film. Especially nice is Charlie Martin Smith, playing Terry the Toad, the butt of everybody's joke, who ends up a bigger winner than you expect. It is worth noting that the music track plays virtually continuously through the film. At the time of theatrical release, it was part of the movie's appeal. Interestingly, although the songs are dated, they aren't distracting. You may find yourself singing "Sixteen Candles" or "He's So Fine" in the shower.

If you want to get your mind off the news of this decade, go back in time and savor the foolishness, the rituals, the outsider-insider turf tensions, and the hot rods. If you're off to a high school reunion from a mid-'60s year, consider this a refresher course. This is an American classic whose success enabled Lucas to follow his own destiny. Nonetheless, *American Graffiti* remains solidly a part of his own personal and cinematic history.

And what about that girl in the T-Bird? Choose your own metaphor.

EXTRAS:

The extra that matters here is the documentary entitled "The Making of *American Graffiti*." It's new material, not rehashed clips with old audio overlays. Lucas, producer Francis Ford Coppola, and most of the stars are in it. If you know the film well, or even if you don't recall it all that well but did see it initially, watch this documentary first. It makes viewing the film again all the more enjoyable and meaningful. For those born in '62 and beyond, though, we advise watching the film first.

An American in Paris

CAST: Gene Kelly, Leslie Caron, Oscar Levant, Nina Foch, Georges Guetary
DIRECTOR: Vincente Minnelli
SCREENWRITER: Alan Jay Lerner
RELEASED: 1951 (114 minutes)
RATED: Not rated

In 1951, Americans wanted to be happy. Why not? Hitler was vanquished. The war was over. Men were back home, and just about everybody loved Americans, even the French.

Overjoyed by victory and the end of the war, Americans flocked to theaters to see this upbeat film. The Academy also loved *An American in Paris*. It deservedly won lots of Oscars, including Best Picture. A special Oscar went to Gene Kelly's choreography, which closes the film. Few remember the plot, largely because there isn't much of one. But everybody remembers the closing ballet. Vincente Minnelli gave Kelly the freedom to try things that were daring at the time. With the combined talents of Minnelli, Kelly, writer Alan Jay Lerner, and the Gershwin brothers, it was hard to miss.

Americans lost their innocence in the horrors of World War II, but they were more than ready to get it back again in the 1950s. *An American in Paris* appealed to just that national mood. Kelly plays a struggling painter. Oscar Levant plays a music student. They are pals who are both in love with the same woman, hardly a fresh plot twist. Trying to take it all in stride, Levant all but immolates himself attempting to drink coffee and light a fistful of cigarettes. His charm was an acquired taste, but if you had acquired it, seeing him again has an aching sadness to it.

From the beginning, you know Kelly will dump his girlfriend (played by Nina Foch), who really isn't very lovable. He will find true love with the younger and totally delicious Leslie Caron. Caron was already a terrific dancer but not much of an actress. Somehow this only adds to her charm; she walks right off the screen as a real-life gamine.

You want this on your "American Musical Comedy" shelf because of Kelly and Caron. You want it because we aren't innocent any longer; the French don't love us as much anymore; wars are everywhere; and we'll never be able to dance with Gene Kelly. The film's ending pas de deux with Caron and Kelly replays their entire courtship. It may be the best romantic dance sequence ever filmed. We love *An American in Paris* because life is hard. Actually, life was never this beautiful, even in Paris, but this film is a kind of "let's pretend" for adults.

As you might have guessed, there aren't any extras. It's a shame, but the restoration looks great. There are subtitles in French and English.

Annie Hall

CAST: Woody Allen, Diane Keaton, Tony Roberts, Carol Kane, Paul Simon, Shelley Duvall, Colleen Dewhurst, Christopher Walken, Donald Symington
DIRECTOR: Woody Allen
SCREENWRITERS: Woody Allen and Marshall Brickman
RELEASED: 1977 (93 minutes)
RATED: PG

Annie Hall is arguably the most successful of Woody's neurotic love stories. It is perhaps the most autobiographical of his movies. He was living with Diane Keaton at the time the film was shot. It's a universal love story, with a Woody Allen slant to such matters of the heart.

It's hard to imagine anyone else as filled with romantic anxiety as Allen, but we all respond to the fragile quality of love found, love lost, and love mourned. Testimony to the film's resonance is that it won the Oscar for Best Picture—in the same year *Star Wars* was nominated. It also won for Best Director and Best Screenplay. Keaton won for Best Actress; Allen was nominated for Best Actor.

Allen plays Alvy Singer, a Jewish comedian whose jokes are more Borscht Belt than sly urban wit. As in: Did you hear the one about the two women vacationing in the Catskills? "The food is terrible," says one. Her friend agrees: "Yes, and the portions are so small."

In a role that would shadow her career for years, Keaton is Annie Hall. She's midwestern and decidedly not Jewish. She's filled with a fresh enthusiasm for life that the jaded Alvy finds irresistible. Allen parodies Jews so ruthlessly that he can almost be forgiven for doing the same to Gentiles. His take on Jewish attributes could be branded anti-Semitic if he weren't Jewish himself, or if he weren't so funny. Allen's fascination with misunderstandings between Jews and WASPs unfolds here in a particularly amusing yet realistic manner. Everyone has a favorite scene from the movie. For many, it's the lobsters in the kitchen. For us, it's Easter dinner with the Hall family.

Allen employs a wide array of cinematic devices in chronicling the rise and demise of the romance between Alvy and Annie. The film uses flashbacks, a split screen, animation, and other techniques to explore the feelings of the characters and the reasons their relationship finally fails. It's a Woody Allen film, so you know it can't last, but getting there is a good ride. In a hilarious directorial conceit, Allen employed subtitles to clue the viewer in on what is really going on in the heads of the protagonists. Some say that this is Allen's best comedy; it surely is one that turns up on almost everybody's list of the top hundred romantic comedies of the twentieth century.

There's no question about the movie's staying power. Halfway through it, you even begin to wonder why women gave up that copycat Annie Hall look, involving meticulously chosen layers of scarves, blouses, sweaters, jackets, all worn at once and appearing to be casually tossed on.

Keaton and Allen didn't make it together in real life, either, but we have this lasting memoir of a relationship that reached a zenith both on and off the screen. We also have a treasure of an American film in which people have sustained conversations and intellectual debates about real issues. That's almost as passé as Keaton's layered wardrobe.

EXTRAS

No goodies. We can hope that in the future, Allen might provide commentary and more. The menu does offer gobs of scene selections. Also included are subtitles in many European tongues.

The Apartment

CAST: Jack Lemmon, Shirley MacLaine, Fred MacMurray, Ray Walston, Edie Adams, Jack Kruschen, David White, David Lewis, Hope Holiday, Joan Shawlee, Naomi Stevens, Johnny Seven, Joyce Jameson, Willard Waterman

DIRECTOR: Billly Wilder

SCREENWRITERS: Billy Wilder and I. A. L. Diamond

RELEASED: 1960 (125 minutes)

RATED: Not rated

Junior executive Jack Lemmon hopes to rise to the top of his profession by loaning out his bachelor apartment to higher-level executives. We never find out exactly what he does. He works in a building full of rows of desks with other people doing the same thing. He makes the mistake, however, of falling in love with Shirley MacLaine, who has just been dumped by her boss. Fred MacMurray makes a terrifically sleazy philanderer. He's not the jovial father in the silly sitcom *My Three Sons* here. Actually, he's a bit sinister in his callousness. MacLaine is in top form. It's one of her best roles.

MacLaine and Lemmon as a couple were, as Lemmon liked to say, "magic time." There isn't a single frame you want to change about their time together on camera. There's a piece of dialogue near the end of the film involving a Christmas fruitcake that continues to delight anyone who has ever seen it.

Billy Wilder combines the sexual cynicism of *Double Indemnity* with the unabashed romanticism of *Love in the Afternoon* and adroitly pulls it off. He won Oscars for Best Picture, Best Director, and Best Screenplay.

Like so much of Wilder's work, the older *The Apartment* gets, the more you want of it. Wilder belongs not in your cellar like a fine wine but on your DVD shelf. His sense of timing and pacing is a constant source of wonderment and delight.

EXTRAS

The only extra is an educational lesson in the original trailer in which you can see what you would be seeing if the film had not been restored.

Apocalypse Now Redux

CAST: Martin Sheen, Marlon Brando, Robert Duvall, Frederic
      Forrest, Dennis Hopper, Aurore Clement, Laurence Fishburne,
      Albert Hall, Harrison Ford
DIRECTOR: Francis Ford Coppola
SCREENWRITERS: Francis Ford Coppola and John Milius
RELEASED: 2001 (202 minutes)
RATED: R

Francis Ford Coppola couldn't let go of *Acocalypse Now* in much the same way that LBJ couldn't get out of Vietnam.

Because of that fact, we have *Apocalypse Now Redux*. The flaws in the original 1979 release remain, but seeing the *Redux* version is a reminder that this is one of the most important films ever made. Within the war genre, it is at the very top. If you doubt that, watch the latest entries on the battlefield, from *Pearl Harbor* to *Saving Private Ryan*. *Apocalypse Now* is the war film that refuses to take hostages. It is, and undoubtedly will remain, the definitive Vietnam film.

Vincent Canby's original review, which appeared in the *New York Times* on August 15, 1979, compared the film to David Lean's *The Bridge on the River Kwai*. To produce these films was to mount a war of one's own. Canby said: "Both productions were themselves military campaigns to subdue the hostile landscapes in which they were made. *Kwai* was shot in Ceylon; *Apocalypse Now* in the Philippines, which became, for Mr. Coppola, his Vietnam, swallowing men, money and equipment as voraciously as any enemy."

Coppola took Joseph Conrad's novel *Heart of Darkness* and moved the setting and its crazed Colonel Kurtz from Africa to Vietnam. The literary conceit itself is a daring risk. To some extent, the movie is flawed by the Conrad overlay, but it is also ennobled by the conceptual and artistic links to the novel. Ideally, watching *Redux* should be paired with a viewing of the stunning 1991 documentary *Hearts of Darkness*, which is the story behind the movie. It was conceived and coproduced by Coppola's wife, Eleanor. She had kept extensive notes and journals, realizing *Apocalypse* would have a singular place in film history. (Unfortunately, Coppola didn't choose to include the documentary as a feature on either DVD release.)

Conrad's Kurtz, while hardly benign, is not the same character as Coppola's Kurtz, played by Marlon Brando. Brando's Kurtz has gone mad, with the special madness invoked by the Vietnam War, and has created his own kingdom in Cambodia. In an insane situation, the only sane response might be insanity. That is part of Coppola's theme, and perhaps why he was so committed to using Kurtz as a vehicle to tell the story of what had become of the American vision for a "free" and "democratic" Southeast Asia. Martin Sheen, who now serves as our Wednesday-night television president residing in the *West Wing*, is Captain Willard, who must go on the river to find and assassinate the renegade Kurtz. It is on Willard's journey (as it was for Marlow in *Heart of Darkness*) that the beginnings of moral consciousness develop. Along the way, Willard sees what ravages have come because of U.S. involvement in this region of the world.

Even after twenty years, for many viewers, Robert Duvall's performance remains freshly imprinted. As Kilgore, he is the other face of war's insanity as he leads a chopper attack in order to find a surfing beach and engages in other unspeakable atrocities with a spirit that could be described accurately as carefree and mindless. Children are wiped out with their families. It doesn't feel like a depiction of war, it feels like actual war. What keeps you from turning away in total disgust is the introspection of Willard and the ghastly surprises he encounters as he goes forward. The film has a surreal quality but at the same time awakens you to what this war was about, which was confusion and gore. Dennis Hopper portrays a drugged-out news photographer who has fallen under the spell of Kurtz. He serves as an eerie epilogue to Willard's journey and to the damage the war brought to our national ethos.

EXTRAS

Vietnam is history, but its story is a recurring nightmare in our minds and souls. Coppola has referred to *Apocalypse* as his "personal Vietnam." It wasn't finished for him. *Apoca-*

lypse Now Redux is the attempt to end his inner war and to put his creative demons to rest. *Redux* is a full forty-nine minutes longer than the 1979 release (that's a lot of footage). Much of it centers on a visit of Sheen and his men to a French plantation house, somehow mysteriously surviving in the midst of the war. It's not critical to the movement of the film or its impact, but it was terribly important to Coppola to restore that deleted segment. We honor his decision and feel that it is *Apocalypse Now Redux* that should be on your shelf. It's Coppola's last word; it should be seen in the same light as an author's revised edition of a classic book. It is the river journey, however, that continues to be the primary text of the film. That journey is reason enough for the film's position at the pinnacle of cinematic achievement. The rest of *Apocalypse* serves as a series of footnotes, some more helpful and illuminating than others.

The other restored footage is not as significant and doesn't bear much comment. The real reason to own *Redux* is that the transfer to this generation of DVD is breathtaking. The sound is now more ear-shattering than before. Everyone talks about the helicopters, but you won't believe it until they enter your house. Coppola and his editor, Walter Murch, began again in the editing room. It wasn't a splice-and-add operation; it was a completely fresh look with decisions made and remade.

Redux does not have a full director's commentary this time around, either. Coppola does share his feelings in a few scenes and attempts to put to rest the rumors of an alternative ending. "War and rumors of war" will attend this film for all time; the story of the making of the film is as much a part of artistic legacy as the end product. But that isn't what matters. This seminal work is now available in a technically perfect version, and that's what matters.

Apollo 13

CAST: Tom Hanks, Bill Paxton, Kevin Bacon, Gary Sinise, Ed Harris,
  Kathleen Quinlan, Jean Speegle Howard, Tracy Reiner
DIRECTOR: Ron Howard
SCREENWRITERS: William Broyles, Jr., and Al Reinert (based on
  the book *Lost Moon* by Jim Lovell and Jeffrey Kluger)
RELEASED: 1995 (140 minutes)
RATED: PG

Ron Howard's film is about the almost tragic mission of
Apollo 13. The nation, indeed the whole world, held its
breath while the spacecraft *Odyssey* struggled to come
home. The film begins in 1969 with the walk on the moon.
Jim Lovell (Tom Hanks), along with his wife, Marilyn
(Kathleen Quinlan), and fellow astronauts Fred Haise (Bill
Paxton), Ken Mattingly (Gary Sinise), and Jack Swigert
(Kevin Bacon), have gathered to watch the momentous
event. The space program is very new, its significance still
exciting and controversial. In the opening sequences, you
experience again the first thrills we all had at the audacity
and glory of it all. For those who weren't yet born or were
too young at the time to remember the 1969 lunar landing,
the film does a wonderful, realistic job of allowing viewers
to experience that time in history.

Shortly after the moon landing, astronaut Lovell is no-
tified that he and his crew have been bumped up to Apollo
13, another lunar mission. Lovell, who has already flown
around the moon several times, is overjoyed. His wife, on
the other hand, feels guarded in her enthusiasm. She is
frightened, having experienced three previous space mis-
sions, and is not fond of the number 13.

With launch only two days away, astronaut Mattingly is
removed from the team because of an exposure to measles.

Swigert from the backup crew replaces him. Swigert, not expecting to be able to go, feels that he is the luckiest man alive. Devastated by the change, Mattingly sees a lifelong dream evaporate before his eyes.

On the thirteenth of April, at 13:13 hours, Apollo 13 blasts off. Shortly after breaking from its initial orbit, the now-dreaded line is spoken: "Houston, we have a problem." What turns out to be a faulty wire in one of the oxygen tanks causes an explosion in the spacecraft that debilitates almost all of its systems. As if on a sinking ship, the crew of Apollo 13 struggle to stay afloat. They are in outer space in a free fall. Oxygen is being lost at an alarming rate. The entire craft has to be shut down in a daring attempt to get the astronauts back to Earth alive.

In Houston, flight director Gene Kranz (Ed Harris) struggles to maintain focus and morale among his crew and "work the problem." They work around the clock figuring out how to create a new air filter, how to save power. They have to place Apollo 13 in a flight pattern that will bring it back to Earth without guidance systems. (Watching the scientists work with slide rulers and prehistoric computers makes the movie even more terrifying.)

Mattingly, at Houston, works the flight simulator to develop a reentry plan. It is here that Howard's attention to detail is most evident. The intensity is palpable as we watch the crew on board read through procedure manuals, transmit data back and forth to Houston and struggle to find the problem and fix it. We watch Marilyn Lovell valiantly struggle to stay calm for her family, while listening to increasingly upsetting news broadcasts.

The cast is uniformly spectacular. The phenomenal Harris portrays Kranz with a clear respect for the real-life flight director. Hanks as Lovell is Hanks at his ultimate. (Apparently, Lovell felt Hanks was the ultimate Lovell, which is what really matters.) Paxton, Bacon, and Sinise all bring strong characterizations to their roles. Quinlan underplays her part in a manner that makes her role as a distressed but determined wife of an astronaut more believable.

Howard collaborated with Jim Lovell in making this film. He researched old documentary footage and followed every detail of the story, from the design of Houston Control and the Lovell house to the launching of Apollo 13 to the floating tape recorder. The film could not have attained its degree of authenticity without the cooperation and assistance of NASA, which allowed Howard and his crew to use the KC-135 antigravity jet. By performing 612 parabolas over the Gulf of Mexico, they were able to film the movie in a real antigravity environment.

Howard has gone forward in his career. There are strange but telling similarities in the attention to detail in his magnificent portrayal of mental illness in the story of John Nash, *A Beautiful Mind,* and his precise representation of the crisis on the space mission, *Apollo 13.*

EXTRAS

A one-hour documentary on the making of the film includes cast and director interviews, along with Jim Lovell, Gene Kranz, and many of the Houston Flight Control team members. You also get original footage from the Apollo 13 mission, along with old interviews and a clip from Johnny Carson's *Tonight* show. There are two commentary options: one with director Howard and the other with Lovell and his wife. Howard talks about the making of the film and the difficulties encountered in production. He is amusing as he talks offhandedly of the great fun they all had together. The Lovells share their admiration for the film and how representative it is of the actual events. Lovell adds more information about the dramatic events that occurred during the mission.

Editing our manuscript for publication, we often pushed late into the night to proofread and polish. On the January 31, 2003, at just after midnight, we made our last changes to this review. The last words we wrote appear above. On the morning of Februrary 1, 2003, we awoke, along with the world, to the tragic news of the loss of the shuttle *Columbia* and its seven crew members. It is a surreal reminder of the magnitude of the dangers astronauts face each time they undertake a mission.

The Apostle

CAST: Robert Duvall, Farrah Fawcett, Billy Bob Thornton, June
  Carter Cash, Miranda Richardson, Todd Allen, John Beasley
DIRECTOR: Robert Duvall
SCREENWRITER: Robert Duvall
RELEASED: 1997 (133 minutes)
RATED: R

Redemption isn't a word you usually fling around in movie reviews, but that's the notion at the core of this fine film. Bringing the project to fruition became Robert Duvall's personal quest, and he underwrote a big chunk of the budget himself. *The Apostle* charts the spiritual and very human journey of Euliss Sonny Dewey, Southern preacher and one complex critter.

Don't mistake this for a revision of *Elmer Gantry*. Duvall's character has demons, but they are as real as the character he portrays. The passion in Sonny's soul drives the plot. Whether you come from this religious tradition or none at all, you can't help but be pulled into the story. At times despondent, at others euphoric, Sonny never wavers from his personal relationship with God. He often screams at God, not unlike a Hebraic prophet. (God doesn't answer, at least not that we can hear.) Marital betrayals, a bad temper, and the law on his heels notwithstanding, Sonny stays on his path.

He moves from place to place, holding revivals and saving souls. Yet you sense that it is his own soul he is hoping to save as much as the congregants'. Sonny finally puts down roots in a small Louisiana backwater town and is reborn as "The Apostle E.F." He becomes the head of a small black church by making a deal with its retired preacher. The old preacher is too wise to mistake Sonny for a saint, but he sees into the soul of an imperfect man who has the gift of spiritual rhetoric and the blessing of a deep belief. E.F. is redeemed but not in the way you might expect.

This is a must-own for all Duvall lovers. The scenes with Miranda Richardson as a new love interest are added testimony to the brilliance of Duvall's direction. It's a likely path to Duvall conversion if you're not already there. It's a double journey, the one on the screen and the one that led Duvall down road after road in his determination to make the film. Film historian David Thompson called it "one of the events of the decade."

EXTRAS

As director, writer, star, and banker, it's not surprising that Duvall has a great deal he wants to say in the audio commentary. The extras in the interior church scenes were residents of the rural communities where the film was photographed. Duvall seems to remember where each was found and how he put each into the film. He has great respect for rural preachers and refused to make a film that was condescending. He confesses that his charismatic preaching scenes came directly from the sermons of actual preachers.

"The Journey of the Apostle" is a thirty-minute mini-documentary that provides excellent behind-the-scenes footage. This feature is somewhat redundant, however, after Duvall's commentary, which is by far the best extra here.

Country singer Steven Curtis Chapman has his own featurette (which lasts less than five minutes). We weren't aware of the musical contribution of Chapman, engrossed as we were with the preaching. Nonetheless, it's a nice touch.

As Good As It Gets

CAST: Jack Nicholson, Helen Hunt, Greg Kinnear, Cuba Gooding, Jr., Shirley Knight
DIRECTOR: James L. Brooks
SCREENWRITERS: Mark Andrus and James L. Brooks
RELEASED: 1997 (138 minutes)
RATED: PG-13

Melvin Udall is a complete mess. He's hateful, aggressive, cruel, and trapped inside a disorder known as obsessive-compulsive. Mostly, he's a mess in the way that only Jack Nicholson could be a mess. By this we mean he's less text-book obsessive-compulsive and more purely bad-boy Jack. Yet it is convincing, if at times overplayed. Obsessive-compulsive disorder can be a disabling disease in its most extreme manifestations. While depression can be romanticized, especially in literature and films, nothing about obsessive-compulsive disorder is romantic. It's annoying, enraging, and confusing. Nicholson does well with the enraging and annoying part. It's to his credit that he takes us deep enough into Melvin's character that our sympathy begins to build for his plight. In the beginning, however, it's rough going. He insults everyone; he's a racist, a homophobe, and a misogynist. Having found his niche as a romance novel writer, he's also very wealthy.

As a novelist, Udall has many fans, but he doesn't want them. In fact, he hates them. During a visit to his publisher, he has the opportunity to express himself fully to one of them. He rarely leaves the apartment, except for his habitual meals at a particular restaurant, the only one he will patronize. He takes his own plastic utensils (for fear of germs) and proceeds to antagonize everyone there. There's only one waitress with the patience to deal with him, and she's the only one he will allow to wait on him. She's the harried, somewhat saintly Carol Connelly, played by Helen Hunt. Carol's life hasn't been a romance novel; she probably doesn't have the time to read the pulp Melvin turns out. She's a single mom with a very sick kid. Hunt's performance is terrific.

One day, Melvin goes too far with Carol, as he eventually does with everyone. She refuses to serve him ever again. This presents a crisis for Melvin, who can manage only one restaurant, one waitress. At first, one assumes his contrition is based solely on his own needs, but we begin to rethink his monstrous conduct when he finds a doctor for Carol's asthmatic son and pays for the boy's treatments.

The rest is pretty standard romance comedy, with politically correct subplots. Melvin throws a neighbor's dog down the trash chute, but he ends up taking care of the dog after its owner, Simon, a gay artist (Greg Kinnear), is beaten badly by one of his model-subjects. Cuba Gooding, Jr., plays the artist's agent who just about mops the floor with Melvin in a scene that's too exaggerated to be as funny as it should be. How it happens that Carol and Melvin fall in love is pretty much a mystery, which keeps the action going. The plot doesn't make all that much sense.

There are great sight gags; the most amusing is Melvin's training of the dog. (We won't spoil that surprise if you didn't see this in the theater.) What makes the film memorable is the talking. Remember that stuff called dialogue? What drives this film isn't just the star power but the lines the stars are given. The ever-glorious Shirley Knight plays Carol's mother, who brings common sense and rationality to her daughter's otherwise impossible relationship. Kinnear's portrayal of a gay man afraid to tell his family about his sexual orientation is full of tenderness and humor. The car ride to the moment of truth with Hunt, Nicholson, and Kinnear is the most cohesive part of the plot.

Not everyone loved this movie, but that didn't stop the Academy from rewarding the effort with nominations and awards. We forgive it its sins and transgressions because there's so much terrific dialogue and because the acting is first-rate. Nicholson won the Oscar for Best Actor, and Helen Hunt was Best Actress. Come to *As Good As It Gets* with the belief that love happens and that everybody deserves acceptance. There's enough going on to make you enjoy watching more than once.

EXTRAS

The commentary track features director James Brooks, Nicholson, and Hunt, as well as Kinnear and other production members. It's more entertaining than informative, although the secret to why the dialogue worked so well is revealed. In places, Nicholson is screamingly funny. Stay on this until the very end, and you're in for a purely Jack remark. There's a French-language option for the film itself.

Babette's Feast

CAST: Stephane Audran, Birgitte Federspiel, Bodil Kjer, Vibeke
    Hastrup, Hanne Stensgard, Jarl Kulle, Gudmar Wivesson, Jean-
    Philippe Lafont, Bibi Andersson, Pouel Kern, Asta Esper Hagen,
    Thomas Antoni, Ghita Norby (narrator)
DIRECTOR: Gabriel Axel
SCREENWRITER: Gabriel Axel (adapted from the short story by
    Isak Dinesen)
RELEASED: 1987 (102 minutes)
RATED: Not rated

Winning the Oscar for Best Foreign Film, *Babette's Feast* was
a foodie's delight. It's still our favorite food movie, although
A Chef in Love would be next if it were on DVD. *Babette's
Feast* isn't just a film about food as an art form; it's about
ways of loving, ways of giving, and ways of letting go.

The movie is based on a short story by Isak Dinesen.
This time, she mines her homeland, not her adopted
Africa. The setting is a dreary and faraway part of Denmark
called Jutland. It's a tiny fishing village inhabited by an odd
sect of Protestants who are joyless and extremely pious.
Two older unmarried sisters carry on in the tradition of
their father, who was the minister who founded the sect.
Their total obedience to his wishes has cost them the
chance to have different lives. Each had a love. Martine's
was a handsome military officer. Filippa fell in love with a
French opera star she met while he was on a holiday in Jutland. It is Filippa's unfulfilled love that forms the vehicle for
the story (when the aging Frenchman sends a waif to the
cottage door).

You would really need a place to hide to want to come
to Jutland. Babette arrives during a winter blast, carrying a
letter. She is played by the luminous Stephane Audran. The

letter is from Filippa's old beau. He simply asks that the sisters allow Babette to stay with them because she has lost both her husband and her son in the Paris commune uprising. The sisters don't have money, but they do have a safe haven to offer. Babette offers to cook and clean for them. She keeps her distance and her dignity.

The story has a floating mystery to it. You're not sure where it's really going. There's a lot of subtitle reading to do, because there's a lot of conversation. Please don't choose the English-language version; it absolutely destroys the quality of this film.

After many years in their company, Babette has a plan of some sort, and commodities that have never before been to Jutland begin to arrive by boat. The feast is not just about the meal; it is about the transforming power of giving without expecting anything at all in return. How Babette, the unpaid cook, comes to be able to prepare the meal is a surprise we refuse to spoil for those who don't know.

EXTRAS

If you own or rented the original Orion video of the film, you might not think it's worth your time to get the DVD. But MGM's DVD is a pleasure to watch. The color and sensuality of the food are back. (The quality of the video was quite poor.) Although there's dubbed English, French, and Spanish, leave the clicker alone! Stay with it in the original version, which is a combination of Danish and French. If you speak either of those languages, you can remove the English subtitles.

There are no other extras, except the trailer. It doesn't matter. Savor, cherish, keep, and then go out to a wonderful dinner. Or better yet, prepare a version of your own feast, and then watch the DVD. Don't watch this with an empty stomach.

A Beautiful Mind

CAST: Russell Crowe, Ed Harris, Jennifer Connelly, Paul Bettany,
     Christopher Plummer, Judd Hirsch
DIRECTOR: Ron Howard
SCREENWRITER: Akiva Goldsman (based on the book by Sylvia
     Nasar)
RELEASED: 2001 (129 minutes)
RATED: PG-13

A Beautiful Mind is the fascinating journey of Professor
John Nash, Nobel Laureate and survivor of schizophrenia.
His victory over the disease is as laudable as his achieve-
ments in mathematics. It's the story of genius and madness,
a chronicle of the power of hope and the determination of
love against all odds.

At the darkest moment, Alicia Nash, played by Jennifer
Connelly, says, "I need to believe that something extraordinary
is possible." That's what guided Ron Howard and producer
Brian Grazer to make a film about what isn't understood and
can't be seen. Unlike other films about mental illness, this one
is made from the point of view of the afflicted person. Russell
Crowe doesn't simply play a role, he becomes John Nash.
Connelly is also transformed into the heroic Alicia.

Through Nash's eyes, we see the seduction and betrayal
of this tragic disease. Few actors can communicate with
only a glance or a twitch as much feeling and information
as Crowe. Nash's ideas seduce his brain to take breathtaking
leaps into the then-unknown world of game theory. Later,
this same engine of a mind, in partnership with the power
of full-blown schizophrenia, betrays Nash. We meet very
real hallucinatory characters. When the psychiatrist, played
by Christopher Plummer, dismantles Nash's delusional
world, viewers are reluctant to accept the truth.

The delusional world is made believable by the cinematic alchemy of Howard and his actors. You root for Nash's sanity because so much of it seems plausible. Even when clues are given, viewers don't pick up on them. Distinguishing the real from the imaginary is precisely the dilemma of the person in the grip of schizophrenia. When the disease chooses a genius as its host, it's particularly complex. One of the most evocative scenes in the film is with Plummer and Crowe. Plummer explains to a weakened Crowe that he can't reason his way out of the illness because his mind is the problem. Unbowed, Crowe says, "I can work it out." The delusional reality in which he's trapped has become a mathematical problem; he'll find the solution. That one scene is as heartbreaking and life-affirming as any.

Howard adds tension by shooting many of the most terrifying delusional scenes in film-noir style. Nash became very ill during the paranoid cold war era. Akiva Goldsman's script captures the period and uses it as a backdrop to complement, rather than to contrast, Nash's decline. At times, the film is a spy thriller; at others, a tender love story. Small moments of cinematic perfection should not be overlooked. In total anguish, Alicia smashes a bathroom mirror. The next morning, Nash carries out the shattered glass in a box, and the camera catches his reflection on the shards. It's rare to say a film is flawless; this is one time when the word truly applies.

EXTRAS

Disc One contains two features worth viewing. The commentary by Howard is rewarding and meaningful to the content of the film in a way not often seen. Howard made the audio track less than two months after the film was released.

* * *

Don't miss the deleted scenes for a fuller understanding of the particular directorial talents of Howard.

On Disc Two, watch "Meeting John Nash," not expecting to understand game theory but because, as Howard says, "it makes clear the miracle of Nash's recovery."

"The Process of Age Progression" is a show-and-tell with makeup wizard Greg Cannom. Crowe and Connelly aged about forty-five years during the film's progression. You'll actually see how the facial appliances were crafted.

"Creation of Special Effects" is superb. Our favorites are the baby in the bathtub and the pigeons.

"The Development of the Screenplay" is the best of Goldsman and better than his audio commentary on Disc One. Goldsman gives much deserved credit to the original book's author, Sylvia Nasar.

"A Beautiful Partnership" is an unexpectedly delightful conversation between director and producer. The film began because of Grazer's love of the Nasar book.

The "Bonus" option yields a hidden gem: composer James Horner on his original score and selection of Charlotte Church as the vocalist. Horner summarizes the majesty of the film when he says he felt Nash's mind was like a fast-changing weather system.

Being There

CAST: Peter Sellers, Shirley MacLaine, Melvyn Douglas, Jack
    Warden, Ruth Attaway
DIRECTOR: Hal Ashby
SCREENWRITER: Jerzy Kosinksi (from his novel)
RELEASED: 1979 (130 minutes)
RATED: PG

Chance (the obvious pun on his name becomes a bit arch) spends his entire life doing two things: watching television and caring for the garden of a rich, eccentric man. He has no interaction with the outside world. You are tempted to ask: Did he crawl from under a rock at birth? You forgive the plot's sloppy inattention to those details because of Peter Sellers. This is the film Sellers should be remembered for but probably won't be. It's the last film he made before he died, and he got an Oscar nomination for his role as Chance the gardener. Melvyn Douglas won for his supporting role as a gullible millionaire who takes a liking to him and befriends him, believing he is something other than what he is.

Hal Ashby directed this film with a light touch that enabled it to say things of a much deeper nature than later films that have attempted similar subject matter. The subject is just how ready we are to believe in someone or something if it looks right or sounds mildly spiritual. We think of *Being There* as the thinking person's *Forrest Gump*. Whereas Gump was also about a simple-minded person, he was celebrated and congratulated in the film in a way that added to the debate about how much we can "dumb down" our population.

Being There is a different take. Chance is suddenly homeless when his boss dies. He is thrown out of the manor house he has known his entire life. But he's dressed well and speaks simply but exceedingly elegantly. Shirley MacLaine, as Eve Rand, bruises him with her automobile and takes him home to her ailing patrician husband, Benjamin Turnbull Rand (Douglas). Somewhere between the collision and the entrance to her home, Chance the gardener, as Sellers introduces himself, is misheard and becomes Chauncey Gardner. Now his name matches his suits, and you're off on a wonderful satiric adventure.

When he wasn't gardening for his previous employer Chance watched endless hours of television. Those two experiences comprise all that he is. Chance is a character without character, something just this side of a moron who has spent more than fifty years inside one house and its garden. Once he's kicked out, he doesn't have a clue about what to do in the real world. In a scene where he is hassled by street toughs, he points a remote control at them. He believes he can just click them off his personal life screen.

His "lucky" accident with Mrs. Rand sends him into an increasingly surreal existence, where he meets powerful people, including the president of the United States. He doesn't say much, but those in power transfer to him wisdom and an almost divine presence. He becomes all things to all people.

The film is still very funny. More than ever, it has something important to say about the deadening effects of television and some forms of popular culture. It's more of a challenge to media-driven news than it was intended to be at the time it was made, in the prehistoric world before we had all news all the time. The last scene of the film is surrounded by much conjecture. Just what is he doing out there on the water? Is it a joke? Is it a metaphor? Are we to believe Chance is a supernatural being? It's been debated for almost twenty-five years. There are far more interesting things in the film to discuss, but you can vote about its meaning, if you like.

EXTRAS

The supplements here are skimpy, but this DVD is one you'll want in your collection in spite of this flaw. There's a large scene selection menu as well as a theatrical trailer, the usual European subtitles, and standard cast profiles.

Best in Show

CAST: Christopher Guest, Eugene Levy, Jennifer Coolidge, John
  Michael Higgins, Michael Hitchcock, Jane Lynch, Michael
  McKean, Catherine O'Hara, Parker Posey, Fred Willard
DIRECTOR: Christopher Guest
SCREENWRITERS: Christopher Guest and Eugene Levy
RELEASED: 2000 (90 minutes)
RATED: PG-13

Best in Show is a mockumentary, a wildly funny technique
perfected by Christopher Guest with his team of improvisational actors. This sophisticated send-up focuses on dog
shows. Using the real Westminster show as its model, this
"dogumentary" portrays the fictional Mayflower Dog
Show. Dog owners from all over the country converge,
united only by their obsession with their canines, and their
determination to win.

Guest previously teamed with Eugene Levy (see below),
but this is their finest work to date. Guest's credits include
NBC's *Saturday Night Live* and *This Is Spinal Tap*. No dog's
dignity was injured during the making of the movie. It's a
tougher call with regard to the humans. However, with artful improvisational work, the actors manage not to cross
the line into ridicule that is overly cruel.

First, a distressed Parker Posey is in her shrink's office
listening to her hostile husband. The camera pans to Beatrice, a Weimaraner, sprawled out on a miniature Freudian
couch. It gets better. Wait for the doggie bee-toy scene. Jennifer Coolidge as Sheri Ann Cabot and Jane Lynch as
Christy Cummings provide sidesplitting scenes, as owner
and trainer.

Everything goes wrong for Cookie and Jerry (Catherine
O'Hara and Levy), but they win your heart as their dog,

Winky, has won theirs. Stefan and Scott are an urban gay couple, played by Michael McKean and John Michael Higgins, whose banter proves irresistible, especially in the hotel scenes.

The movie belongs to Harlan Pepper (Guest) and his bloodhound, Hubert. When the two of them take to the road, laughter might overtake you. Be prepared for the "nut" sequence, or you might require emergency oxygen. Fred Willard is flawless as a moronic master of ceremonies.

This movie is less about dog shows than about humans and their dreams, however misplaced or distorted. It's about the pursuit of the gold ring or the chocolate dog biscuit.

EXTRAS

Another movie is wrapped up in seventeen deleted scenes. We suggest you group them by character, starting with Harlan Pepper (1, 4, 7, 12, 15). Number 12 is the best— Harlan driving and singing a tune called "Turtle Woman." Stefan and Scott are strong enough characters to base a film on, so select 2, 8, 13, and 14. Other scenes are amusing, but these are gems. Guest and Levy's commentary is uncensored and fairly goofy. It's less a commentary, and more a performance. We learn Guest really did fall in love with Hubert the hound and tried to adopt him. Guest and Levy explain that because of the improvised script, the actors took classes with professional dog handlers.

A filmography is available by clicking the ribbon next to cast names printed in yellow.

Big Deal on Madonna Street

CAST: Vittorio Gassman, Marcello Mastroianni, Toto, Renato
    Salvatori, Carla Gravina, Rossana Rory, Tiberio Murgia
DIRECTOR: Mario Monicelli
SCREENWRITERS: Suso Cecchi d'Amico, Agenore Incrocci, Furio
    Scarpelli, and Mario Monicelli
RELEASED: 1958 (91 minutes)
RATED: Not rated

Here's an evening you'll want to organize. Invite some
friends over who still have their funny bones, and watch *Rififi* followed by *Big Deal on Madonna Street*. If you aren't
rolling and scratching and gasping for air by the end, there
is little hope for you.

Big Deal on Madonna Street is an unabashed Italian parody of *Rififi*. American director Jules Dassin helmed and
coauthored that suspenseful 1956 French robbery yarn
about a heist in a swanky Parisian jewelry shop. Dassin was
working in Europe at the time because he was blacklisted in
his native America. He later married Greek actress Melina
Mercouri and briefly made her an international star playing
a prostitute with a refined sense of humor in *Never On Sunday*. Dassin also has a major on-camera role in *Rififi*, portraying Cesar, using the phony name of Perlo Vita.

This enduring nail-biter boasts one of the most taut
robbery sequences in the history of film. After the closing
credits, press the "play" button on your DVD of *Big Deal*.

Film buffs everywhere correctly think this is one of the
funniest movies ever made. It's an art film with subtitles
and a cult following; that's hard to beat. A ridiculous group
of characters have decided they can pull off the perfect
heist. Only one problem exists. Not one of them can think
his or her way out of the proverbial paper bag. It's a spoof

of a caper gone wrong. Whatever you want to call it—slap-stick, vaudeville, or delicious Italian comedy—it's irresistible.

Marcello Mastroianni is adorably inept as Tiberio, a temporarily single father. His wife is in jail. Peppe, played by another great Italian star, Vittorio Gassman, is a former fighter with an eye for the ladies instead of the safe that needs to be cracked. Ferribotte, played by Tiberio Murgia, has a hot temper and is not glued down all the way; he won't let his sister outside. There's more, but you get the picture.

It's not a movie about wanna-be criminals. It's about Murphy's Law and how everything can go wrong all at once. The acting is superb, the mishaps priceless.

EXTRAS

There really aren't any extras, except an original trailer, but thank the muses and the distributor that it's on DVD at all. If, like most of us, you've seen this on television (with inter-ruptions) or on very grainy video, the DVD is a wonderful new way to enjoy a glorious classic comedy.

The Big Sleep

CAST: Humphrey Bogart, Lauren Bacall, Martha Vickers, John
    Ridgely, Dorothy Malone, Elisha Cook, Jr., Charles Waldron
DIRECTOR: Howard Hawks
SCREENWRITERS: William Faulkner, Leigh Brackett, and Jules
    Furthman
RELEASED: 1946 (114 minutes)
RATED: Not rated

There was Tracy and Hepburn, and there was Bogie and Bacall. Both couples had real-life romances that added an extra dimension to their on-screen fictional relationships. We just got a lot more of Tracy and Hepburn than we did of Bogie and Bacall because Bogie left us all too soon. But before he did, he and Bacall left a cinematic history of one of the most electric love affairs to hit the big screen. Their relationship on screen was a tango to the waltz of Tracy and Hepburn. Both couples graciously left us some lovely duets to watch for all time.

Sadly, some Bogie and Bacall films that ought to be on DVD are not yet. Happily, *The Big Sleep* is, and so is *Key Largo*.

Before Roman Polanski directed Jack Nicholson and Faye Dunaway in *Chinatown,* Howard Hawks directed Humphrey Bogart and Lauren Bacall in the adaptation of Raymond Chandler's novel. (We recommend viewing this film **before** *Chinatown* if you're doing a noir sort of night.)

Bogie stars as Chandler's tough but soft-around-the-edges gumshoe, Philip Marlowe. He moves through a tawdry universe of violence and corruption in his effort to unravel an impossibly complicated series of goings-on. There are more than the requisite murders, of course, but the real action is with two sisters, Carmen and Vivian. Martha Vickers is Carmen, and a sultry Bacall plays Vivian. Carmen's got a thing about sex and sucks her thumb to boot. Vivian is a society type who has gotten a bit frayed around the edges. There's blackmail and betrayals and just about everything else.

Although William Faulkner had more than his share of troubles in Hollywood, he was one of our greatest novelists. However, he just couldn't get this screenplay written. Help was brought in with the addition of writers Leigh Brackett and Jules Furthman. It didn't much help. It might be one of Hollywood's most convoluted scripts. Midway through the production, everyone involved realized that nobody knew who had committed one of the murders. Chandler reportedly said he didn't know, either. Who cares? It doesn't matter.

You might be interested to know that it mattered a great deal to *New York Times* critic Bosley Crowther, who reviewed the movie in 1946. He didn't like it, he didn't get it, and Bacall didn't turn him on: "Miss Bacall is a dangerous-looking female, but she hasn't learned to act."

EXTRAS

Here's what you get in the way of supplements. The disc contains both the 116-minute 1944 version and the 1946 theatrical version. If you weren't around in 1946, you might not know what the fuss is about. The fuss is about the intensity of the Bacall-Bogart love affair. The fireworks made this film worth watching and continue to do so. Studio boss Jack Warner knew what he was sitting on and wanted to capitalize on the fire between his stars. That's why there are two versions.

Be sure to watch a short but highly informative mini-documentary, "The Big Sleep Comparisons." Robert Gitt, of the UCLA School of Film and Television, tells the story of the behind-the-scenes drama. Bacall's agent had to get involved to force Warner to release the film.

A cautionary word: There's another *Big Sleep* out there that must be avoided at any cost. It's a remake done in 1977 and produced in Great Britain. It stars Robert Mitchum, Sarah Miles, Joan Collins, and James Stewart. Michael Winner directed it, but it's far from a winner. It's not a big sleep, either. It's not a nod, a snore, or a nap but rather a rotten-film-induced coma.

Billy Elliot

CAST: Jamie Bell, Julie Walters, Gary Lewis, Jamie Draven, Jean
  Heywood, Nicole Blackwell, Stuart Wells
DIRECTOR: Stephen Daldry
SCREENWRITER: Lee Hall
RELEASED: 2000 (110 minutes)
RATED: R (unfairly; it's the *f* word, no serious violence)

Before this film passes into history as the one Stephen
Daldry made *before* he made *The Hours,* a few words
should be said on *Billy*'s behalf. Initially seen by some as too
sweet and implausible, it's become a very big hit on DVD.
It was also a box-office success despite the dismissal of
many critics.

It's about a young boy who gets sent off to boxing class,
which he abhors. Across the room in Town Hall, he sees
something he does like. It's ballet class for girls, but Billy
just knows it's right for him. He has many obstacles to
overcome, despite his natural gift for the dance.

He doesn't live in sophisticated London but in a
working-class coal-mining town. Most of the men are on
strike. Both Billy's father and his brother are active in the
strike. His mother has died; Billy's sort of on his own. Dance
transforms him under the tutelage of the not at all motherly
Mrs. Wilkerson, the ballet teacher. She gives Billy his chance.
There are lots of stops and stumbles before he can fly, however. His father doesn't have the money to send his son to
ballet school in London; besides that, there's the horror of it
all within the town's cultural context. The father and brother
are convinced Billy's a sissy (read: gay). Billy isn't, but his dear
friend Michael is. There's a tender cross-dressing sequence
that won't alarm anyone but the very young. There's also a
very delicate scene between Billy and his teacher's daughter.

The movie about a little boy who lives to dance and ultimatley triumphs has become a favorite for girls about the same age as Billy (eleven to twelve years old). The girls obviously see the importance of a broad definition of gender roles. Watch it with a young girl, and see the delight in her eyes. Show it to a young boy in your life, and explain just why it's fine for a boy to dance. Either way, you won't lose.

There's a cameo appearance by Barbara-Leigh Hunt, an extraordinarily gifted veteran British actress we rarely have the opportunity to see on film. She's one of the judges on the panel at the admissions audition. It's her one crucial question that saves the day for Billy. Wait for it, because it's a telling moment and lends some authenticity to the story. The closing scene of Billy onstage as a star is just enough, but not too much, sugar. It's our cup of tea for an entertaining and delightful child-based film. You won't see hints of what Daldry has in store for us with *The Hours*. But what you will see is an accomplished debut film from a director on the move.

EXTRAS

There's a delightful "making of" feature entitled "Breaking Free," which includes some discussion about the inspiration of the story, especially about the coal miners' strike of 1984. This was the worst strike in post–World War II British history. It marked the beginning of the end of the mining industry in England. With interviews from the cast and filmmakers, it's an entertaining behind-the-scenes look at this touching film.

There is also a brief segment of "Production Notes" that reveal something about the original idea of the film and the casting process, specifically the inspired casting of Billy Elliot (Jamie Bell). In addition, there's a short, but well-done theatrical trailer.

A DVD-ROM feature will give you more background information about the story, as well as a photo gallery.

Boogie Nights

CAST: Burt Reynolds, Julianne Moore, Mark Wahlberg, John C.
Reilly, Heather Graham, Don Cheadle, Luis Guzman
DIRECTOR: Paul Thomas Anderson
SCREENWRITER: Paul Thomas Anderson
RELEASED: 1997 (152 minutes)
RATED: R

If you are prepared for a riveting and sober look at the underworld of porn films, *Boogie Nights* is a compelling film.

The setting is the San Fernando Valley in California. This is a locale that director Paul Thomas Anderson returns to in his later film *Magnolia*. Although some think *Magnolia* is a better film, we choose *Boogie Nights*. Burt Reynolds is Jack Horner, a small-time pornographer with an elevated opinion of his importance and his "art." Reynolds's performance is a tour de force and was highly acclaimed at the time of the theatrical release of the movie. Julianne Moore plays the star of his films and also serves as a surrogate mother figure to the assembled crew of actors and technicians. Moore's portyayal of Amber Waves brought her deserved recognition. In this film, she takes the seemingly impossible role of porn star, coke head, and runaway mother and makes her character one we root for and cry over.

Heather Graham is a lost girl who should be on the back of a milk carton but instead never takes her roller skates off. She is known only as "Rollergirl."

Although it is about pornography, there is nothing sen-

sual or erotic about the film. Remember, this is not Hugh
Hefner at the Playboy Mansion; this is the Valley and a
low-budget porn movie production company. It's also
about drugs, especially cocaine addiction.

The action revolves around Horner's discovery of a
young man named Eddie who comes from a family of domestic horror. For him, any ticket out looks like a good option. Horner finds him working as a busboy and
dishwasher in a nightclub and suspects from the lump in
his Levi's that he might have what Horner needs. What
Eddie has is a foot-long penis. He is soon reborn as Dirk
Diggler, porn star.

All this may sound amusing, but it's mostly sad. At
times, it's shocking. The time period is from 1977 to about
1983. In the 1970s, the porn industry flourished in places
like Horner's garage studio because the films were shot
cheaply and packaged quickly for release in porn theaters
across the country. By the mid-1980s, the world was turning to video, and any "artistic" flourishes were simply re-
placed by raw sex acts. It's the end of Horner's empire and
the demise of much of anything for Dirk Diggler.

Part of the appeal of *Boogie Nights* is its format. The
characters are set up as a family. You could say it's the dirty
little family of choice. Losers and the lost cling together
with one thread of connection that makes them believe that
they have something worthy to do and that somebody cares
about them. By the end of the film, any pretense of family
love is gone. All is unveiled, even Dirk Diggler's equipment. As all illusions drop away, Horner's enterprise is seen
for what it always was.

Although *Boogie Nights* is a period movie about the
changes that occurred in pornography as it moved from
theaters to the home, it's still relevant today. Its success lies
in Anderson's ability to condense so much into one film

(even if it runs for 152 minutes) and to work with such an enormous ensemble cast. While *Boogie Nights* surely isn't for everyone and should not be seen by children, it is one of the major film accomplishments of the 1990s.

EXTRAS

There are a couple of DVD releases of *Boogie Nights* available. You should make your choice depending on your desire for supplements. The earlier release (1998) is of excellent quality but does not have the array of features contained in the 2000 two-disc release. Both versions offer Anderson's commentary, which is thoughtful and richly peppered with his experiences and information he gathered during the preparation and shooting of the film.

The commentary by the cast sounds like a better party than any of those depicted in the film itself. If you still want more, buy the two-disc set.

In the second disc are some outrageous outtakes, as well as deleted scenes. There's also one hidden treasure. If you're longing to know whether Diggler's equipment was enhanced or not, stay around through the biographies and then to the color bars. After that, you'll have your answer.

Born on the Fourth of July

CAST: Tom Cruise, Willem Dafoe, Kyra Sedgwick, Raymond J. Barry, Caroline Kava, Jerry Levine, Frank Whaley, Josh Evans, Jamie Talisman

DIRECTOR: Oliver Stone

SCREENWRITERS: Oliver Stone and Ron Kovic (based on the book by Ron Kovic)

RELEASED: 1989 (145 minutes)

RATED: R

Born on the Fourth of July is based on the true story of Ron Kovic, whose birthday is indeed July 4. It is hard to rank the many fine films about the war in Southeast Asia, but this is surely one of the most important. Unlike Oliver Stone's fictional recreation of JFK's murder, *Born on the Fourth of July* is Stone at his barest and his most honest. *Platoon* borrowed from Stone's own war experience, but this is Kovic's story, and Stone respects it.

The movie is not about what Americans did to the Vietnamese; it's about what the war did to Americans. Kovic is a standard-issue regular guy. He's blindly patriotic, eager to serve his country, and, like so many others of his generation, he became cannon fodder. Vietnam was fueled from hometowns just like Kovic's. The opening scenes send chills down the spine of anyone of a certain age and childhood experience. The movie follows Kovic's life from high school graduation, to enlistment, to active duty in Vietnam, to the horrific injuries he sustained. His return as a war hero with severe disability (he's completely paralyzed) is his own personal wake-up call. There isn't another film about the atrocities of the war that better portrays the devastating effect it had on the young men who served.

Stone chose Tom Cruise to play Ron Kovic; it remains his most significant role. There's nothing in Cruise's Kovic that isn't portrayed perfectly, from the middle-class kid who didn't ask enough questions to the bitter antiwar activist. By the end, you don't think of Cruise as anyone other than Kovic. The film is an indictment not just of American involvement in Vietnam but also of the overworked Veterans Administration medical system, which simply couldn't cope with so many destroyed lives.

This is a shattering movie. The effect of viewing it has not been diminished in the years since its release. Innumerable scenes are etched in your memory. The scenes at the VA hospital are harrowing. Mrs. Kovic's ridiculous line about not saying the word *penis* in her home when her own son's doesn't function for any purpose is particularly jolting.

The saddest parts of the movie are perhaps those in Mexico, where other disabled veterans hang around drinking, taking drugs, and pretending to have sex with prostitutes. In these segments, we see the work of the extraordinary Willem Dafoe (who was also in *Platoon*). The aimless and hopeless quality of their lives is directed by Stone with both tenderness and righteous rage about what happened to many thousands of young men.

The Oscar for Best Picture in 1989 went to *Driving Miss Daisy*. Stone received the Oscar for Best Director. Cruise lost the Oscar to Daniel Day-Lewis for his role in *My Left Foot*, which is a hard call as Day-Lewis delivered an incredible performance. But maybe it's just possible that we find it easier to deal with deformity than with atrocity.

EXTRAS

Despite multiple releases, the DVD of *Born on the Fourth of July* has yet to receive the technical attention it should. This movie deserves the best, and it hasn't gotten it. However, the soundtrack is in far better shape than in the previous issues.

You will want the latest version, because, at last, there is a commentary track with Stone. That's what "Special Edition" means. What is special about the extras is the opportunity to hear Stone talk about his own experiences and the making of the film. It's one of the few times you aren't bored for one second by the director's audio track.

Bread and Tulips

CAST: Licia Maglietta, Bruno Ganz, Marina Massironi, Giuseppe
    Battiston, Felice Andreasi, Antonio Catania
DIRECTOR: Silvio Soldini
SCREENWRITERS: Doriana Leondeff and Silvio Soldini
RELEASED: 2000 (114 minutes)
RATED: PG-13

Whenever we go to Venice, we take a water taxi from the
airport. When we arrive, there is always a large black-and-
white cat waiting for us. He escorts us through San Marco
and then disappears; he owns the square. He may own
Venice; he may be one of the lions of Venice in domestic
size. "This isn't possible," our friends insist. "The same cat
can't be there each time, when months, and sometimes a
year or two, separate your visits." Despite the many cats of
Venice, we insist that he is there. He is the same cat.

Venice is an illusion that cannot exist. If it's really
dying, it does so with a kind of grace we would all do well
to replicate. If you can believe in the reality of Venice, then
you can believe in the cat who greets us and the possibility
that absolutely anything can happen to you in Venice.

The Italians have given us a fantasy in *Bread and Tulips*
that makes complete sense within the realm of magic that
exists for the asking inside Venice's watery world of wonder,
art, and love.

Rosalba (Licia Maglietta) is about as much of a doormat of a wife as we've encountered. She lives in comfortable
quarters in Pescara, where her sons and her husband enjoy
the life she makes for them. Her family doesn't abuse her as
much as ignore her. She's such an afterthought, they leave
her behind at a roadside restaurant. The tour bus pulls out
before anyone, even her husband, notices she's not on it.

When he does notice, he is furious with her and calls on the cell phone. She picks up a ride in order to catch up with them. Then, without warning, she decides to go to Venice. There, without much money, she finds a nondescript small restaurant to have a meal and is greeted by an even more forlorn-looking waiter, Fernando. Fernando is played by the graceful actor Bruno Ganz, who can make sad and lonely look like a noble calling better than almost any other European actor we know. There's no cook and therefore no possibility of dinner, but Fernando prepares a plate of cold cuts and serves them to Rosalba. We see the shock in her face as she relishes someone serving her for a change.

Rosalba isn't beautiful—she's rather chubby, and her years show—but as she gets further and further away from her husband, she begins to become a beautiful woman. The story turns into more of an escapade when Rosalba decides to stay in Venice. She becomes Fernando's boarder, gets a job in a florist's shop, and finds a true friend in Marina, a "holistic" masseuse. Fernando has troubles and secrets; his noose is always at the ready. Rosalba's husband sends a private investigator to find her, who's actually a plumber. The movie moves between frolic and absurdity with such smoothness that you never stop to say, "This can't be true."

If you can believe in the cat who owns San Marco, you will appreciate the dreamlike vision of happiness that concludes the film. When you choose to be in Venice, illusions are reality.

EXTRAS

None. Please provide your own bread and tulips.

The Bridge on the River Kwai

CAST: Alec Guinness, William Holden, Sessue Hayakawa, Jack Hawkins, James Donald, Andre Morell, Geoffrey Horne, Peter Williams, John Boxer
DIRECTOR: David Lean
SCREENWRITERS: Michael Wilson and Carl Foreman (adapted from the novel by Pierre Boulle)
RELEASED: 1957 (162 minutes)
RATED: PG

The Bridge on the River Kwai is about a crew of British prisoners of war held in Burma. They are ordered by their captors to build a sprawling, strategically important bridge. It's mostly about the efforts of their leader, Colonel Nicholson (Alec Guinness) to maintain his own pride and the pride of his soldiers. For the colonel, it means that they will build a better bridge than the Japanese would build for their own war effort.

This war epic is about relationships under the strain of battle, as much as it is about war itself. The real battle is in the heads of the men who must continue on in their roles as enemies but also find a place to exhibit human honor and dignity. This is a truly memorable World War II film. The visual images alone make it stand out in a class by itself. The film was shot on location in Sri Lanka (then Ceylon).

This is a many-faceted story. Watching *The Bridge on the River Kwai* will provoke a thoughtful discussion among you and your family or friends. You'll find that the sentiments about war resonate with equal impact in today's world.

Sessue Hayakawa plays Colonel Saito, the Japanese martinet in charge of the POWs and in charge of Nicholson. His performance has both subtlety and complexity. William Holden is Major Shears, an American POW who escapes and returns with a demolition commando, Major Warden (Jack Hawkins). Their mission is to destroy the bridge. This film, like a few other great war epics (*Apocalypse Now* comes to mind), illustrates the shifting boundaries of insanity and sanity during combat. "Madness" is what Guinness calls it in the film. There was no madness in David Lean's superb direction. He had a piercing clarity of purpose as he chose to shift the points of view in the story.

In 1957, *Bridge* was awarded the Oscar for Best Picture. The other contenders that year included *Sayonara, 12 Angry Men, Witness for the Prosecution,* and *Peyton Place.* Guinness won for his role as the mad but prideful Colonel Nicholson against Marlon Brando in *Sayonara* as well as his other rival, Charles Laughton, in *Witness for the Prosecution.* You'll learn in the extras, if you didn't already know, that Lean's first choice for the part of Colonel Nicholson was Laughton! Fortunately, Lean was persuaded that Laughton was too portly to be effective in the part. Hayakawa was nominated as Best Supporting Actor, but the Oscar went to Red Buttons in *Sayonara.* Lean won for direction, beating out Joshua Logan for *Sayonara* and Sidney Lumet for *12 Angry Men.*

Pierre Boulle was awarded the Oscar for the screenplay adaptation of his novel. He didn't write it, however, and didn't turn up at the Oscars ceremony. The false reason given was that he spoke only French. The actual screenwriters, Michael Wilson and Carl Foreman, were blacklisted. Their names were not on the original credits. In 1984, the Academy posthumously awarded the Oscars to these talented writers.

The Bridge on the River Kwai is the first of the trilogy of epic films that Lean directed between 1957 and 1970.

(*Lawrence of Arabia* in 1962 and *Doctor Zhivago* in 1970 would follow.) The American Film Institute lists *Bridge* as one of the greatest movies ever made, and they're right.

EXTRAS

In 2000, Columbia/Tristar released the "Limited Edition" of *The Bridge on the River Kwai*. It has plenty of extras to keep you happy, but even if it didn't have anything at all, you should own this epic. The restoration is immaculate. In fact, it is breathtaking. If you've seen this on videocassette, you'll really appreciate the difference.

This edition comes with two discs, as well as a replica of the original souvenir program sold in theaters during the initial release. Remember, this film was an important event in 1957, barely a full decade after the war.

You won't get a director's commentary, of course, as Lean died in 1991; the majority of the leading actors also have left us. An audio commentary by a film scholar is always a difficult choice for production companies to make. The matching of scholar to film isn't an easy task. The comments of some our most distinguished scholars are best read and not heard, in any event. We think they made the right choice not to add an audio commentary to the film.

The feature attraction of the extras is a new documentary on the making of the movie. Norman Spencer, who was long associated with Lean, discusses the movie in a compelling way. You'll hear from Peter Newbrook, one of the cameramen, and Donald Ashton, who was the art director. There are others, as well, who add memories, technical information, and, of course, the ubiquitous Hollywood gossip. At the time, there was considerable jealousy toward Holden, who negotiated a million-dollar contract and a percentage of the take. The Laughton "mistake" is noted with good humor. How the bridge was created and blown up is meticulously discussed. (Come on, Jim Cameron, give us this, with footage, for *Titanic*.) There's some behind-the-scenes footage here, too, but not as much as we wish had been preserved.

A few other goodies consist of photos, stills, posters, and a music-only option.

The older features should be given their due as well. Although they are dated and can't compete with what we know about filmmaking now, don't pass them up. You won't want to miss the opportunity to hear Holden narrate "Rise and Fall of a Jungle Giant."

We're not fans of war games on the computer, but you've got one in the interactive feature if you're set up to do that. It's called "Trivia Sabotage," and it is better than most. The animation is quite good. Additionally, the menus on the DVD itself have been animated very well.

This great film belongs on your shelf by director (Lean) or by genre (war), or by actor (Guinness). Whatever your personal system is, *The Bridge on the River Kwai* must become part of your personal collection.

The Bridges of Madison County

CAST: Clint Eastwood, Meryl Streep, Annie Corley, Victor Slezak, Jim Haynie, Sarah Kathryn Schmitt, Christopher Kroon
DIRECTOR: Clint Eastwood
SCREENWRITERS: Robert James Waller and Richard LaGravenese (based on Waller's novel)
Released: 1995 (135 minutes)
RATED: PG-13

Robert James Waller wrote an enormously successful short novel of the same title as the movie. In certain intellectually chic circles, you couldn't even admit to reading it, let alone liking it. The book was slight, yet it hit on a theme we're all drawn to repeatedly: perfect love might be found but can't always be retained without harming others. The film is larger and more profound than the book. It's on our list of DVDs worth buying because the love story has "legs," but mostly because Clint Eastwood's direction and acting are superb.

Eastwood is a director and actor whose depth and complexity finally have been recognized fully. He's come a long way from his days as the cowboy of choice. He saw something in Waller's novel and bought the rights to it. He cast Meryl Streep as his leading lady, which is about as odd a match for him as the characters in the book were for each other. That's the alchemy of film. The plot revolves around four days in the life of a farm housewife, Francesca (Streep), and her chance encounter with a *National Geographic* photographer, Robert Kincaid (Eastwood). Francesca is an Italian woman who married an honest and good man who is long on work and short on talk. Of course, she's trapped, but the story works because nobody is a victim. People make choices. Their lives usually don't turn out as they might have dreamed they would. This is called real life. But once in a rare time or two, something extraordinary happens to two people. If it's meaningful enough, the memories of even four days might just be enough to get you through the hardest days of the rest of your life.

Francesca isn't moping around looking for love; Kincaid has made his own deal with life as well. In the one case, there is the honesty of a life on the farm; in the other, the excitement of world travel and recognition. Yet both are essentially lonely. There's a building recognition that these two people connect in a way far deeper than a chance encounter. Eastwood's direction is subtle and evokes both the impossibility and the complete rightness of these two coming together.

He wants her to leave her husband and come with him; she won't. You know that, and it's one of the reasons the book was so popular and the movie lasts in your mind. What endures forever is the scene where she grabs the door handle of the car with her husband sitting next to her and has that moment to consider breaking free and breaking up a series of other lives. Kincaid just stands there in the rain looking piercingly and directly at her. Eastwood gets very high marks for being willing to look like a drowned rodent instead of a Hollywood icon. He gets high marks in general for taking this project on and making it something much more than it might have been.

EXTRAS

Although thousands have ventured to the real Madison County to see the place, the house, and all those bridges, the "scene of the crime" feature will save you travel, time, and money.

There's also a Diana Krall music video, which saves you a nightclub tab as well.

Brief Encounter

CAST: Celia Johnson, Trevor Howard, Stanley Holloway, Joyce Carey, Cyril Raymond, Everley Gregg, Dennis Harkin, Margaret Barton

DIRECTOR: David Lean

SCREENWRITERS: David Lean, Noel Coward, and Anthony Havelock-Allan (adapted from Coward's play *Still Life*)

RELEASED: 1946 (86 minutes)

RATED: Not rated

The story is simple and the setting homely. A middle-class woman on a routine shopping excursion encounters a handsome doctor who assists her by removing a piece of coal dust from her eye. They are total strangers; both are married. Most of what happens occurs in an ugly little railroad station in the English countryside. They know their love is doomed in spite of its intensity. They break it off, because they must. The performances of Trevor Howard as the doctor and Celia Johnson as the woman are sublime in the spare, controlled qualities they bring to their screen interpretations. David Lean directed the love scenes as well as any have ever been directed. The canvas of their lives is solidly boring; it's proper and English. In their brief encounter, they transcend their surroundings.

In 1946, Lean could break your heart in precisely eighty-six minutes. By 1965, it would take him 197 minutes to do it in *Zhivago,* and it wouldn't hurt as much. Lean is usually associated with those epic films, *Lawrence of Arabia, The Bridge on the River Kwai,* and, of course, *Doctor Zhivago.* But this lean Lean from 1946 stands as one of the greatest love stories ever filmed.

The casting of Howard and Johnson is part of the magic, but one must always be mindful that the original spark was ignited by the best word magician of them all, Noel Coward.

EXTRAS

This black-and-white beauty has made it to DVD with a transfer that was taken from its original negative. If you've become accustomed to *Brief Encounter* in other formats, you'll be very pleased with how it looks now. If you've never seen this film before, you come to it at the right time.

Bruce Eder is a serious film historian who provides the commentary. He's a bit stiff, but his expansive knowledge makes up for his flat style. He has a number of interesting theories about what Lean was doing in this film, which add up to an enjoyable and highly informative experience. Besides talking about *Brief Encounter*, he shares his thoughts about films of the 1940s in general.

The segment entitled "Restoration Demonstration" is pretty much what we have come to expect with these features. In the case of this film, however, the before-and-after frames look like the scrapbooks in the office of a Beverly Hills plastic surgeon. It's great fun to see.

Butch Cassidy and the Sundance Kid

CAST: Paul Newman, Robert Redford, Katharine Ross, Strother Martin, Henry Jones, Jeff Corey, George Furth, Cloris Leachman, Ted Cassidy, Kenneth Mars, Sam Elliott
DIRECTOR: George Roy Hill
SCREENWRITER: William Goldman
RELEASED: 1969 (111 minutes)
RATED: PG

Butch Cassidy and the Sundance Kid created an archetype for male relationships in American movies. It was an archetype whose perfect obverse was Dustin Hoffman and John Voight in *Midnight Cowboy* (also released in 1969). It was a template that would overlay Robert Redford and Paul Newman's later film, *The Sting*, which was also directed by George Roy Hill and won several more Oscars than *Butch and the Kid* did.

It's an adventure film with romance and comedy. Butch and the Sundance Kid were real characters circa 1901, who, together with Sundance's girlfriend, Etta (Katharine Ross), took off for South America. There's more than a little fictional makeover done to the real-life story of two cheerful bank robbers, but the basic structure is true. It's sheer entertainment. The dialogue by William Goldman is superb and won the Oscar for him. There's extraordinary photography of the American West, hardly a surprise, as the cinematographer was the remarkable Conrad Hall, whose final film was the visually stunning *Road to Perdition* more than thirty years later.

We hadn't seen *Butch Cassidy* for some years and were surprised at the photographic "collage scrapbook." We had forgotten how hauntingly beautiful it is. It depicts the threesome in turn-of-the-century New York and on their way, via steamship, to Bolivia. It's a brief but wonderful interlude in the film.

Interestingly, however, not all of the activities of Butch, the Kid, and Etta still hold up in the twenty-first century. There's a troubling scene where the viewer is set up to believe that Etta is going to be raped. It really doesn't work anymore. It's more than a little misogynistic. And outlaws and crime have far less appeal than they might have in the more innocent days of 1969. But, all in all, watching Butch and the Kid have so much fun together and make so many foolish mistakes is still great viewing. If you really want to pick on something, start with the "blow up the world and everybody in it" action films we have to endure these days. Then you'll come back with a grateful heart to this beloved classic.

EXTRAS

The beginning of our new century was a good time for the studio distributors to release some of our favorite films in special editions that are truly wonderful. Fortunately, this is true for *Butch Cassidy and the Sundance Kid*.

The special edition has an audio commentary that includes not only Hill but Hall as well. The Oscar-winning song "Raindrops Keep Falling on My Head" plays a role in this audio because the lyricist, Hal David, also comments. The music was by Burt Bacharach.

The "making of" documentary is more than worth your time, if for no other reason than the realization that this was the film that started the lifelong friendship between Redford and Newman. It's an original in every definition of the word.

The interview material is from an earlier DVD release but is of better-than-average quality and includes quips from Newman, Redford, Ross, Goldman, and Bacharach. More than anything else, this transfer is wondrous. It will have to tide you over on the Newman-Redford front until *The Sting* is released in a deluxe DVD edition.

Cabaret

CAST: Liza Minnelli, Joel Grey, Michael York, Helmut Griem, Fritz
     Wepper, Marisa Berenson, Elisabeth Neumann-Viertel
DIRECTOR: Bob Fosse
SCREENWRITER: Jay Presson Allen (based on the musical by Joe
     Masteroff; adapted from the play *I Am a Curious Camera* by
     John Van Druten and *Berlin Stories* by Christopher Isherwood)
RELEASED: 1972 (124 minutes)
RATED: PG

Sally Bowles is a decadent young American living in Berlin in the early 1930s who doesn't really understand what's going on around her. She finds it all divine. Bob Fosse's provocative film sets the story of this young nightclub entertainer against the solemn and sobering political backdrop of Hitler's rise to power. Liza Minnelli's captivating portrayal of Sally remains her trademark performance.

Joel Grey won Best Supporting Actor for his role as the emcee of the Kit Kat Klub. He's a sinister and ambiguous presence. In fact, he's a metaphor for Berlin at the time. Michael York, too beautiful for his own good, plays a bisexual who is involved with Minnelli and her German boyfriend. Helmut Griem plays the sophisticated Maximilian von Heune, who isn't as sophisticated about sexuality as he thinks he is. The entire film drips with an uneasy and dark sexuality and with the notion that everything is about to collapse unless you keep on dancing and singing. The film can still produce goose bumps as you watch them all feverishly spinning around. The characters are memorable, and so are the songs by John Kander and Fred Ebb, especially "Cabaret," "Money/Money," and "Mein Herr."

The garish quality of Grey's makeup intensifies the mood of chaos and confusion. The atmosphere is evocative and provocative. The acting and singing are fantastic. It's a piercing film about a dangerous and deadly time. It doesn't sound as if it all should have worked so beautifully in one film, but it surely did. *Cabaret* is essentially a drama with music, not music tied together by a flimsy plot. Fosse's genius was never more apparent.

It's important to note that at the movie's release in 1972, the American public was presumed to be long finished with the musical. But Fosse turned the musical into a wholly new phenomenon with *Cabaret*. The film version of the successful Broadway show remains a classic. Testimony to the endurance of the play is that it had a smash revival in Manhattan in the late 1990s.

Besides Oscars for Grey and Minnelli, the film won for Best Art Direction/Set Decoration, Best Cinematography (Geoffrey Unsworth), Best Director (Fosse), Best Film Editing (David Bretheron), Best Musical Score (Ralph

Burns), and Best Sound (Robert Knudson and David Hild-yard). It was nominated for Best Picture (*The Godfather* won) and for Best Screenplay (adaptation).

EXTRAS

Make sure that you've gotten the special edition that was released for the twenty-fifth anniversary of the film.

It's all on one disc, but there's quite a goodly amount, so don't despair. The documentary is filled with tidbits. There's interesting conversation about the history of the movie and Fosse's steadfast loyalty in bringing the play to the screen. You'll learn some fascinating details about the complexity of weaving Christopher Isherwood's stories into the film and the challenge of getting the intimate look of the club on film. There are really three small documentaries on the disc, including a series of clips by stars and crew called "Kit Kat Klub Memory Gallery" and the "Recreation of an Era," which sounds like more than it ultimately delivers.

An interesting companion film for your library is *Aimee and Jaguar,* which depicts Berlin at the end of the war through the eyes of women.

Casablanca

CAST: Humphrey Bogart, Ingrid Bergman, Paul Henreid, Claude Rains, Conrad Veidt, Sydney Greenstreet, Peter Lorre, Dooley Wilson, S. Z. Sakall, Leonid Kinskey

DIRECTOR: Michael Curtiz

SCREENWRITERS: Julius J. Epstein, Philip G. Epstein, and Howard Koch (adapted from the play *Everybody Goes to Rick's* by Murray Burnett and Joan Alison)

RELEASED: 1942 (102 minutes)

RATED: PG

"They have used Mr. Bogart's personality, so well established in other films, to inject a cold point of tough resistance to evil forces afoot in Europe today. . . . In short, we will say that *Casablanca* is one of the year's most exciting and trenchant films. It certainly won't make Vichy happy—but that's just another point for it."

So wrote *New York Times* film critic Bosley Crowther on November 27, 1942. Of the many things that are constantly repeated about this classic of all classics, it is rarely mentioned that the events it depicts were happening right that minute. It was, in a manner of speaking, shot in real time. It's the love story between Humphrey Bogart and Ingrid Bergman that has captured every generation since its release. Yet when it was made, it was as much a political film as a romance. In retrospect, it was quite a daring topical film to make in 1942.

Now we tend to see it only as a timeless romantic favorite. When the audiences in the theaters at the time watched Bogart give up his one true love, it wasn't fantasy; it was reality. The Nazis weren't history; they were the terrorists of today's headlines. Danger was everywhere. Bogart played a tough-living, tough-talking, big-drinking man, but one who had unselfish courage and strength. He wasn't just a suave guy with a memorable parting line.

Bogart plays Rick Blaine, the strong but also vulnerable proprietor of Rick's Café, a safe haven for wartime refugees. Luminous and ever enigmatic, Bergman plays Ilsa Lund, the woman he loved and lost in Paris and will lose again.

The script was written and revised as the shooting progressed. Nobody knew exactly how the story would end until the film was almost completed. It was just a Warner Brothers studio picture; there wasn't fanfare or hype during its production. The play on which it was based was mediocre. Nobody involved was prepared for what happened. But Michael Curtiz's balanced and subtle direction and the passionate yet subdued performances of an entirely outstanding cast resulted in one of the most unforgettable of all Hollywood dramas. *Casablanca* won three Oscars, for Best Picture, Best Director, and Best Screenplay.

Most of us have seen *Casablanca* at least once. It was a favorite late-night television movie for decades. Much was lost to the deteriorating print quality and insufferable commercial interruptions. If you've never seen it before, now is the time to verify that its legendary position in film history is deserved. Even with countless viewings, one never tires of the mood, the intrigue, or Bogie and Bergman.

EXTRAS

Of course, you have to have *Casablanca,* but you already know that. Unfortunately, there still isn't a release completely worthy of the film's longevity or legend. There may never be; nobody can predict the whims of the distributors. If you don't want to wait it out, we suggest you make your choice with all the facts at hand.

There's no question that *Casablanca* looks much better on DVD than it did on video, to say nothing of late-night television with used-car commercials every fifteen minutes. That said, this film would benefit from a total restoration and obviously deserves it. For about twenty-five bucks, you can purchase a DVD that has one quite decent feature. It's hosted by Bogie's widow, Lauren Bacall, and is called "You Must Remember This . . ." The earth won't move for you, but you will hear remarks from two of the folks who were around at the time of the production, Julius Epstein (one of the screenwriters) and Murray Burnett (one of the playwrights). If you don't know the amazing trick about the airplane and the mechanics at the end, you'll learn about it.

The scene selection segments are well done. If you don't

have time for the whole movie but just need to hear Bogie say that very last line, it's an easy-access no-brainer.

The DVD Rip-off of the Century Award goes to the *Casablanca Collector's Edition* that retails for about eighty dollars and gives you the exact same DVD transfer. There are no surprise extra features, but it's in a fancy case and includes "limited edition" lobby cards. There's also a movie poster and a booklet. The advertising and the case say that the DVD inside is a special edition, but that's a lie. You must remember this.

Charade

CAST: Cary Grant, Audrey Hepburn, Walter Matthau, James
 Coburn, George Kennedy, Ned Glass
DIRECTOR: Stanley Donen
SCREENWRITERS: Peter Stone and Marc Behm
RELEASED: 1963 (113 minutes)
RATED: Not rated

Stanley Donen's classic faux-Hitchcock thriller isn't all that faux. In the forty years since its release, *Charade* holds up as well as many of Hitch's best. Donen's take on murder is a stylish one, and it served him well as a device that put a bit of frosting over some fairly grisly murders.

If you've never seen *Charade,* you're in for a thrill. Audrey Hepburn plays a young widow living in Paris who is stalked by a gang of thugs (even if they are the likes of some our greatest actors). Enter Cary Grant, suave (far too handsome for sixty) and quite mysterious. Will he save her, or is he part the problem? It seems her hubby left a fortune that wasn't his; the dear departed was a thief. There's a great deal of suspense. You are never all that frightened, of course, because Grant and Hepburn are too lovely to watch. The scenery is a free trip to Paris and Switzerland. It was all shot on location in Europe. There are very amusing moments, which still make you laugh out loud. Grant takes a shower fully clothed. And Hepburn delivers a line that women can actually use as a pickup gimmick. She asks Grant, "Do you know what's wrong with you?" He can't reply. She does: "Absolutely nothing."

Although there are a few sloppy plot twists, there's nothing so out of whack that you won't be captivated by the story and the performances.

If you haven't seen it for a while, perhaps you've even forgotten the terrific ending. The score was by Henry Mancini, and few will ever forget the haunting melodies he provided. In short, the movie still has legs, and if you're a fan of the kind of radiance that Grant and Hepburn projected on screen, you'll want this.

Here's a DVD tip, however. If you're one of those fans who really couldn't wait until this one came out on DVD and grabbed the first things out there, you know what you got. So toss it out; don't even recycle it for charity. Buy the only one worth watching, to say nothing of owning. It's the Criterion release, *Charade: Special Edition*. There are several other discs out there, but the quality of the transfer on the others is, simply stated, a total charade.

EXTRAS

The best extra is the commentary by Donen and screen-writer Peter Stone. They are comfortable with each other and in their conversational style reveal many tidbits that provide delightful viewing. If you watch the full feature, there's a little surprise for the dutiful that involves a cameo performance by Stone. Filmographies on Donen and Stone also provide "factoids." This release of *Charade* is gorgeous to watch, and the extras are worth the added expense. What you are really paying for is the vast amount of engineering that went into producing a flawless transfer. In this case, we are happy to say it's well worth it.

Chinatown

CAST: Jack Nicholson, Faye Dunaway, John Huston, Diane Ladd, John Hillerman, Perry Lopez, Darrell Zwerling
DIRECTOR: Roman Polanski
SCREENWRITER: Robert Towne
RELEASED: 1974 (131 minutes)
RATED: R

Chinatown is a film noir about 1930s Los Angeles made in 1970s Los Angeles. It tells the story of a two-bit private eye, an ex-cop named J. J. Gites, who is hired to investigate a suspected adultery and ends up in the middle of a murder mystery, a potential romance, and a heartbreaking revelation. Mostly, however, the story is about the lack of water and Southern California's greedy need for it, with millions to be made from land development.

Chinatown endures primarily because of the virtually perfect script by Robert Towne and the way director Roman Polanski interacted with the actors in making the film. As Jake Gites, Jack Nicholson moved from mere movie star to legend. The importance of the role haunted him for years. (You'll do yourself a major favor if you don't watch the failed sequel called *Two Jakes,* which was made without Towne's deft touch.) John Huston, in a rare and searing acting role, plays the father of Faye Dunaway's character, Evelyn Cross Mulwray. As Evelyn, Dunaway is manipulative, mysterious, and vulnerable; this performance stands as one of her best. It's a layered story with twists and turns and politics and sex at its core but without cheap tricks. It's been hailed for twenty-five years as one of the best films ever to come out of Hollywood. Hollywood seldom takes chances with scripts as sophisticated and demanding as this one. That's a shame, because viewers are up to the challenge.

The ending is without mercy. Towne was unable to persuade Polanski to use his softer and more hopeful conclusion. It often has been said that Polanski was still raw from the murder of his pregnant wife, Sharon Tate, by the Manson family. Some say the film's ending was a footnote to his personal tragedy. That's unfair to the artistry of Polanski's direction. The ending was as it should have been. *Chinatown* is a story about how deep and how far the decay spread in the building of the urban chaos called Los Angeles from the lands once known as California. This is where the story ends. We have Nicholson in other great roles. You'll never get Towne's writing at this level again or Dunaway more luminescent.

EXTRAS
The twenty-fifth-anniversary DVD highlights the contributions of John A. Alonzo's cinematography in this widescreen edition. Jerry Goldsmith's score benefits greatly from the digital remastering from mono sound to stereo.

The theatrical trailer is a nice touch, if only because the production quality was higher than we are now accustomed to seeing. The scenes are suspenseful and put together in a clever way.

The much-touted interviews with Polanski, Robert Evans (then head of Paramount), and Towne could have been better but are still very interesting. It's great to hear that Polanski hoped the film would conjure up the era of private investigator Philip Marlowe (of Raymond Chandler's works), even if we already knew that.

All three confess they doubt a studio would make such a film now. Towne reveals who inspired the character of Jake. Although it's mostly old news, it's wonderful to hear the stories from the sources themselves.

Chocolat

CAST: Juliette Binoche, Lena Olin, Johnny Depp, Judi Dench, Alfred Molina, Peter Stomare, Carrie-Anne Moss, Leslie Caron, John Wood, Hugh O'Conor, Victoire Thivisol
DIRECTOR: Lasse Hallstrom
SCREENWRITER: Robert Nelson Jacobs (adapted from the novel by Joanne Harris)
RELEASED: 2001 (120 minutes)
RATED: PG-13

Wake up and smell the chocolate. For all of us who have been insisting for years that chocolate has healing, if not magical, powers this is our film. Directed by Lasse Hallstrom, whose *My Life as a Dog* remains a favorite, this is a tale about tolerance versus rigidity. That's if you want to take a deeper look and are intent on coming up with a message in order to impress your friends. Otherwise, take this movie on its own terms for pure enjoyment.

The ever delightful Juliette Binoche mysteriously arrives in a provincial town in France during a windstorm. She opens a chocolate shop. It doesn't appear so threatening until we learn that she might be a pagan worshiper or at least a witch. She also has the bad timing to open during Lent, when the town's religiously observant residents have sworn off treats. Alfred Molina is cast as the town's awful mayor, the Comte de Reynaud. (This was before his liberating transformation as Diego Rivera in *Frida*.) The Comte rules with an iron hand and even writes the priest's sermons. He's just the kind of repressed municipal official you would want to pick a fight with, if you knew you could win. He's got a match in Vianne (Binoche). She won't give up; she won't go away.

The chocolates are like medicines or magical potions. They contain properties capable of changing your life. A shy old man takes the chocolate cure and confesses his love to the local widow (Leslie Caron). Everything Vianne makes melts in your mouth, and your troubles seem to melt away as well. Judi Dench plays an unexpected role that is both believable and quite poignant.

It's not all spun sugar and melted cocoa. There's mystery about who Vianne is and where she came from. It keeps you guessing long enough to stay interested in what will happen. Johnny Depp, as Vianne's love interest, brings an element of diversity to the town's stultified population. There's a crime; there's domestic sorrow. But the open-minded chocolate eaters win out over the cruel rules of the Comte de Reynaud, and there's quite a surprise at the film's end.

Some dismissed *Chocolat,* but it wasn't supposed to be a psychological thriller or *King Lear.* Give yourself a break, and enjoy. Make sure to have a supply of excellent chocolates at the ready when you watch.

EXTRAS
The audio commentary features Hallstrom along with his producers, David Brown, Kit Golden, and Leslie Holleran. There's a bit too much Brown for us and not enough Hallstrom. However, Brown does have a lifetime of experience in the industry.

We especially like the short interview clips with Depp and Dench. There's also a little historical bon-bon about chocolate. The deleted scenes are as lovely as the rest of the film.

The costume feature, although too brief, is definitely worth watching, and the animated menu amuses without confusing the technologically challenged.

Citizen Kane

CAST: Orson Welles, Joseph Cotten, Dorothy Comingore, Everett Sloane, Ray Collins, George Coulouris, Agnes Moorehead, Ruth Warrick
DIRECTOR: Orson Welles
SCREENWRITERS: Orson Welles and Herman J. Mankiewicz
RELEASED: 1941 (119 minutes)
RATED: G

Some say that *Citizen Kane* is the greatest movie ever made. A twenty-five-year-old, Orson Welles, known as a New York theater and radio director, changed the language and grammar of film. The movie remains a benchmark of cinematic achievement. Books have been written about it, as have countless dissertations and essays. Warner Home Entertainment has put together a superb two-disc package that is a required entry for every personal DVD library.

When Welles arrived on the RKO set, he said, "This is the best toy train set a boy ever had." He made use of that train set in miraculous ways. On a budget of barely a million dollars, he made an epic by using stock footage, still photographs, and existing sets. He was a genius at innovation and at direction. He was the first to use deep-focus photography, as well as a variety of other brilliant tricks never before seen. The cast included unknown actors from Welles's Mercury Theater, and their performances are dazzling.

The story revolves around newspaper magnate Charles Foster Kane, based on William Randolph Hearst, who was still very much alive when the film was made. Although Welles included elements of other famous men, such as Joseph Pulitzer and Chicago's Colonel Robert McCormick, nobody much believed that the movie was about anyone other than Hearst, especially Mr. Hearst. In fact, the telling of the tumultous life of the fictional Kane cut too close to the bone for Hearst. Attempts were made to keep the film from ever being released.

Citizen Kane opens with a newsreel parody of Henry Luce's popular "March of Time," which chronicles the life of Charles Foster Kane by way of his obituary. It is a fast-forward glimpse of the entire movie, which enabled Welles to expand the film itself in economical ways. The first scene is of Xanadu, Kane's estate, modeled directly on San Simeon, now called the Hearst Castle. Dorothy Comingore plays Kane's young wife. Her character is an unflattering version of Hearst's longtime mistress and companion, Marion Davies.

The film is legendary for many reasons, but one of the most curious is that it is known for one word, "Rosebud." Even if you have never actually taken the time to view this extraordinary work of art, you know that this was Kane's last word as he lay dying. In the extra features, you will find a much more tantalizing possibility than the film's revelation.

EXTRAS

In Disc One, for fun, begin by clicking on the red sled. (Yes, it's an egg.) You will hear an interview with Ruth Warrick, who played Kane's first wife. It's a warm-up for what's to come.

Peter Bogdanovich was a close personal friend of Welles. The commentary by Bogdanovich is an appealing feature because he tells of his intimate conversations with Welles about the film and its aftermath. Bogdanovich is a superb film scholar as well as a director.

Roger Ebert is a scholarly popular critic appearing both on TV and in newspaper syndication. His commentary is worth watching, as he seems to know every camera shot in this enduring cinema classic.

The production, postproduction, and production notes are entertainment for the film buff. There's a harvest of stills, deleted scenes, storyboards, original posters, the souvenir program, and a three-second look at opening night. Return to the red sled under "Production Notes," and there's an interview with Robert Wise, film editor, later the director of *The Sound of Music,* and the co-director of *West Side Story.*

On Disc Two, the real bonus of the set is the 1996 PBS American Experience documentary entitled *The Battle over Citizen Kane.* Welles is heard from in some interviews filmed before his death in 1985.

If you are familiar with the film, you might want to watch this first. It details the struggle with Hearst and the "Hearst machine's" attempt to destroy the film. Welles rather wistfully says he wasn't really fair to Davies—an odd confession, as that was precisely the cause of Hearst's intense rage. The program does a very good job of differentiating the real-life Hearst from his fictional counterpart, Kane.

Associates and friends of Welles contribute thoughts and memories. In the end, the story about the movie is as compelling as the film itself. Unfortunately, Welles's last days imitated those of Kane, not Hearst. Yet history remembers Hearst as much for Welles's portrayal of him as for his castle and his life.

City Lights

CAST: Charles Chaplin, Virginia Cherrill, Florence Lee, Harry
    Myers, Al Ernest Garcia, Hank Mann
DIRECTOR: Charles Chaplin
SCREENWRITER: Charles Chaplin
RELEASED: 1931 (87 minutes)
RATED: Not rated

Let's begin by noting that if you're not on a budget, there's a boxed set of Charlie Chaplin's classics for approximately a hundred dollars. Image Entertainment presents *Gold Rush*, *City Lights*, *Modern Times*, and *The Great Dictator*. These are old films, so don't expect tremendous amounts of bonus material.

If you're not going to make that sort of investment but still want to enjoy the genius of Chaplin, *City Lights* stands alone. Made as a silent film in 1931, just after the dawn of the "talkies," it's an essential element for any serious collector. The story is a simple one and features Chaplin as his recognizable alter ego, the Little Tramp. Virginia Cherrill plays a poor blind flower seller with whom the Tramp falls hopelessly in love.

The story warms the heart and is the sentimental favorite of Chaplin's legions of admirers around the globe. Don't let the sweetness of the story blind you to his mastery of the art of cinema.

What might be less obvious than the sparkling story of a tramp and a blind girl is the beautiful organization of the film's parallel stories. The poignancy of the blind girl who doesn't know her hero is a tramp is echoed in the low-comedy story of the eccentric millionaire (Harry Myers) who makes a fast friend of the Tramp. But when he wakes up in the morning cold, stone sober, he doesn't even remember the Tramp's face.

The Little Tramp struggles throughout the movie to raise money to help the blind girl. Of course, the irony is that thousands of dollars are squandered in the exploits with the drunken millionaire. *City Lights* includes many classic Chaplin set pieces. If you've never seen it before, prepare yourself for the rescue of the millionaire from attempted suicide. There's also the often-viewed scene between Chaplin and an enormous boxer (Hank Mann). The very last sequence is still, after seventy years, a genuine heartbreaker.

Although there's no dialogue, the film is elaborately scored with music effectively used to create a vast range of emotion and action.

EXTRAS

Image Entertainment offers an affordable single edition of *City Lights*. The supplements are spare. The only feature you'll care about taking a repeated look at is the interview with Carl Davis, the conductor and composer. He reconstructed the music in 1989 (the Chaplin centennial). The story notes, production data, and other business items aren't much to talk about. We prefer to see the film accompanied by the new digitally recorded stereo version of the musical score. For purists, the original soundtrack option is provided on the menu.

A Clockwork Orange

CAST: Malcolm McDowell, Patrick Magee, Adrienne Corri, Aubrey
     Morris, James Marcus, Warren Clarke, Michael Tarn, Sheila
     Raynor, Philip Stone, Miriam Karlin, Godfrey Quigley
DIRECTOR: Stanley Kubrick
SCREENWRITER: Stanley Kubrick (adapted from the novel by
     Anthony Burgess)
RELEASED: 1971 (137 minutes)
RATED: R

With the death of Stanley Kubrick in 1999, it's comforting
to be able to report that his most controversial film is now
on a new DVD that has been digitally restored. There aren't
any extras, except the trailer, but this release is a superb
transfer of a truly great and complex film. If you appreciate
Clockwork, you'll want to buy this one for the quality of the
transfer alone.

A Clockwork Orange is a hypnotic futurist film that is
far less shocking now than it was when it was released. It is
set in England in a future, but not distant, time. It is a
parable that has grown less outrageous yet more provocative with the passing years. The episodic narrative follows
Alex, a reckless gang member, played by Malcolm McDowell. McDowell's character is buoyant and winning. Kubrick
uses his usual pyrotechnics as an emotional focus, so that
Alex is so charismatic at times that liking him becomes
your own moral dilemma.

Alex's gleeful rendition of "Singin' in the Rain" as he
rapes an author's wife and assaults the author remains the
most unsettling and shocking sequence in the film. (The
author, played by Patrick Magee, was reportedly based on
writer Anthony Burgess.) Alex is sent to prison for his
crime. Rehabilitation turns him into a passive robot of a

human, incapable, one assumes, of committing further crimes.

The film is Kubrick's statement about the boundaries between justice and punishment. It's also his social commentary on the state of modern society and the humans who function within the system. *Clockwork* never completely captures the eccentric power of the novel, which contains its own futuristic language, used only minimally in the movie.

This is a major film by one of the greatest directors in film history. It's well worth seeing. The memorable musical score is the work of Walter Carlos, also known for his *Switched-On Bach*.

Cries and Whispers

CAST: Harriet Andersson, Kari Sylwan, Ingrid Thulin, Liv Ullmann, Erland Josephson, George Arlin, Henning Mortizen
DIRECTOR: Ingmar Bergman
SCREENWRITER: Ingmar Bergman
RELEASED: 1972 (95 minutes)
RATED: R

This is a mature masterpiece from the legendary Ingmar Bergman. *Cries and Whispers* eschews the straightforward movement of narrative and works by means of a continually shifting series of images clustered around a central theme. It's a complicated film artistically as well as emotionally. *Cries and Whispers* merits more than a casual once-over.

The story revolves around a trip home by two married sisters to the deathbed of their unmarried sister in rural Sweden at the turn of the twentieth century. Maria is played by Liv Ullmann and Karin by Ingrid Thulin. It's typical Bergman terrain: the interplay of individual isolation and the guilt over failed communication. The pain and dysfunction are amplified by the isolated closure of the country manor, the unsparing revelation of the relations of sisters, and the grim end game of a death watch. The two sisters are too consumed by their own demons and unresolved lives to be able to comfort their dying sister. In both her life and her suffering, Agnes (Harriet Andersson) has somehow managed to live unrestricted by the confines of recrimination and acrimony.

Each image becomes amplified, diminished, and changed by every other image. There's a devastating fantasy image of the loyal servant. Anna is the only one able to face the reality of the moment. Her loss of a child earlier in her life makes her more compassionate. Also, she in fact loves Agnes, but her status as a servant is never forgotten by the other sisters. Anna is played by Kari Sylwan, and her role is a central one. Agnes, in death, cuts through the earlier scenes of alienation between the sisters, giving the film a wrenching emotional climax. This is a beautiful, pensive work of art, a story of almost unparalleled sadness. If you think you've got a dysfunctional family or sibling problems, watch this one. You'll either feel better about things or start to mend family fences.

EXTRAS

We're not sure that *Cries and Whispers* looked any better in its theatrical release. The transfer to DVD is extraordinary. It's appropriate, as the film won the Oscar for Best Cinematography (Sven Nykvist).

In 1999, Swedish television made *Ingmar Bergman: Reflections on Life, Death, and Love with Erland Josephson*. (It played on a few public TV stations in the United States, but didn't receive wide attention.) This is an hour-long interview documentary with Bergman and his long time collaborator and friend, Josephson. He's the doctor in *Cries and Whispers*. Bergman is mostly out of our range of view as anything other than an artist. It's quite exciting to hear him speak about personal feelings, spirituality, and his craft. He is far from the celebrity culture of Hollywood, and so it is a refreshing change of pace. Josephson balances Bergman's more serious personality with anecdotes and a lighter touch. This is a special treat for anyone who loves Bergman's artistry. Note that the documentary is not specific to *Cries and Whispers,* however, but to the Bergman oeuvre and its method and philosophy.

Crouching Tiger, Hidden Dragon

CAST: Chow Yun-Fat, Michelle Yeoh, Zhang Ziyi, Cheng Pei Pei
DIRECTOR: Ang Lee
SCREENWRITERS: James Schamus, Wang Hui Ling, and Tsai Kuo
    Jung (based on a novel by Wang Du Lu)
RELEASED: 2000 (119 minutes)
RATED: PG-13

We weren't onto this magnificent film from the jump. We waited until it received a number of Oscar nominations. Even then, one of us went to the theater kicking and screaming, assuming it would be all kicking and grunting. Martial arts films aren't to our taste; we went because friends badgered us. We came away wondering if we should have a sandwich and return to see it again the very same afternoon.

What happened to us happened to millions of others. Ang Lee took the basic martial arts format and turned it into a film about power, destiny, magic, and love. He also put women in charge. This is a film you want your daughters to see.

Much has been said about the flying sequences, but you need to see them to understand that this isn't *Peter Pan* for adults in a Chinese landscape. The fighting and flying scenes are magisterial; there isn't another word that adequately describes what you will experience. We were at the store waiting for the first DVD release (usually a mistake) and quickly bought the better one when it was out.

The setting is nineteenth-century China. Like many allegorical tales, the story revolves around a magic sword. The sword is called Green Destiny. Li Mu Bai, played by Chow Yun-Fat, is a warrior who wants revenge for the murder of his beloved master. He has loved only one woman his entire life, the warrior Yu Shu Lien, played by the entrancing Michelle Yeoh. They put their personal lives behind the noble calling. The sword must be recaptured; justice must be served. Part of the problem with viewing the movie is that you become so taken with the ballet of the martial arts that you lose the sequence of the story from time to time (all the more reason to own this DVD). The journey of the sword brings another human element into the film in the person of a beautiful young woman, Jen Yu, played by Zhang Ziyi. Her life has been determined for her, but she has other plans.

The villain is another powerful woman who is deliciously evil. Jade Fox is the seemingly insurmountable barrier between justice and love.

Director Lee (*The Wedding Banquet, Eat Drink Man Woman, Sense and Sensibility, The Ice Storm, The Hulk*) is well known for his ability to transcend genres. But it is in *Crouching Tiger, Hidden Dragon* that we have the opportunity fully to appreciate his rare talent for synthesizing diverse elements into one glorious feast for the eyes. *Crouching Tiger, Hidden Dragon* is a choreographed wonder of fantasy, skill, and poignancy. Where have you seen that combination lately?

EXTRAS

Warning: Do not select the dubbed English version available on the disc. It's simply dreadful and literally ruins the movie.

The director's commentary includes James Schamus (screenwriter) and is a playful audio filled with tidbits about the filming. It's enjoyable and informative, although we felt they could have told us even more about the stunts.

"Unleashing the Dragon" is a documentary made by Bravo, which is very helpful for those who are new to the martial arts film world. If you're already a fan, you'll love it. Yeoh gives an interview that suggests that her on-screen character shares many attributes with the real woman. High marks go to Lee for this segment of the feature; it's crucial to see the movie from Yeoh's point of view.

Dead Man Walking

CAST: Susan Sarandon, Sean Penn, Robert Prosky, Raymond J. Barry, R. Lee Ermey
DIRECTOR: Tim Robbins
SCREENWRITER: Tim Robbins (based on the book by Sister Helen Prejean)
RELEASED: 1995 (120 minutes)
RATED: R

Why would you want a movie about a nun, capital punishment, and rape on your DVD shelf? The answer is that this is one of the best serious films Hollywood has made in a long time. It's a film that might have gone wrong in so many ways but didn't. It could have become commercially sloppy, politically extreme, or do-good sentimental; it didn't do any of those things.

Tim Robbins had the benefit of working with excellent material. The memoir written by Sister Helen Prejean is an account of her experience with a Death Row convict. Although he follows the book closely, the movie is even more powerful. Prejean, a nun who works with poor inner-city children, begins a pen-pal correspondence with a convicted rapist and killer played by Sean Penn. Matthew Poncelet waits his fate but asks the nun to come to see him. She does so with humility and Christian charity but not artifice. Susan Sarandon plays Prejean with natural dignity; her performance gives the film its focus as well as its authenticity.

Poncelet, whether innocent or guilty, is not a man you want to come across in your life. Robbins carefully directs the film's progression so that we have to work through our own prejudice. He looks just like the kind of person who would attack and kill two young kids on Lovers' Lane. He claims he's innocent; he blames his pal for the crime. Prejean listens and decides to help him with a last-minute appeal. She does so because she is a committed Christian, in the deepest sense. She believes all people must be treated as Christ would treat them. If all of this sounds like a Sunday morning sermon, it isn't. This is a tough, relentlessly honest film, which dares to look at all sides of the morally unresolved death penalty issue.

Sarandon plays Prejean with a quiet intensity, different from but equally as affecting as her role in *Lorenzo's Oil*. She acts, looks, and speaks as an intelligent, "worldly," and modern nun. When Poncelet makes what would qualify as a sexual pass at her, she responds not as an offended victim but as an exasperated, tired professional. Robbins makes us see the other side too. The film portrays the parents of the victims and the ruin of what is left of their lives. We follow Prejean's journey of self-evaluation, when she must face the possibility that Poncelet is, in fact, guilty.

There's no escaping the truth of this film and the power of the performances. Poncelet is shown within the context of his own family, and the scenes at the end are as difficult as the scenes with the families of the young victims. Robbins doesn't look away from what capital punishment means, nor does he look away from the meaning of violent acts. Prejean stays with Poncelet, hoping for his spiritual awakening. This isn't about the simplicity of forgiveness and salvation, though, but rather about its profound dilemmas. The performances by Penn and Sarandon are breathtaking to witness. Sarandon won the Oscar for her performance, and Penn was nominated for his.

EXTRAS

The feature that makes this worth the purchase price is the audio commentary by Robbins. He unfolds the story of Prejean, who served as a consultant on the film project. Robbins tells his own story about how he and Sarandon became interested. The evolution of the relationship between Robbins and Prejean would make a film itself. Much of what Robbins says is as important to know as the content of the movie. *Dead Man Walking* was a watershed in Hollywood, as well as in Robbins's career. The audio commentary makes you fully aware of the magnitude of the achievement. It also enhances your understanding and appreciation of the theatrical release.

Do the Right Thing

CAST: Danny Aiello, Ossie Davis, Ruby Dee, Richard Edson, Spike
Lee, Joie Lee, Sam Jackson, John Turturro, Paul Benjamin,
Giancarlo Esposito, Frankie Faison, Robin Harris, Rosie Perez,
Roger Guenveur Smith, Bill Nunn, Rick Aiello, Miguel Sandoval,
John Savage
DIRECTOR: Spike Lee
SCREENWRITER: Spike Lee
RELEASED: 1989 (120 minutes)
RATED: R

This film grabs you from the first frame. You can sense the
unbearably hot New York summer in a racially tense neighborhood. Spike Lee sets the mood in the same way that
Woody Allen instantly gave us his New York in the opening
frames of *Manhattan.* Allen and Lee live in very different
cities of the same name. However, both men have an unerring ability to tell the story of the city from their particular
experience, the African American experience in Lee's case
and the New York Jewish experience in Allen's.

This film sets you on fire. It's that good, and it's that
unforgettable. What ultimately explodes on the screen
could be a news article in yesterday's paper. This is one of
the most important films to be made in the last part of the
1980s. We believe it is one of the most important American
films ever made about race, class, and prejudice. Lee is a
multitalented man, combining acting, writing, and directing in one powerful, insightful, and creative energy force.

Do the Right Thing is visually interesting because it
combines the feature film with the texture of the documentary and doesn't do a disservice to either genre. The presence of Ossie Davis and Ruby Dee could feel iconic or
labored if they weren't such good actors. As it is, however,

Davis gives one of his finest performances as the character called Da Mayor. This is a lacerating drama about Bed-Stuy in Brooklyn, mostly fabled by outsiders as a place of violence, drugs, and racial hatred.

Lee shows a neighborhood that has moved from ethnically diverse to predominantly African American but with some vestiges of the previous demographics. Danny Aiello owns the pizzeria that has framed photographs of Frank Sinatra on the walls. He doesn't get it; his sons don't get it; the residents don't get the Italians, either. Lee plays Mookie, who works for Sal (Aiello) as a deliveryman. Samuel L. Jackson, credited then simply as Sam Jackson, is the local DJ, whose handle is Mister Señor Love Daddy. Music pulsates through the film, adding to the ever-mounting tension.

The cultural abyss opens, and you know it is going to end badly. Lee's astute direction and writing keep this film from becoming a diatribe against either race. It is in the character of Sal where we can see the depth of Lee's understanding of the human condition, regardless of racial identity. Aiello was nominated for Best Supporting Actor, and Lee received a nomination for his screenplay.

This film blends characters and situations seamlessly. The result is shattering, but it contains as much compassion as it does passion. Lee is a director with a clear eye and a razor-sharp intelligence. *Do the Right Thing* reports on America's most painful dilemma with as much or more impact than virtually any documentary. It is also a milestone artistic achievement.

EXTRAS

There are two versions of *Do the Right Thing* currently available. One is the Universal release, and the other is part of the Criterion Collection. We strongly recommend the Criterion. The Universal version doesn't have any features.

On the Criterion release, you'll receive two discs, lots of options for background material, and a closer look at Lee and his craft. The audio commentary has four voices: Lee and his sister Joie as well as cinematographer Ernest Dickerson and designer Wynn Thomas. Lee talks mostly about the public's reaction to the film and less about the making of the film. But both Dickerson and Thomas fill in fascinating details about their techniques and approaches to the film.

Disc Two has most of the other supplemental material. Lee introduces the features. The bonus here is a sixty-minute documentary by St. Clair Bourne, "The Making of *Do the Right Thing,*" which makes neighborhood sociology as interesting as it will ever get. The film was shot on location, and many extras were residents. There's behind-the-scenes footage that is extensive (more than you need). Most enjoyable were the interviews with the actors.

Lee and his producer, Jon Kilik, take you on a tour of the neighborhood a decade later. You might be startled by what you learn; we were.

Lee and others (including Davis and Dee) are on the segment from the Cannes festival. Lee handles some fairly inane questions with skill and grace and more patience than frustration. There's also a more candid Lee on a tiny feature at the end of his narrated introductions, called, aptly enough, "Final Words." It's actually a riff on the critics of the film.

If you are a storyboard fan, you'll be justly rewarded on this DVD. The riot sequence storyboards captured our attention. There's also a music video, "Fight the Power," by Public Enemy.

We're still waiting for *She's Gotta Have It* to come out on DVD. Until it does, you can rent or buy another good Lee flick, *School Daze.* This film was made in 1988 and stars

Laurence Fishburne, Lee, Giancarlo Esposito, Tisha Campbell, Joe Seneca, and a touch of Branford Marsalis. It never got the attention it warranted. It's a good, solid comedy, with serious racial issues raised. It's set at a black college and involves the hazing that goes on in fraternities. The audio commentary (the disc's only extra) is valuable. In it, Lee divulges what he was after and why he felt the need to take what is an unflattering look at a part of college life. The actual college was Morehouse, but the administration there was so upset by the very notion of the film that they refused to cooperate with Lee. You'll see a handsome and much younger Fishburne playing Dap Dunlap. This DVD is of purchase quality, if you're attracted to the work of Lee. If not, buy *Do the Right Thing*, and rent *School Daze*.

Despite mixed reviews, we also suggest *Jungle Fever* on DVD to round out your Spike Lee collection. *Jungle Fever* takes on the taboo of interracial attraction, and it does so without blinking. As you might imagine, Lee puts an interesting class spin on the topic. Wesley Snipes, playing Flipper Purify, is a successful, well-educated, and married architect. Annabella Sciorra plays Angie Tucci, a not very successful, working-class, temporary office worker. Their attraction is purely sexual and magnetic. The affair, such as it is, isn't terribly romantic, unless you think architectural blueprints are seductive.

Lee is going for something else and, as always, something deeper. It's in the fallout of the affair where you'll find the genuine action in the movie. It's where Lee's real motivation for making the film is disclosed. Besides Lee, Snipes, and Sciorra, the rest of the knockout cast includes Ossie Davis and Ruby Dee, Samuel L. Jackson, John Turturro, and Anthony Quinn. Lonette McKee plays Drew, Flipper's betrayed wife. McKee gives a stellar performance. There are few predictable outcomes in this film; the surprises can be jarring. But *Jungle Fever* is always thought-provoking. It isn't as perfectly polished a film as *Do the Right Thing*, but we include *Jungle Fever* on our list without hesitation.

We aren't suggesting a purchase of Lee's controversial and powerful film *Malcolm X*. At press time, it's still in a bare-bones edition, which is out of sync with the impact of the film and the importance Lee has always attached to it. We hope that a bigger, better *Malcolm X* DVD might be coming down the road. Rent it; don't purchase at this juncture.

Doctor Zhivago

CAST: Omar Sharif, Julie Christie, Geraldine Chaplin, Tom Courtenay, Rod Steiger, Alec Guinness, Siobhan McKenna, Ralph Richardson
DIRECTOR: David Lean
SCREENWRITER: Robert Bolt (adapted from the novel by Boris Pasternak)
RELEASED: 1965 (197 minutes)
RATED: PG-13

It's over the top. It's too much snow, too much revolution, too much sorrow, too much beauty, too much Russia. And, by the way, it's too damn long. It's got to be David Lean. Seeing *Lawrence of Arabia* and *Doctor Zhivago* again in their DVD releases, it's hard to remember that this is the same man who made the incomparable *Brief Encounter* in 1946. But the big screen was made for the epic format. (The success of *The English Patient* attests to the fact that we haven't lost our taste for the sweeping romantic tale.)

If you don't know the basic plot line, here it is: Omar Sharif plays Zhivago, a doctor and poet who is married to

Tonya (Geraldine Chaplin). She is the daughter of Anna and Alexander Gromeko (played without much distinction by the otherwise wonderfully talented Siobhan McKenna and Ralph Richardson). Zhivago was raised by Anna and Alexander, and little Tonya was a sort of sister. Suddenly, as in a *Gigi* moment, he notices her, and they are married.

Not far away in Moscow, a less genteel drama plays out involving Lara Antipova (Julie Christie), the daughter of a dressmaker (Adrienne Corri). Zhivago's and Lara's paths cross a number of times early on, most significantly when he is called to her mother's bedside. But nothing occurs until the accident of fate puts them together during the war in a field hospital, she as a nurse and he as a doctor.

The love story of *Doctor Zhivago* is the backdrop for Lean's expansive concept of what a movie should look like. It contains some of the most glorious visual material available—war scenes, winter scenes, revolutionary conflicts, the countryside, and, yes, those beautiful actors. There's a reason it won the Oscar for Best Cinematography. It's also Lean's last picture of real merit.

Boris Pasternak's novel was political and romantic; the movie is less than the book. Screenwriter Robert Bolt took a piece of the novel, and Lean created the rest, much of which belongs to cinematic history. The movie is especially impressive when you consider it was made in the days before computer-generated images. The set designers and crews had to perform yeoman's services now completely unthinkable, such as painting leaves different colors overnight to signify the changing of seasons. Or how about the trick of spraying sets with freezing water over hot wax to get the effect of a Russian *dacha* encased in ice? The supplements here are very explicit in letting you in on the production secrets.

It's not a great film, but it's one we cling to, partially for the memory of who we were and where we were when it was first released. There was tremendous excitement surrounding the release of *Zhivago;* the book was still banned in the Soviet Union. It would be decades before Russians would be permitted to view the film. Some of the performances are flawed. Sharif was too passive, but everyone forgave him because he was so impossibly handsome. The camera adored Christie. American women wanted to look like her and wear clothes that looked like Russian costumes. Chaplin was too sweet not to love, and we wondered why Sharif didn't. (But then he couldn't, because there was also Lara.) The plot was impossibly convoluted, and the running time was close to three hours. Nobody much cared; people saw it several times. Theaters turned up the air conditioners during the winter scenes so it would be more realistic . . . well, that's the lore.

Watch this with someone young enough not to have seen it before.

EXTRAS

Besides the entertaining supplements, the quality of this DVD is exceptional. It's a joy to see it again, thanks to the very high-quality production of the two-disc set. The features are terrific. There's audio commentary by Sandra Lean (the director's widow), Sharif, and Rod Steiger. Sharif's remarks are the most compelling. His enthusiasm for the movie has a childlike quality to it that is endearing. He talks about how he is still called Zhivago by people who see him.

"The Making of a Russian Epic" is an hour in length. It's on Disc Two. Here we think the true bonus of the package is the story of the real-life Lara, who was punished by the authorities. It's also on Disc Two that you will learn of the intricate and involved creation of the sets and atmosphere of the movie. It's a miracle that it could be pulled off at all.

Remember to highlight microphone icons for Sharif, Christie, and Chaplin. As usual, they're located in "Cast and Crew."

"Vintage Documentaries" includes a series of profiles with Lean, a short biographical glimpse of the life of the novelist, and some close-up portraits with the leading actors. Like all the other features here, it's rewarding.

Dr. No

CAST: Sean Connery, Ursula Andress, Jack Lord, Joseph Wiseman, Bernard Lee
DIRECTOR: Terence Young
SCREENWRITERS: Richard Maibaum, Johanna Harwood, and Berkely Mather (from the Ian Fleming novel)
RELEASED: 1962 (110 minutes)
RATED: PG

This is the first of the James Bond films. It isn't necessarily the best, but it's fast-paced fun without all the later gadgets. Who knew in 1962 that this would be the beginning of a franchise that would last into the new century? Sean Connery was an unknown Scottish actor who took the world by storm with his fearless and slightly dangerous good looks. He was too cool to be true. But he was James Bond, Special Agent 007, and the world's very best super-spy. We think it's the classic 007, because the forces of evil and good are unhampered by the later fancier pyrotechnics. Here it's the acting and the plot. And it's the beginning of it all, so it's our vote for your Bond shelf.

Dr. No, played by Joseph Wiseman, is a nefarious force

that Bond has to vanquish. Dr. No is the first of the evil forces who will come across Bond's path in the next decades. Shot in the photogenic West Indies (so that Ian Fleming, who lived in the "neighborhood," could help supervise), the landscape adds to the suspense. Ursula Andress is but the first in a long, luscious line of Bond women. We still favor the young Connery as the absolute 007.

EXTRAS

The "Special Edition" release of *Dr. No* is worth purchasing. If you're a serious follower of the Bond saga, you'll want to consider a boxed set, which is pretty pricey. It includes *The Spy Who Loved Me, On Her Majesty's Secret Service, The Man with the Golden Gun, Moonraker,* and, of course, *Dr. No.* But if you want the first in the series with good supplements for your library, we suggest buying *Dr. No* separately.

"Inside Dr. No" is a fairly long (forty-five minutes) documentary about the history of the Bond movies. There are lots of interviews, including one with Andress. Unfortunately, director Terence Young "moved upstairs" some years ago, so his comments are not recent. They are interwoven in the right places, more or less.

As for "Terence Young: Bond Vivant," if you can move past the hopeless pun in the title of this mini-documentary, you will like the profile of the director.

The printed book inside the case is a keeper.

Yes, yes, the martini. No, you don't get one, it's virtual. Special features, click remote down, hit martini glass. You get a recipe and a somewhat accurate record of how the martini came into existence. Go into the kitchen or bar area of your residence, make your own version, sip, relax. Remember we were all young and chic once. If you are still young and chic, you'll probably be drinking the apple version. But Bond wouldn't; and just so you know, Dr. No wouldn't, either.

Driving Miss Daisy

CAST: Morgan Freeman, Jessica Tandy, Dan Aykroyd, Patti LuPone, Esther Rolle, Joann Havrilla, William Hall, Jr., Alvin M. Sugarman, Clarice F. Geigerman

DIRECTOR: Bruce Beresford
SCREENWRITER: Alfred Uhry (from his play)
RELEASED: 1989 (99 minutes)
RATED: PG

Driving Miss Daisy tells us as much about the difference between North and South and racial attitudes in America as any sociology textbook will. Miss Daisy (Jessica Tandy) is a fairly wealthy Jewish woman, who is driven around and looked after by her chauffeur, Hoke Colburn (Morgan Freeman).

Over their years together, things change, but the entrenched notions of place and status are difficult to alter. It is important to note that Jews in the South are as much outsiders as Blacks in many ways, and so the dynamic of social class between two marginalized people is particularly complicated and layered. The only thing that doesn't work for us in this film are the over-the-top characterizations of Daisy's son, Boolie (Dan Aykroyd), and daughter-in-law, Florine (Patti LuPone). Their performances (despite Aykroyd's Oscar nomination) detract from what might have been a much more serious look at a particular time and sensibility among Blacks and Jews in the South.

Look for the subtle manner in which the two lead characters are attached but dare not be. It's an often quoted line but worth noting here: "The Southern white is very comfortable with individual African Americans but often uncomfortable with the group. Northerners are very comfortable with the concept of African Americans but are often exceedingly uncomfortable with individual African Americans."

Miss Daisy was the Academy's favorite in 1989, being named Best Picture. Tandy won for Best Actress. Alfred Uhry won for Best Screenplay (adapted); since he also wrote the play, you might say he won twice. Even the makeup team won; although some might think that's a stretch, these makeup artists had to age the characters more than thirty years during the course of the film's ninety-nine minutes. Freeman was nominated for Best Actor, Aykroyd was nominated for Best Supporting Actor, and there were also nominations for Best Art Direction, Best Costume Design, and Best Film Editing.

Driving Miss Daisy was hugely popular because it made us feel good about race in America and because Tandy and Freeman were so fine together. It isn't as sentimental as it seems on first viewing. The fact that the horrible racial conflicts of the day were largely ignored is more or less the story of writer Uhry's life. Southerners truly understand *Miss Daisy;* sometimes others don't.

EXTRAS

In the special edition, the mini-bio section features the cast members and the crew. You can scroll through the pages on screen and read about all the film accomplishments of each cast member.

The original theatrical trailer makes you want to see the movie all over again.

Screenwriter Uhry, along with director Bruce Beresford and producer Lili Fini Zanuck, offer personal commentary.

Uhry talks about his excitement when Freeman and Tandy agreed to star. He reveals the personal story behind *Miss Daisy*, which is based on the life of his grandmother and her chauffeur. He discusses similarities between the story and his adaptation for stage and then screen.

"Jessica Tandy: Theater Legend to Screen Star" is an appropriate tribute. Members of the cast and crew talk about working with Tandy and about her qualities as a friend. Clips from the movie as well as production photos of Tandy are also shown.

An original featurette offers a behind-the-scenes look at *Driving Miss Daisy* with producer, director, and author interviews as well as a look at the sets and off-screen shots of the cast. This section is not digitally remastered; notice the difference in the footage quality.

If you watched the commentary, most of the information in "Miss Daisy's Journey: From Stage to Screen" is redundant. The most interesting gossip is about the problems getting the movie funded and getting backers to agree that Freeman was the right man for the role. He was the original cast member in the play but had just made a movie about being a pimp called *Street Smarts*. There was considerable worry about his portrayal of such a gentle role. A segment about costume and makeup is rewarding.

Easy Rider

CAST: Peter Fonda, Dennis Hopper, Jack Nicholson, Karen Black, Warren Finnerty, Luke Askew, Luana Anders
DIRECTOR: Dennis Hopper
SCREENWRITERS: Peter Fonda, Dennis Hopper, and Terry Southern
RELEASED: 1969 (94 minutes)
RATED: R

Before millions of baby boomers were checking to see how much their social security checks were worth, many were angry and smoking dope. Some of the rest were getting shot in Vietnam. Some were in training to become the current Republican leadership or the previous Democrat administration. The rest were living their lives, while perhaps affecting a general disdain for anything that looked as if it was "Establishment" or American. It was cool to spell America with a *k* in the middle of it. *Easy Rider* is one of the best cinematic records of that time. To say it's a period movie is to state the obvious. Two guys high on dope most of the time aimlessly wander through the U.S.A. on motorcycles, fueled by a cocaine deal they made before they left Los Angeles.

Sound like a convincing story? Well, maybe you had to be there. At the time of its release, *Easy Rider* and what it meant were discussed by everyone, everywhere. It was said to define the decade. It didn't. There wasn't anything at all easy about the ride the characters took or the times themselves. On their big choppers, purchased with their dope score, Billy and Wyatt (Dennis Hopper and Peter Fonda) roar through the country. By 1969, the drug counterculture was about finished, but the film became a landmark. Hopper and Fonda play contemptuous characters, who, as the advertisement said, "went looking for America and couldn't find it anywhere." In the 1960s, those sorts of remarks were recited like mantras; their meaning was elusive and unimportant. One could say the portrait of America in *Easy Rider* is romantically harsh. *Easy Rider* is a jumpy, nervous film that finally criticizes its alienated subjects by revealing their complete lack of values.

George Hanson, a rich Southern delinquent played by Jack Nicholson, finds himself way out of his depth with the wild antics of Wyatt and Billy. Once the Nicholson character is dispensed with, the film loses some of its appeal. However, *Easy Rider* is still an all-time favorite for millions of people. Finally, there's a version worth buying. It was released for the thirtieth anniversary of the film's theatrical opening.

We should warn you that *Easy Rider* could be a dangerous weapon in the wrong hands. If you're a boomer and are either a parent or a grandparent and have been judgmental with your younger family members, you might want to lock this one up. "What was it you said you were doing in the 1960s, Grandpa?"

EXTRAS

It's the "Special 30th Anniversary Edition" you want. This release was digitally remastered, so that the print is absolutely perfect. The hard rock soundtrack is appropriately deafening, if you've got the right sound system on your television.

If you've followed the details behind the story of *Easy Rider*, you'll know not to expect to hear Fonda's voice on the audio track. Hopper and Fonda have feuded for decades about whose idea it was. Apparently, Hopper never learned how to share. We find the Hopper commentary annoying on that basis alone, as well as the fact that Hopper has such an elevated sense of his own importance. It's Hopper on Hopper. If you're a Hopperite, you'll love it.

What's worth the admission price is the documentary entitled "Easy Rider: Shaking the Cage." This is for real; it's not a studio promo piece fattened up to look like something else. It's more than an hour long and features plenty of clips from the movie and new interviews with cast and crew, actress Karen Black, production manager Paul Lewis, cameraman Seymour Cassel, and both Hopper and Fonda (but not at the same time). It's here that you'll hear Fonda's stories about the motorcycles, which were apparently more show than go, designed to look great but not to travel distances with any comfort. We won't give away Fonda's amusing punchline. There's good material from Black and Luke Askew, as well as an interview with the immensely talented cinematographer Laszlo Kovacs. It's a tonic after Hopper's self-serving audio. You'll get an uncensored look at how he behaved during the filming. "Shaking the Cage" is excellent, better than many stand-alone feature-length documentaries we've seen.

8½

CAST: Marcello Mastroianni, Claudia Cardinale, Anouk Aimée, Sandra Milo, Rosella Falk, Guido Alberti, Barbara Steele, Jean Rougeul
DIRECTOR: Federico Fellini
SCREENWRITERS: Federico Fellini, Tullio Pinelli, Ennio Flaiano, and Brunello Rondi (adapted from a story by Fellini and Flaiano)
RELEASED: 1963 (140 minutes)
RATED: Not rated

Just by uttering the name of Federico Fellini, we invoke respect and mystery. If you're a serious aficionado of the man's works, you will want to fill your library with everything he made that is available on DVD. For those who want a great Fellini film but not a shelf of them, we suggest that you pick his semiautobiographical 8½, a challenging and at times aggravating film. It is not one you will tire of easily, nor is it one that you will regret purchasing. It's been released in the Criterion Collection, with all the attention to quality and extras that it deserves.

8½ tells a story that mirrors Fellini's life at the time it was made. It's fragmentary and elusive in places, but the overall impact is a wallop. It holds its status as a landmark masterpiece about a famous director who has reached an impasse in his art and his life. His dilemmas revolve around his wife, played by Anouk Aimée, ever chic and elegant, and his mistress, played by Sandra Milo. Carla (the mistress) excites him, although he is ashamed of this passion. She's common and tacky, and he knows he shouldn't want her so intensely, but he can't help himself.

He's stuck creatively, he's in pain emotionally, and so he escapes into his memory and dreams. For his alter ego, Fellini chose Marcello Mastroianni to play Guido Anselmi, the tormented and driven director. Who wouldn't want to be played by Mastroianni on screen?

The plot is sometimes hard to follow, but that's not what the intent was. It's a frantic twister of fantasy and reality. It's actually a brilliantly imaginative effort to portray the search for creative inspiration and inner peace.

It's often a bit of a wild ride, and the juxtapositions of psychoanalytic insights with sheer fantasy and hard reality can have you looking for the Valium. Nonetheless, this is one of the greatest of the genre of autobiographical or memoir films made by one of the greatest and most inventive directors of the twentieth century. More than forty years after its debut, 8½ is still astonishing and riveting. It's Mastroianni's vehicle as much as it is Fellini's story. Both of these giants pulled the very best from their fellow actors.

If you want a definitive look at the art of filmmaking, this is it. While it might occasionally be self-indulgent, it isn't a romp through Hollywood's machine; it's a deeper look that leaves traces of its presence in your memory.

8½ won the Oscar for the Best Foreign Film and another for Best Costume. Fellini was nominated for Best Director. He and his team of writers were nominated for the original screenplay, and Piero Gheradi received a nomination for set and art decoration.

EXTRAS

Presented as part of the Criterion Collection, the two-disc set is rich in bonus material and well worth the rather steep price.

The transfer is from a digitally restored print, and therefore you are seeing 8½ as few have ever seen it for many years. The DVD format enhances the cinematography. There isn't an imperfection in this rendition of the masterpiece.

Now for the extras. Let's begin with a small book, not the usual cheap little throwaway. It is more than twenty pages in length and has important commentary by film scholar Alexander Sesonske, Fellini biographer Tullio Kezich, and Fellini himself.

There are many hours of bonus material in this package. The real-life Carla has her own interview section— really Milo on Milo with Fellini overlay. It's a fascinating piece of history; she tells everything she did, everything she felt, everything she still feels. It's very personal and sometimes a little too intimate, but you will be delighted you've got it available.

Cinematographer Vittorio Storaro is featured in an interview. His mastery of the camera and his association with Fellini provide a rare glimpse inside the workings of a Fellini film. Director Lina Wertmuller talks about her admiration for Fellini and his work. She's a little stilted and not entertaining, but God didn't give us Lina Wertmuller for entertainment.

There's a lot more to discover, but, as always, we want to note the best of the best. In late 1968, NBC television made a documentary about Fellini. Few people we know ever saw it. It's *Fellini: A Director's Notebook*. Unfortunately, the print isn't pristine, and you have to be willing to put up with the imperfections. But it is a treasure.

There's some behind-the-scenes material from the personal archives of Gideon Bachman, who was Fellini's friend.

The audio commentary is well presented, with narration by actress Tanya Zalcon, who has a lovely voice.

For any fan of Fellini or of international cinema generally, this is a must-have DVD.

Erin Brockovich

CAST: Julia Roberts, Albert Finney, Aaron Eckhart
DIRECTOR: Steven Soderbergh
SCREENWRITER: Susannah Grant
RELEASED: 2000 (130 minutes)
RATED: R

The setting is small-town America, where a power plant's reckless dumping of toxic waste over many years has slowly but relentlessly poisoned its residents. That's the text, but the action is the story of a woman who refuses to let it go unpunished. The movie is based on the life of a real person whose determination and intelligence didn't change the whole world but surely changed one corner of it. Julia Roberts plays Erin. She has a great deal of attitude, which she is happy to share with anyone in the way of progress.

Brockovich makes an uneasy alliance with Ed Masry, a small-time lawyer played by Albert Finney, who finds her as aggravating as she is impressive. She's broke, has no legal training, and wants desperately to reclaim her life. Her own resilience leads her on the journey that will ultimately help others. Finney, one of our finest actors, is well featured in this film. He was nominated for Best Supporting Actor. Julia Roberts won the Oscar for Best Actress.

It was director Steven Soderbergh's artistic choice to focus more on Erin than on the details of the tragic story of the people in this small California town. He was roundly criticized by environmentalists for making too much of Roberts and not enough of the plight of the people. In fact, the film did attract needed public attention for this issue. Soderbergh's call was the correct one because the story of Erin Brockovich's life is not only absorbing but illuminating. (*A Civil Action* and *Silkwood* were more overtly political in their message.)

It is obvious from the first that Erin Brockovich, although she might indeed be in deep personal trouble, is a survivor. She's also witty, intelligent, sarcastic as needed, and unsinkable. After being denied yet another job, she is involved in an automobile accident. She is not at fault, but the results are devastating for her. Her car is totaled, and she has minor injuries. This is our first introduction to Finney as the low-end lawyer. You might call him a generic ambulance chaser. He seems fairly inept at handling her case, although, in fairness, she doesn't make it too easy for him.

Erin loses the case, still has no job, and doesn't even have a car. She shows up at Masry's office announcing he owes her a job in his firm. Roberts plays these sequences well. She combines her natural comedic talent with a growing flair for handling dramatic parts with guts.

None of the other women want Erin anywhere around. They protest vehemently to Masry. Yet, against their wishes, he installs her as a lowly file clerk. She's not intimidated by them. Soon they will be quite threatened by her. Roberts is given more than her share of good dialogue, and she makes it memorable. The job she is given might be mindless, but our hero is not. While filing, she comes across a case involving a small town that has a peculiarly high rate of cancer. It intrigues and troubles her. Acting as a legal assistant, Erin takes her charm and miniskirts to do some digging. Roberts flashes the hallmark smile and talks her way into everyone's home, hearth, and heart. PG&E (the utilities company) is not at all charmed by her activities.

When's she confronted by the officials for having her nose where it doesn't belong, she gives plenty of red, hot, angry lip. One of the more famous lines of the movie is directed at an overweight nemesis: "Bite my ass, Krispy Kreme." It's just the kind of line you would like to pop to an officious representative of some sleazy company. Unfortunately, you need to look like Roberts to make that quip work. Erin rallies the town to fight and convinces Masry to take on the lawsuit.

Roberts and Finney make a divinely ill-matched pair as employee and employer. Their work together is worth the whole movie. This isn't the film of the century, but it's worth owning because it's about something that matters. It's also a good watch, the way a book is a good read. You come back to it again and find more in it to appreciate.

Soderbergh was nominated for Best Director for both *Traffic* and *Erin Brockovich;* he won for *Traffic.* Not too bad for a boy who started out with a tape recorder in *sex, lies, & videotape.*

EXTRAS

"Spotlight on Location: The Making of *Erin Brockovich*" is a pretty standard short feature about the making of the film and the location shoots. What makes this a bit special is to hear just how the story came to Soderbergh's attention. You'll also meet the real Erin Brockovich and understand her deep commitment to the work she did. The next selection gives you a fast but more personal look at her.

"Erin Brockovich: A Look at a Real-Life Experience" is a documentary about the real Brockovich's life and her experience, including an interview. It lasts only about five minutes, which seems a pity.

There are thirty minutes of compelling deleted scenes, some of which probably should have been left in. You can watch them with or with out commentary. In the commentary, director Soderbergh describes the difficulties he had in the cutting room.

For reasons that are hard to fathom, Soderbergh didn't make an audio commentary, so we suggest you listen to this, because it's all you're going to get.

In 1989, a young director came to the world's attention with a quirky daring film called *sex, lies, & videotape*. His name was Steven Soderbergh, and the work was a dark, emotionally exhausting examination of infidelity. It was more than another art film, more than a young indie director. It was hard to know where this talented young man would go. If he could do all he did in *sex, lies, & videotape* in about a month and with a million bucks, what might be next?

Now we know who he is and where's he's been, although we still wonder where he's going. If anyone has a powerful eraser, would you loan it to him so that he can rub out the *Ocean's Eleven* remake next to his name?

Let's take a look back at the first serious Soderbergh. *sex, lies, & videotape* takes an overdone topic, adultery, and does something utterly fresh with it. Soderbergh succeeded in making the act of betraying a spouse far more shocking than it had looked in decades.

Andie MacDowell plays Ann, a wife without a sexual urge for anyone, especially her husband, John (Peter Gallagher). He is a slithering sort, a successful high-powered lawyer who doesn't seem to inspire her but seems just the right package for her sister, Cynthia. Here is the stuff for a lifelong session on Freud's couch, which is the underlying theme of the film.

Everything becomes oddly sexual when a friend of John's arrives, played by James Spader. What makes the sensuality odd is that Spader's character, Graham, is reportedly impotent. Not so odd after all—there's the conquest of the unavailable man that plays across the sisters' dialogue without actually being directly enunciated.

The talented actress Laura San Giacomo, who has never made it to the top rung, plays Ann's sister. She's a forceful actress, and one might have thought this movie would have taken her where she belongs. (If you want a truly offbeat film, try to track her down in *Nina Takes a Lover,* sometimes available on video. You'll see where she's trying to go; although the film is flawed, her acting is superb.)

More than a decade later, watching *sex, lies, & videotape* has its moments when you remember why you thought it was so groundbreaking. At other times, it looks dated and labored. The film was important because it put Soderbergh on the map. The more subtle reason is to realize again that Soderbergh's unique perspective on sexuality, marriage, and relationships has not spawned a generation of new films that take it to the next dimension. Consequently, *sex, lies, & videotape* still stands out as an achievement not just for a young director but for any director. We found the film more affecting and much sadder this time around.

There's not a great deal of bonus material, but there's commentary with Soderbergh, which we recommend.

E.T. The Extra-Terrestrial

CAST: Henry Thomas, Dee Wallace, Drew Barrymore, Peter
    Coyote, Robert Macnaughton, K. C. Martel, Sean Frye, Tom
    Howell
DIRECTOR: Steven Spielberg
SCREENWRITER: Melissa Mathison
RELEASED: 1982 (120 minutes)
RATED: PG

Adjacent to a completely ordinary housing development in
an average California town, something odd is going on. In
the woods, a spaceship lands, and small but efficient creatures descend and begin to gather specimens. Something
startles them, and they quickly return to their craft, scramble up the ramp, and leave.

They forgot somebody. They forgot E.T., and that was
a lucky break for all of us. The story of *E.T.* is the story of
an alien and the little boy who comes to his aid. In no time
at all, his entire family is involved in his care and feeding.
In 1982, *E.T.* mania was everywhere. It's lovely to come
back to this film without all the hype and toys and other
marketing gimmicks.

We wondered how *E.T.* would play after twenty years.
Would it still have the ability to move us as it did then?
Strangely and happily, it does. The special effects are still
exquisite, but there is a lovely innocence to the story that
dates it in a tender way. The children who conspire to keep
E.T. are still as lovable as they were when we first encountered them. Henry Thomas, as Elliott, E.T.'s benefactor
and true soul mate, remains as edible a little boy as he was
then. Drew Barrymore as Gertie, the youngest child in the
family, still delights as she waddles around and plays dress-
up with E.T. Robert Macnaughton is the older brother who

is at first resistant and then a willing partner. Dee Wallace plays an overworked, stressed single mom who doesn't even notice E.T. at first. Her role isn't dated at all; single mom syndrome is as timeless as E.T.

E.T. is just about as ugly as he was when we first met him, although you can view him in his altered state, where he hops around a little more freely. He still wants to go home, and it's that longing for home that works, perhaps even more now than it did in 1982. The bicycles still fly, and E.T. still returns to the planet he loves, a place called home. Seeing E.T. again is like running into a dear friend you haven't seen for two decades. You remember most things about him but not everything. The scene with the children when they attempt to have him communicate where he's from is even more wondrous than we had remembered. We're awfully glad he's returned to delight an entirely new generation of children and their grown-up friends and relatives.

EXTRAS

The two-disc set contains two versions of the movie. Disc One has the original 1982 theatrical release just as it was when last we saw it. Disc Two has an enhanced and edited version. There are two completely new scenes. E.T's face is more expressive, and he moves with a touch more grace. The bicycle sequence has been modified slightly. The largest difference between the two versions is a sign of what's happened in twenty years. The police have lost their guns and use walkie-talkies instead. Some dialogue has been changed.

We prefer *E.T.* as it was released originally, but it's a personal decision. Frankly, for all the hype about the changes, they aren't significant.

Steven Spielberg introduces the movie on Disc One,

but the big bonus on this disc is the twentieth-anniversary premier. E.T. had his birthday party at the Shrine Auditorium in Los Angeles with John Williams conducting a full orchestra. This orchestration is available on split screen with the movie.

The last feature on the first disc is a space exploration segment for children narrated by E.T. It's about the solar system and is clever and engaging.

Disc Two contains "A Little Piece of Wonderment in My Life," in which Spielberg narrates a documentary about the experience of making E.T. initially and what led him to return to it. He says that it was necessary for him because he was never completely pleased and had to "satisfy the perfectionist in me." How E.T. was "born" is fascinating, from its initial creation to the digital enhancements of today.

"Designs, Photographs, and Marketing" is not the best of the lot. It's done in a PowerPoint format, with no sound. You can miss this one.

"The Reunion" is a group interview with the cast plus co-producer Kathleen Kennedy. This feature is interwoven with clips from the making of the movie. Barrymore talks about how much she actually loved E.T. and became attached to him as to a favorite pet or stuffed animal.

There's a Steven Spielberg moment we won't betray, but it involves a Halloween costume from a cast party.

By the way, does anybody remember that Debra Winger was one of E.T.'s voices?

The French Connection

CAST: Gene Hackman, Fernando Rey, Roy Scheider, Tony
LoBianco, Marcel Bozzuffi, Frederic de Pasquale, Bill Hickman
DIRECTOR: William Friedkin
SCREENWRITER: Ernest Tidyman (adapted from the novel by
Robin Moore)
RELEASED: 1975 (119 minutes)
RATED: R

William Friedkin's superbly executed cop thriller remains one of this genre's best in the modern era. Gene Hackman as tough, foul-mouthed narc Jimmy "Popeye" Doyle took home the Oscar. The movie involves the pursuit of an international heroin ring and its multimillion-dollar cache of very pure heroin, inconveniently hidden in an automobile that has been shipped from France. The handler on the American side of the business is Fernando Rey as Alain Charnier, too elegantly French to be a real crook. Ernest Tidyman's taut, furiously paced script structures the entire movie as a series of chases, the most memorable being a car-versus-subway race through Brooklyn that must be one of the most nerve-racking vehicle duels on film.

The novelty of cops who look and sound like real people has diminished since *The French Connection* was released, partly because of the host of imitations and rip-offs it inspired. But this is where it all began; the rest is but a footnote. *The French Connection* still packs a wallop as dynamic action entertainment, masterfully handled on all levels. Eddie Egan and Sonny Grosso, the former cops whose real-life exploits inspired the film, appear as Simson and Klein. The movie won Oscars for Best Picture, Director, Actor (Hackman), Screenplay (Tidyman), and Film Editing (Gerald B. Greenberg). Roy Scheider was nominated as Best Supporting Actor for his role as Detective Buddy Russo.

When *The French Connection* was released, Friedkin was not known for particularly stellar work. Perhaps the impact and power of what he directed stunned even him. Friedkin made *The Exorcist* in 1973.

EXTRAS

When Detectives Egan and Grosso busted the heroin deal, it was the largest bust in history. The true-life story was almost as good as the movie. In the new Fox Special Edition of *The French Connection*, there are two excellent documentaries. "Poughkeepsie Shuffle: Tracing the French Connection" was made in 2000 for the BBC. The other is "Making the Connection: The Untold Stories," which is a Fox Productions feature made in 2001. We prefer the British show, but you need to see both. There are some nice touches to the Fox-produced feature, which shouldn't be overlooked; especially good are some of the comments by the two real-life detectives.

There's audio commentary with Friedkin, Hackman, and Scheider, as well as photo stills and way too many deleted scenes with too much Friedkin chatter.

Overall, this is excellent, with superb extras.

Funny Face

CAST: Fred Astaire, Audrey Hepburn, Kay Thompson, Michel Auclair
DIRECTOR: Stanley Donen
SCREENWRITER: Leonard Gershe
RELEASED: 1957 (103 minutes)
RATED: Not rated

Don't look for any message beyond the sublime joy of this film. It was 1957, and boys didn't make passes at girls who wore glasses. Fashion was more important than being an intellectual, if you happened to be a young woman. This isn't about what would happen to women's lives; this is only about two things: Astaire and Hepburn. Nothing else counts, not this time.

Funny Face weaves a romantic yarn about the life of an ugly ducking, Jo (Audrey Hepburn), who works in a bookshop and is involved in an esoteric, philosophical approach to life. The notion of Hepburn playing a totally plain and even somewhat unattractive young woman is a stretch from the beginning, but she's made to look frumpy enough for you to suspend disbelief until she is "transformed." Maggie Prescott, played to brittle glass-breaking perfection by Kay Thompson, is a fashion editor who wants a new look for her magazine. She knows she wants something different and new. She's not sure what. Famed photographer Richard Avedon was a consultant to the film.

Fred Astaire happens into the bookstore where Hepburn works and selects her as the one he will promote to fashion heights. She wants to go to Paris to study with Professor Flostre (Michel Auclair). Of course, you know the ending, even if you've never seen the movie. Astaire falls for her; she might be in love with him, but there's the odd professor. It all ends the way a fairy tale does. It's fairly subtle, but if you do look between the scenes, you might find that screenwriter Leonard Gershe was writing an ever so gentle parody of both the New York fashion trade and the Greenwich Village bohemian hyperintellectuals.

You'll love this film for the Gershwin music alone. Astaire was close to sixty when he made *Funny Face,* but he was as elegant and youthful as ever. Astaire was one of those men lucky enough never to look young, so that when he was old, we hardly noticed. The visuals are unforgettable. There's Paris, a delicious lakeside dance, and that "funny face" popping up in the developing trays of the darkroom. You love them both, and now that we've lost them both, be grateful we have this beautifully restored DVD. "Let's Kiss and Make Up" is the best dance routine in the film. Also, you get to hear Hepburn's actual singing voice, limited as it was, rather than having her dubbed. *Funny Face* is a near-perfect love story wrapped in a musical.

When Astaire died, the *New York Times* ran a small article on the editorial page headed, "When Fred Astaire Leaves the Room." It was unthinkable that he would go away. Astaire wasn't a typically handsome leading man, yet he was one of the great ones. It wasn't only about his dancing; it was something else that can't really be defined. It was enough for Hepburn, and it's enough for us.

EXTRAS

There's nothing much on the supplements to note, except for a photo selection at the very end of the disc. It contains several stills from the production. If *Funny Face* doesn't break your heart, you've been dealt one of the granite versions.

Funny Girl

CAST: Barbra Streisand, Omar Sharif, Kay Medford, Anne Francis, Walter Pidgeon, Lee Allen
DIRECTOR: William Wyler
SCREENWRITER: Isobel Lennart (based on her play)
RELEASED: 1968 (155 minutes)
RATED: G

William Wyler's rendition of the life of Fanny Bryce is a meandering musical biography pulled together by the power of Barbra Streisand's comic talent and voice. She sings what would become standard Streisand hits such as "People," "Don't Rain on My Parade," and "My Man."

You don't ever really believe that Streisand is Fanny Bryce, because she can't let go of her own charismatic personality, which is just as grand to watch. More than the first half of the film depicts the beginnings of Bryce's career and subsequent celebrity. It's amusing and lively, and you want more. Then *Funny Girl* bogs down in the glop of her personal woes. Her marriage to the debonair Nicky Arnstein is overlong and overdone. Omar Sharif plays the part with verve, however. He's much more alive than he was in *Doctor Zhivago* (maybe Omar was too cold in that Russian winter).

Walter Pidgeon does a credible job as Flo Ziegfeld. But it's deservedly all about Streisand. It's her show. She electrifies. In 1968, she shared the Best Actress category, tying for an Oscar with Katharine Hepburn for *The Lion in Winter*.

Give yourself the present of *Funny Girl,* but stay away from its sequel, *Funny Lady.*

EXTRAS

We were quite surprised that the extras on the DVD release are so sparse. Maybe there's going to be a big birthday party for it soon. What you get is the film in a restored edition. At the time of the release, there were two short promotional pieces made, "Barbra in Movieland" and "This Is Streisand"; neither is much to see. There are the usual filmography and scene selections. This is a movie we would like to see get the deluxe treatment.

Gentleman's Agreement

CAST: Gregory Peck, Dorothy McGuire, John Garfield, Anne
  Revere, Celeste Holm, June Havoc, Albert Dekker, Jane Wyatt,
  Dean Stockwell, Nicholas Joy, Sam Jaffe, Harold Vermilyea,
  Ransom M. Sherman
DIRECTOR: Elia Kazan
SCREENWRITER: Moss Hart (based on the novel by Laura Z.
  Hobson)
RELEASED: 1947 (118 minutes)
RATED: Not rated

In polite conversation about reservations, club member-
ships, and the like, the word was *restricted*. In real estate
deals, the word was *covenant*. What they meant was "no
Jews allowed." Based on the novel by Laura Hobson, *Gentleman's Agreement* took a searing look at anti-Semitism for
the first time in a major studio film. Just as lighter-skinned
African Americans sometimes "passed" as whites, Jews
without obviously Semitic features sometimes chose to
"pass" as well. In this enduring classic, a WASP's WASP,
played by Gregory Peck, decides to expose the prevalence of
anti-Semitism by posing as a Jew. He slips into his identity
easily, moving from Phil Green to Philip Greenberg. Suddenly, his privileged life becomes difficult as he is denied
access to any number of things and places he had been accustomed to and never really thought about.

Peck plays an established journalist who is asked to do
a series of articles about anti-Semitism for *Smith's Weekly*.
The editor is a fighter for good causes named John
Minify (Albert Dekker). Green gets the idea that the only
way to break through the barriers and tell the truth is to
pose as a Jew. Green is a widower who comes to New York

with his small son, Tommy (Dean Stockwell), and his
mother (Anne Revere).

Green tells Minify that the hook for the series will be
his deception scheme, "I Was Jewish for Six Months."
Minify loves the idea and puts together a meeting with the
magazine's staff. Celeste Holm plays Anne Dettrey, fashion
editor. Present at the meeting is an important tycoon who
is Jewish. He hates the idea and says it will only cause harm
to Jews.

His secretary, played by June Havoc, uses the name
Elaine Wales but reveals that her actual name is Estelle
Walovsky. It's not that these things didn't exist in plenitude,
but the device now seems a bit too handy. The love interest
is Minify's beautiful divorced niece, Kathy Lacey (Dorothy
McGuire). She's understanding and lovely and believes herself to be accepting and unbiased.

It all becomes much more involving after a few somewhat awkward setup scenes. Then the movie really clicks
along. Director Elia Kazan gets to the discomfort people
have with Jews and Jewishness in a most convincing manner. The movie is at its most believable in the performances
of McGuire and John Garfield, who plays Green's Jewish
friend Dave. McGuire is convinced of her open attitudes,
but out of her mouth pop her true feelings, without her
even realizing what the words reveal. When Tommy is hassled at school as a "dirty Jew," she immediately hugs him
and comforts him. She tells him that of course it isn't true,
he's not a Jew. A later scene in a restaurant with Garfield
and McGuire, absent the stilted manners and 1940s décor
and clothing, could happen today.

Garfield's performance was a brave one. Part of the joy
of this new DVD is in the extras. Peck's character is forever
changed by his experiences as a temporary Jew. His naïveté
is over; he emerges at the end of the film as a far more multi-

dimensional character than he was at its beginning. The Academy rewarded the film with the 1947 Oscar for Best Picture. Holm won as Best Supporting Actress, and Kazan won for Best Director. Peck was nominated for Best Actor, but Ronald Colman won for *A Double Life*. An interesting part of Hollywood history is that Peck and Garfield competed with each other in the Best Actor category that year, although neither won. Garfield also was nominated for his starring role in *Body and Soul.*

EXTRAS

The audio commentary with Holm, Havoc, and critic Richard Schickel brings the movie into sharp perspective. Peck felt that he was carrying the world on his shoulders when he made this film. He cared passionately about its message. Revere was later blacklisted. The irony of Kazan's direction of this film and his later behavior during the blacklisting hearings in Washington in the 1950s is not lost. The scene in the magazine's offices was apparently Kazan's jab at the studio power players who didn't want this film to be made. Just about everyone in power in Hollywood was Jewish, but they felt, as did the Jewish industrialist in the movie, that it was a bad idea to make the movie.

It was Darryl F. Zanuck who believed in the film. Zanuck, although not Jewish, was often mistaken for a Jew because of the sound of his last name. His sympathy for the plot had personal aspects to it.

Fellow cast members appreciated Garfield's talent as a "wonderfully natural actor." He was proud of being Jewish and took the role knowing that it might have adverse effects on his career. Garfield died at the age of thirty-nine in 1952, but not before the House Committee on Un-American Activities stirred up enough trouble for him that

he found employment difficult. Unlike Kazan, he coura-
geously refused to testify about anyone else.

"Backstory" is a superior feature. It goes into far more
depth about the mood and political climate at the time of
the making of *Gentleman's Agreement.* Particularly moving
and illuminating are the interview clips with Garfield's
daughter, Julie Garfield. She's an actress and acting teacher
who offers an intimate portrait of her father and of his
stand against blacklisting. She talks about his reactions to
the "naming of names" that others engaged in and of
Garfield's struggles to find appropriate work. In a wrenching moment, she says she has always felt her father "died of
a broken heart."

Gigi

CAST: Leslie Caron, Maurice Chevalier, Louis Jourdan, Hermione
    Gingold, Eva Gabor, Isabel Jeans
DIRECTOR: Vincente Minnelli
SCREENWRITER: Alan Jay Lerner (based on the play by Anita Loos
    and adapted from the novel by Colette)
RELEASED: 1958 (116 minutes)
RATED: G

Gigi has had about as many lives as a cat. First and foremost
is the story by French author Colette. In 1948, the French
made their own movie version, also called *Gigi,* but without music. Then it came to Broadway in the Anita Loos
version. However, for most Americans, *Gigi* is synonymous
with the Lerner and Loewe film.

It's the story of a young girl who is the daughter, grand-
child, and niece of elegant French courtesans. The Colette
story has some real spice to it. Gigi is brought up to believe

that the only valid life for her will be the life of a courtesan. It's the tale of a young woman's eventual spirited rebellion against the traditions of her family. It's also a profoundly French slant on questions of love. By the time Alan Jay Lerner and Frederick Loewe and Vincente Minnelli got done with the script and Cecil Beaton dressed everyone, the whole business became so mild it got a G rating. It doesn't matter. In the end, it's a classic American musical with all the trimmings, despite its French inspiration.

If you were a child in the 1950s and saw it, you probably didn't totally understand the plot. It's a dazzling musical with some of the best songs in our songbook: "I Remember It Well," a tribute to old lovers; the moment of love's awakening in "Gigi"; the now impossibly titled "Thank Heaven for Little Girls." It's croissants with too much butter and jam. It's good for a snowy night. It's good when you need a nostalgia fix. Let's cut out the snob appeal and face the facts. It's great just about any time at all.

Leslie Caron, already in her late twenties, pulled off the role as the teenage Gigi with perfection. Her training in the high art of how to be a courtesan is conducted by a cast of female characters who now look so funny you wonder if Dame Edna is hiding out in there somewhere. The songs, the Andre Previn score, those Beaton costumes, and, of course, Paris make it a winner every single viewing.

In 1958 however, it wasn't campy or even slightly silly. It won Best Picture, Minnelli won Best Director, and *Gigi* took away seven other Oscars. It's been endlessly compared to *My Fair Lady* for all the obvious reasons, but it has its own identity. It isn't as much a carbon copy of *Lady* as the press wanted you to believe. There are many who prefer it to *Lady*. We're just sorry so much of Colette's unique flavoring was lost in too much lavish frosting of the cake.

EXTRAS

There is a small booklet, which gives behind-the-scenes information. This one might be ripe for an enhanced release; we certainly hope so.

Gladiator

CAST: Russell Crowe, Joaquin Phoenix, Connie Nielsen, Oliver
    Reed, Richard Harris, Derek Jacobi, Djimon Hounsou
DIRECTOR: Ridley Scott
SCREENWRITER: David Franzoni
RELEASED: 2000 (154 minutes)
RATED: R

The Roman Empire remains one of the most powerful stories of recorded history. Far from romantic, it was a time of savage wars, as well as enlightened civilization and intellectual accomplishments. Circa A.D. 180 was a time of ruthless warfare and bloodshed enough to fill all the rivers of the discovered and yet to be discovered world.

It is the more gruesome side of that period that Ridley Scott depicts in *Gladiator*. Emperor Marcus Aurelius (Richard Harris) is at the end of his life. He is hoping to finish the campaign against the barbarians, the only remaining obstacle to his continued domination of the world. General Maximus Decimus Meridius (Russell Crowe) leads his forces. He's a loyal servant, as well as a trusted friend and companion.

After conquering the barbarians, Marcus Aurelius confides in Maximus that he has selected him to inherit the throne. He wishes to pass over his son Commodus (Joaquin Phoenix) who he fears is too cold and self-serving to be a good ruler. Maximus would rather go home to his family and wheat fields but agrees to the emperor's wishes. When he learns of his father's action, Commodus kills his father before anyone else knows the secret. Once in power, Commodus sentences Maximus and his family to death.

Maximus escapes, but he is gravely wounded by the torture of his captors. He is unable to reach his family in time to save them. A band of slave traders capture Maximus; he ends up in North Africa, where he is sold to Proximo (Oliver Reed). (Reed died during filming. The wonders of computer technology were used to complete the final scenes without his actual presence.) As a former gladiator, Proximo immediately sees the potential in Maximus. He turns Maximus into a fighting star (think *Rocky* in armor with lots more gore).

Just as his father suspected would be the case, Commodus is a lousy and unpopular leader. Thousands in the provinces are dying from the plague or starvation. Hoping to distract them, Commodus lifts his father's ban on gladiator fights. Maximus returns to Rome as a gladiator.

In Rome, Maximus proves to be the greatest gladiator of all time. He conquers tigers as well as multiple gladiators at one time, and nothing can conquer him. He becomes a popular hero and a tremendous threat to the new emperor. Jealousy and rage again fuel Commodus. Politics, intrigue, and more plot and subplot than the film can handle follow, rather haltingly.

Harris and Reed fill their characters with life and mystery. Also superb are the performances of Connie Nielsen as Lucilla, sister of Commodus, and Djimon Hounsou as Juba, Maximus's friend in the gladiator stables. Phoenix is convincing as the hateful and obsessed Commodus. Crowe bursts into vivid life as the lead character. Having suffered the horrific loss of his family, he intends to avenge their deaths and the death of Marcus Aurelius. He brings it all home for the viewer.

Scott brought much emotion to this project. His chosen palette of dark hues encases the depressing nature of the story. It is only in the dreams that Maximus has of his family where more vibrant colors are generously displayed. The action scenes in the Colosseum are remarkable, they are visually chaotic and disorienting. The viewer feels present inside Crowe's body during the gladiator encounters. This isn't a pretty film, filled with beautiful landscapes and people. You must be ready to see it.

In the end, you won't be convinced one way or the other. You either love the movie or hate it. Nobody seems to be in the middle. Many who love it do so because they believe it follows in the tradition of the great epic sagas such as *Spartacus* or *Ben-Hur*. Those who hate it resent that it is compared to those classics, because it doesn't hold up to their standard. It's unfair to compare Scott's *Gladiator* to those cherished films of the past. This is a new time, with new computer and digital technologies; *Gladiator* should and must be taken on its own terms.

Although not every special effect created in this film is of equal impact, the greatest artistic achievement is the recreation of the Rome of the time of the Colosseum.

EXTRAS

This two-disc set has a great amount of added viewing. First and foremost, you'll want to hear the commentary by Scott, along with his editor, Pietro Scalia, and cinematographer John Mathieson. In fact, if you saw this film in the theater, watch it again for the first time with the audio commentary going. You'll get so much more from the film this way. If you haven't seen it, you'll probably want to see the film first, then come back to the commentary later.

(However, most of us don't have the strength or spirit to watch *Gladiator* twice in back-to-back sessions.)

There are eleven deleted scenes that were cut primarily because the film was overly long. We advise watching them with Scott's commentary option on.

"HBO First Look" is a feature focused on the computer-generated aspects of the film. It's not as comprehensive as we imagined it would be but is still worth your selection.

For our dollar, the best feature is a fifty-minute documentary entitled "The Bloodsport of a Gladiator," which was on cable television before the theatrical release. Unless you remember your high school or college Roman history better than we did, you'll find this rewarding. It puts the film in context. The film weaves together truth and fiction, as most films do. This documentary helps unscramble a variety of plot confusions.

A feature on the making of the music for the film is better than most on the subject of matching music to theme and mood.

There are two "eggs," hardly worth the effort, but the effort is minimal. You can figure them out yourself, no doubt, but here they are. The first one is in the trailer section of the main menu. After selecting this section to the left, an eagle will be highlighted in red (subtle). Crack that egg open, and you'll get the theatrical trailer for *Chicken Run*. The other egg is in the "Original Storyboard" section. Select the rhino fight in the deleted sequences, and then highlight the rhino in the middle frame on the first storyboard. Here you can read the scene or view test footage from this deleted sequence.

You should purchase either the "Signature Selection" or the "Collector's Edition," depending on which is available in your area.

Glengarry Glen Ross

CAST: Jack Lemmon, Ed Harris, Al Pacino, Alan Arkin, Kevin
     Spacey, Alec Baldwin, Jonathan Pryce
DIRECTOR: James Foley
SCREENWRITER: David Mamet (from his play)
RELEASED: 1992 (100 minutes)
RATED: R

David Mamet's gruesome but masterful examination of
out-of-luck real estate salesmen transferred to the screen
better than most standard Broadway plays. In some ways,
the film version is even more intense than the play.
Mamet's Pulitzer Prize–winning play makes Willy Loman's
suffering look like the results of an infected hangnail.

Kevin Spacey plays the office manager, John
Williamson, whose motto might well be "Kill or be killed."
It's about closing deals in a dead market with lousy leads.
The story about the tribulations of making a living in sales
is not a new one. Before Mamet wrote this, everyone believed the last word was Arthur Miller's *Death of a Salesman*. It's still a definitive work, and Willie Loman is still a
metaphor for desperation and failure. But it is no longer
the last word on the trials of a salesman. *Glengarry* is an
uglier, meaner version of the way competition for a crumb
can transform a person into a monster. The devil appears
on screen briefly in the person of Alec Baldwin, a motiva-
tional speaker brought in from headquarters. He's there to
inspire the guys to close deals; what he inspires is terror.

A sales contest is put into place. The first prize is a new
car, the second a set of dull steak knives. The third prize is
"You're outta here," and they mean it. The salesmen are
given terrible leads, but must use them to prove their merit.
The real prize is the hope of holding on to the job. Only

two will survive. It's a version of TV's *Survivor* without the adventure scenes. Al Pacino plays Ricky Roma, still at the top of his game. Jack Lemmon is Shelley Levene; once the top closer, he's known as the "Machine." Now, he's a shadow of himself and barely managing. Lemmon plays this role with extraordinary pathos; he's even better in this than in *Save the Tiger*, another outstanding performance in a film with a similar theme. Here the desperation has a softer edge to it, the winding down of a life, not just a career. Ed Harris plays Dave Moss, and Alan Arkin is George Aaronow. Both spout a great deal of attitude but are secretly plotting something almost as sinister as the hand that's been dealt them.

There are many unforgettable scenes in *Glengarry* that portray the fragility of these men, who have been traditional breadwinners, now facing debts, marital problems, and total loss of self-esteem. They look like a species on the brink of extinction, because that is exactly what they are.

Pacino's character tries to put the bite on Jonathan Pryce to buy a property; the interaction is terrifyingly real and superbly executed. Although it's only one scene in the arc of Pacino's career, it will be etched in your memory forever.

Mamet is not known for the elegant turn of phrase but for the force and impact of hammer-driven dialogue and character development. The language used here is incessantly profane. Don't let it get in your way.

EXTRAS

The tenth-anniversary DVD edition offers a variety of supplements of uneven quality.

Disc One offers a commentary by director James Foley that is fragmented. Interestingly, the tension between Baldwin's character and Baldwin himself produced challenges for Foley, which he discusses.

"Magic Time: A Tribute to Jack Lemmon" is the best supplement on the two discs. Just before the cameras rolled on any movie he worked on, Lemmon was widely known to whisper, "Magic time." This is a loving tribute to one of our greatest character actors, whose death in 2001 saddened the movie industry as much as it did his millions of fans. The feature includes interviews with actors, friends, and others who worked with Lemmon through the many years of his career. There's also an interview with Chris Lemmon, his son. Perhaps the best moments of the feature are clips taken from James Lipton's cable television series, *Inside the Actor's Studio*.

Disc Two has interesting background material and historical footage about the tribulations of the salesman's life.

The documentary "ABC" (Always Be Closing) is the best of the lot on this second disc. We especially like it for its attention to the extraordinary documentary *Salesman* made by Albert and David Maysles in 1969.

"J. Roy: New and Used Furniture" is a short documentary about the life of a real salesman named "Diamond" Jimmy Roy. It's in pretty bad shape cinematically. If you are interested in a real behind-the-door look at this life, rent the Maysles brothers' film instead.

There's a bonus commentary by Baldwin, Arkin, and various crew members which we didn't find worth much.

Clips from the Charlie Rose show are of Lemmon discussing the theatrical release of the film as well as a few anecdotes from his life and career. A clip from *Inside the Actor's Studio* is of Spacey and is very humorous.

For theater students, the egg worth the hunt is not so hard to find, although the rest of us won't find it worth the trouble. It's acting students reciting the Blake bit. On special features, go to the main menu and click on "Bar."

The Godfather

CAST: Marlon Brando, Al Pacino, James Caan, Richard Castellano,
     Robert Duvall, Diane Keaton, Talia Shire, Sterling Hayden,
     Richard Conte, Abe Vigoda, Ruby Bond
DIRECTOR: Francis Ford Coppola
SCREENWRITERS: Francis Ford Coppola and Mario Puzo (adapted
     from the novel by Puzo)
RELEASED: 1972 (175 minutes)
RATED: R

Think of *The Godfather* and its sequels as *Gone with the Wind* for the Mafia. Like *GWTW*, it presents a romanticized world that is changing or even dying out. And like *GWTW*, despite the epic length of the three *Godfather* films, there are nuggets of golden sense here and there. *The Godfather* saga has become such a part of our cultural landscape that we don't think much about it any longer. It's the inspiration for the wildly popular HBO *Sopranos* series.

Francis Ford Coppola's *Godfather* has achieved such classic status that many have forgotten the controversies surrounding its original release: the negative representation of Italian Americans and the sympathetic portrayal of gangsters and killers (problems also found, incidentally, in Mario Puzo's bestselling novel, on which the film is based). These difficulties are in many ways reconciled by the sheer power of the filmmaking. *The Godfather* is one of the high points of Coppola's brilliant but uneven career. He paints a vast, dark canvas of characters and events, concentrating on the concerns of Don Corleone (Marlon Brando) about his son who will succeed him as the Godfather. The action begins in the mid-1940s and spans several years (then several more in the sequels, maintaining a remarkable authenticity). The ensemble of Method actors is superb, with

Brando's Oscar-winning Don almost outshined by Al Pacino's likable soldier turned ruthless gangster.

Coppola's problems begin, to some large extent, with the Puzo novel. We believe the 1972 *Godfather* remains Coppola's best artistic effort in this saga of the Corleone family. However, you really do need to see all of them for continuity.

The Godfather, Part II is not really a stand-alone movie. While it considerably enriches the original *Godfather,* it must be seen with it in order to be fully appreciated as the epic that chronicles the rise and fall of the family. In *Part II,* the new Godfather (Pacino) is faced with crooked business partners, disloyal brothers, and a wife (Diane Keaton) who disapproves of his activities. Meanwhile, the film recalls, in extended flashback sequences, how the young immigrant Don Corleone (Robert De Niro) built the now-collapsing empire. Much of the production (which won seven Oscars, including Best Picture)—acting, directing, period design— is as good as, if not better than, the original. It's a must-see film, all the more after a screening of the first.

The Godfather, Part III is a fitting coda to Coppola's epic saga about the Corleone crime family, completing the greatest trilogy in motion picture history. Pacino is exceptional as the aging Don Michael striving to legitimize his family's business by cutting a deal with the Roman Catholic church. The film is rich with the colors of autumn, and it's filled with memories and regret for tragedies past. There are two extraordinary sequences of violence, one set at a mob casino meeting and the other, toward the end, cross-cut between a Palermo opera house and the Vatican itself. Andy Garcia and Talia Shire, as Michael's nephew and sister, give electrifying performances. Co-written by Coppola and Mario Puzo. The film's impact is greatly marred by the poor acting of Sofia Coppola playing Pacino's daughter.

Coppola reached a point of no return with *Godfather III*, and the film does not live up to the promise of the earlier two. However, by the time you get to *Godfather III*, you are practically related to the Corleones, and you simply have to know what happens.

EXTRAS

This is an easy selection. If you like the *Godfather* films, you simply buy the boxed set, which has all three in one package. It's got too much fluff for our taste, but in between the airy hype are some good features.

The three movies with commentary take up four discs. A fifth disc just contains extras. Each film has a commentary by Coppola, who doesn't have to be persuaded to share his experiences. He disarms you with his honesty and willingness to talk about what went wrong and how he might have done certain things differently.

The menus on the fifth disc are among the most user-friendly we've encountered. You'll definitely want to see the documentary "The Godfather Family: A Look Inside." It runs an hour and fifteen minutes and puts into context the entire history of the making of this brilliant, uniquely American saga. Again, like *Gone with the Wind*, it isn't that these Mafia movies are above criticism, either, it's just not the point any longer. *Godfather I, II,* and *III* are events in American movie history, and they continue to provide interesting viewing. With the popularity of the *Sopranos* television series, one suspects interest in the *Godfather* movies will only continue to grow.

Don't laugh at us, but we find the "Godfather Family Tree" and the "Godfather Chronology" exceedingly helpful to follow the story through to conclusion. Why not throw a theme party and watch all three of the *Godfather* films at once, with appropriate rest and refreshment breaks, of course. In "Family Tree," click on Sonny for James Caan extras.

We've been coerced by someone to reveal a really dumb Easter egg. The person in question is in the FBI Witness Protection Plan, so we can't tell you who it is. In the DVD credits, watch through the FBI warning, then zap, and you get the Sopranos doing something mildly amusing. It's not funny enough to be campy, but it does seem to tickle people.

Gone with the Wind

CAST: Vivien Leigh, Clark Gable, Leslie Howard, Olivia de Havilland, Hattie McDaniel, Butterfly McQueen, Ona Munson, Oscar Polk, Thomas Mitchell, Barbara O'Neil, Rand Brooks, Ann Rutherford, George Reeves, Fred Crane, Victor Jory, Evelyn Keyes

DIRECTORS: George Cukor, Victor Fleming, Sam Wood, and Cameron Menzies

SCREENWRITERS: Sydney Howard, Jo Swerling, Charles MacArthur, Ben Hecht, John Lee Mahin, John Van Druten, Oliver H. P. Gerrett, Winston Miller, Johan Balderston, Michael Foster, Edwin Justus Mayer, F. Scott Fitzgerald, and David O. Selznick (based on the novel by Margaret Mitchell)

RELEASED: 1939 (220 minutes)

RATED: G

It's not that *Gone with the Wind* is above criticism, it's sort of beyond it. In 1939, the United States was still a profoundly segregated country, with substantially confused notions about race, gender, and its own history. The Civil War wasn't ancient textbook history. The release of the film was an event of monumental proportion. It remains a perennial favorite for the love story as well as for the sharply defined characters. It took an army of craftsmen, spearheaded by William Cameron Menzies, the designer, to bring it to fruition. "General" David O. Selznick oversaw it all. Ultimately, countless writers became cannon fodder for the campaign leading to its completion (including Selznick himself and F. Scott Fitzgerald). Four different directors were involved. It was Victor Fleming who was able to bring home the victory.

Producer Selznick was determined to make the epic to end all epics. He wanted to realize perfectly Margaret Mitchell's wildly popular Civil War romantic/historical novel. Just as *Gone with the Wind* notes the passing of a way of life, it is a swan song to the Hollywood dream factory. It's not the greatest movie ever made, but it is surely one of Hollywood's greatest productions.

The legendary search for the actress to play Scarlett eventually sent the talented George Cukor off his trolley for a time and finally off the set. Finding Scarlett was a fitting symbol for a crazed commitment to narrative moviemaking. The budget, the effort, maybe even the time spent actually can be seen in the final production. In the end, it was all worth it. Perhaps the most memorable scene is the camera pullback at the train station, where Scarlett walks among the wounded. Of course, there's the ever-popular scene where she and Mammy fashion a dress out of the draperies.

Atlanta burns, as it indeed did. Scarlett yearns for Ashley. Melanie lingers. Rhett, finally, thankfully, doesn't give a damn. Scarlett will worry about it tomorrow.

In many ways, Hollywood never topped this dazzler because it never tried again in quite this way, perhaps until James Cameron's *Titanic*.

Everyone in Atlanta knows that Margaret Mitchell was killed by a car as she crossed the street, but her novel lives forever in this film. Of course, it's a romanticized view of the plantation lifestyle and is about as politically incorrect as you can find, especially today. However, it's also an accurate depiction of the horrors of the Civil War, its bloodshed on both sides, and the brutal punishing revenge of the Union Army as it torched its way through the South.

In the lobby of the Garrick Club in London's theater district, a simple plaque hangs on the wall which commemorates the loss of its members in World War II. There starkly stands the name of Leslie Howard. It always gives us a moment's pause each time we see it. Howard is largely remembered for being a perfectly bland straight man to Clark Gable's glitz in a film about the American Civil War. The real Howard was shot down in a plane in 1943. In England, he is remembered not only as Ashley Wilkes but as a war hero. The details of his death have always remained a mystery. If you would like to see Howard in a much more dynamic role, try *Intermezzo* with Ingrid Bergman, made the same year as *GWTW* (currently available only on video).

EXTRAS

None. Nothing. Bare bones. It's about the film, as we said in our introduction. This print is glorious. We would tell you to hold off for that five-disc set with everything, but we're not sure if it's in the pipeline. (One might assume the sixty-fifth anniversary could inspire something special, but then why didn't the sixtieth?) The original 1998 MGM release has been out of print for quite some time. The 2000 Warner Home edition eliminates even the paper booklet. You can upgrade if and when a new version comes out. That just might take as many attempts as making the movie did. Unless you're a person who has never, ever, even once, eaten dessert first, go for it.

Good Will Hunting

CAST: Robin Williams, Matt Damon, Ben Affleck, Minnie Driver,
   Stellan Skarsgard, Casey Affleck
DIRECTOR: Gus Van Sant
SCREENWRITERS: Matt Damon and Ben Affleck
RELEASED: 1997 (125 minutes)
RATED: R

Matt Damon is Will Hunting, a tough kid who works as
a janitor at MIT. He spends his time drinking, roughing
up people, and generally throwing his life away. His life
has no meaning, no direction, and no purpose. Its
tragedy has a special edge to it, however. Will Hunting,
janitor, is also Will Hunting, secret mathematical genius.
One of MIT's most distinguished professors offers a challenge to his students. Solve a problem previously unsolved,
and he will give that student a prize. In mathematics,
there are solutions and there are solutions. Some mathe-
maticians call solutions that show genius, rather than
mere ability, elegant. Does the notion that numbers in a
line on a chalkboard could be elegant seem odd? It isn't if
you speak the secret language of higher mathematics.
Numbers can be elegant, mind-bending, and sometimes
absolutely beautiful.

A professor named Lambeau, played by Stellan Skarsgard, writes an equation on the chalkboard. An elegant and
precise solution is written on the board when he returns the
next day. But none of his students can provide the answer.
Who did the math?

Eventually, the professor sees the janitor at the board
and understands. Will isn't thrilled to be discovered. He's
angry. There are class issues in this film that are carefully
and honestly portrayed. Will's a kid who doesn't want to

live in an ivory tower. His gift is as much his affliction as anything.

Will thinks that real work is manual work. The more Lambeau struggles to make Will accept what he is capable of doing with his mind, the more he misbehaves. The shrinks call it acting out. Will acts out enough to end up in the slammer and is rescued when the professor bails him out with the obligation that he must be responsible for this angry, confused kid. Enter Dr. McGuire. Robin Williams shines in this role as a complex and sad man who has managed to end up at a third-rate commuter school rather than a first-rate university. He's an old pal of the professor's, and he agrees to take on the job of confronting and counseling Will.

Mathematics is not an acquired skill. Arithmetic is. You can teach a chicken to count to ten and add and subtract. Higher mathematics is not arithmetic. It is art. It comes with your hard drive, if you have that hard drive. It's like the ability to sit down and compose a sonata or paint the Sistine Chapel. Somebody can give you the pencils and the paint and teach you the basics, but you've got it or you don't. The essential and irresistible fact about mathematics is that it can happen in the most unexpected places. While it is true that the gift tends to run in families, it also can come out of nowhere.

This is the screenplay that put Matt Damon and Ben Affleck on the cinematic map. The miracle of this debut screenplay is that Damon and Affleck don't rush the story along. Affleck plays Chuckie Sullivan, Will's best friend, who insists that Will see his genius as the ticket out of Miseryville. It's not all solved in a therapeutic nanosecond. Will isn't ready to be a genius; he isn't ready to be anything at all. He wants to be left alone. There are demons deep in him, and pushing a broom and drinking beer keeps him just about sedated enough to get through the day.

When Dr. McGuire finally cracks the veneer and Will emerges, the scene is so realistic that it can cause a grown man to cry. Minnie Driver plays a British student enrolled at Harvard who has fallen in love with Will. Will can't bear that, either. His self-loathing seems limitless. We won't reveal the ending, in case you haven't seen the film yet or can't quite remember it.

The real-life story of Affleck and Damon is Hollywood lore by now, and the friendship parallels in the film are clearly autobiographically driven. *Good Will Hunting* worked out so well because all the ingredients were right. A large amount of the credit goes to Gus Van Sant's directing, the fine performances from the entire cast, and, of course, the script.

If you're a Driver fan, you'll want to consider her earlier film *Circle of Friends* (1995). It's on DVD in a no-frills version but worth a purchase for her performance. *Circle of Friends* is based on the novel by Irish writer Maeve Binchy.

EXTRAS

The commentary relates the story of the film. Damon and Affleck's personal story is very interesting. It makes the standard-fare audio track a great deal more interesting. Van Sant chimes in as well. However, if you're a behind-the-scenes type, you may be somewhat disappointed. The commentary concentrates heavily on the movie itself. The deleted scenes are best watched twice. Try it first with audio commentary switched off, then go back to your menu and switch on the audio. Elliot Smith's music video "Mrs. Misery" is also available. There is a quick look at the inside story of the movie, but it's a fast-paced series of clips.

The film itself is of such high quality and the film portion of the DVD is well produced, so that this entry gets high marks from us. Despite its rating, it is really appropri-

ate for a larger age group than the rating limits. The rating
has to do with some foul language and some sexual scenes.
It's not appropriate for the very young, however, because a
number of the scenes with Williams and Damon are anguished and deal with issues for mature viewers.

GoodFellas

CAST: Robert De Niro, Ray Liotta, Joe Pesci, Lorraine Bracco, Paul
    Sorvino, Frank Sivero, Tony Darrow, Mike Starr
DIRECTOR: Martin Scorsese
SCREENWRITERS: Martin Scorsese and Nicolas Pileggi (adapted
    from the book *Wiseguy* by Pileggi)
RELEASED: 1990 (146 minutes)
RATED: R

GoodFellas ranks with Martin Scorsese's other top films. It's
certainly become a favorite Mafia movie. It's the meticulous
honesty with which the story is told that seduces you. It's
not as grand or as dramatic as the *Godfather* series. There's
not much flashy stuff in *GoodFellas*. This is a middle-class
Mafia life. *Mobster* would be the word you would write on
the blank line on the census survey for occupation.

Henry Hill (Ray Liotta) wanted to be a gangster from
the time he was a kid, the way some little boys want to be
airplane pilots or firemen. He could never become a member of the inner circle because he was of "mixed" origin, Italian and Irish. Perhaps because of his semi-outsider status, he
sought to please the bosses even more. Ultimately, it also
may have helped lead him to "Ratville" and straight into the
FBI's Witness Protection Program. This is a true story.
Along the way, the real Hill also "sang" for writer Pileggi,
who turned it all into a book called *Wiseguy*. The shocking

details of the activities of the guys in *GoodFellas* are less the focus of this landmark Mafia film than in others.

What confounds and troubles about *GoodFellas* is the rhythmic pattern to the characters' lives. First, you go kill someone. Then you learn you didn't do an efficient job, and it has to be corrected. So, you stop by your mother's house to pick up a good sharp knife. But, since you're there anyway, you might as well enjoy a home-cooked meal. You return to do a better job on the body. You dig it up, drag the decomposing corpse around, and bury it someplace else. It's all in a day's work. The actions are so bizarre that they have a grotesque humor to them. Lorraine Bracco is wonderful as the Jewish wife of Hill, who walks into a life she doesn't fully comprehend.

Scorsese captures the claustrophobic world of the "family" with an unerring and nonjudgmental eye. He grew up in New York's Italian community, quietly observing and obviously making mental notes for later use. Scorsese was nominated for Best Director but lost to Kevin Costner for *Dances with Wolves,* which has not had the lasting influence of *GoodFellas.* Bracco was nominated for Best Supporting Actress. Joe Pesci won Best Supporting Actor. *GoodFellas* also was nominated for Best Picture but lost to *Dances* there as well.

The dialogue between the men in *GoodFellas* crackles with intensity and big-shot foul language. The reason Scorsese's films outlast others is that he insists on placing his characters within the context in which they exist. *GoodFellas* is so upsetting because these are just two-bit criminals willing to risk everything for what turns out to be so little. It is one of the reasons that while the *Godfather* series can be called a truly great epic, *GoodFellas* is far more terrifying.

Would *The Sopranos* exist at all if it hadn't been for Scorsese's dispassionate look at the social structure of mob life? We doubt it. Tony Soprano is just a regular guy who sits at his kitchen table in his underwear eating cold leftover ziti. He's trying to recover from a heavy night of whacking people. You'll see many parallels to Tony's life when you watch *GoodFellas*.

EXTRAS

There aren't any extras to speak of on *GoodFellas*, but the quality of the picture and the sound are first-rate. You'll need to flip the disc over for the second part of the film. There are production notes and the standard trailers. Don't let the absence of bells and whistles keep you from owning this disc. Warner has packaged this film in a Robert De Niro Collection as well, which includes five De Niro films. It is the same *GoodFellas* that you can buy separately; it isn't enhanced in any manner for the special collection. The De Niro five-pack includes *Analyze This, A Bronx Tale, Heat, Wag the Dog,* and *GoodFellas*.

Gosford Park

CAST: Michael Gambon, Kristin Scott Thomas, Maggie Smith, Jeremy Northam, Bob Balaban, Alan Bates, Helen Mirren, Eileen Atkins, Derek Jacobi, Emily Watson, Stephen Fry
DIRECTOR: Robert Altman
SCREENWRITER: Julian Fellowes
RELEASED: 2001 (138 minutes)
RATED: R

The pleasure of your company is requested at a weekend house party at Gosford Park. Time: November 1932. Requirements: Your maid, valet, trunk filled with clothing and jewels. Most important: Proof of membership in the upper class, either by marriage or by birth, or you'll end up downstairs.

Gosford Park is a stunning film, destined to be a classic. If you saw it in the theater, you undoubtedly missed lines and subplots. One viewing isn't enough to enjoy it to its fullest. The DVD is loaded with extras; it even sounds better than it did in the theater.

Although loosely constructed as a whodunit, it's really a Who's Who of the British stage and screen. It's been noted that actors "kill" to work with Altman, as the experience of being directed by him is so unique. In the commentaries, you'll hear these legendary actors explain why.

This pleasantly complex film pretends to be many things. Just when you think you've figured it out, the plot turns, and it becomes something new. Filmed in a real British manor house, *Gosford Park* is an unsentimental look at the British class structure between the two world wars. It's not the romanticized *Upstairs/Downstairs* Masterpiece Theater version but is better entertainment. Maggie Smith, fresh from *Harry Potter,* won't turn from a cat to a person in this one, but you'll watch her apply cucumber eye patches.

Director Robert Altman tells the story from the servants' vantage point. Altman brilliantly contrasts the high energy and systematic life of the servants with the languorous and almost pointless lives of the aristocrats. Despite their leisure, their lives are scripted by rigid rules. Especially provocative is Sir William McCordle (Michael Gambon), the lord of the manor, a self-made man whose vulgarity is almost compelling. To his wife, Lady Sylvia (Kristin Scott Thomas), he is only a crude man with a fat wallet.

Don't look for sainted figures downstairs, and nasty, spoiled brats upstairs. It's subtler than that. You're transported to another time because Altman had all the actors wired and two cameras roving at all times. It feels as if you're eavesdropping.

It's that period of British history when the aristocracy is desperately trying to hang on to its way of life. Screenwriter Julian Fellowes notes that between 1880 and 1920, approximately 450 American "heiresses" married into the British peerage. Self-made British millionaires also found themselves with aristocratic wives who had little to offer but their titles and cumbersome lifestyles. The class system required serious money and legions of loyal and tireless workers downstairs.

The murder in this murder mystery comes late and with an extra twist or two. The motivation isn't who did it but why. It's about the people and their interconnections, or lack thereof. It's the kind of film only Altman can make when he pushes what he calls his "truth button." We reap the rewards of his artistry.

EXTRAS

This disc offers some of the best extras we've seen. "The Making of Gosford Park" has insightful comments by the actors about Altman. You'll learn that the initial idea came from Bob Balaban and how their relationship developed. Eileen Atkins's remarks about her fellow actors are particularly moving.

Another delight is "The Authenticity of Gosford Park." Altman's team located former servants (now all in their mid-eighties), who became technical advisors. You'll meet Arthur Inch, a former head butler, and Ruth and Violet, former house servants. The filmed footage of them working with the actors is amusing as well as poignant.

If you thought the plot was complicated, check out the cutting-room floor in "Deleted Scenes." There's a taped Q and A session with Altman, Fellowes, and some of the cast, which provides more background on the collaborative process.

"Screenwriter's Commentary with Julian Fellowes" is a major highlight. Fellowes is from an upper-class British family. Some of the actual dialogue was taken from his childhood experiences with his great-aunts and uncles and his own parents. Note his comments about the introduction of fish knives, as well as remarks about the amount of information the servants really knew about their employers. This was, we remind you, 1932, when you were unlikely to be paid a few million pounds for a tell-all book about the folks upstairs.

Guess Who's Coming to Dinner

CAST: Katharine Hepburn, Spencer Tracy, Sidney Poitier, Katharine Houghton, Cecil Kellaway, Beah Richards, Roy Glenn
DIRECTOR: Stanley Kramer
SCREENWRITER: William Rose
RELEASED: 1967 (108 minutes)
RATED: Not rated

Spencer Tracy and Katharine Hepburn play a liberal, affluent San Francisco couple. Then their twenty-three-year-old daughter (Katharine Houghton) introduces them to her thirty-seven-year-old fiancé, Sidney Poitier. It was a daring film at the time on interracial romance.

Guess Who's Coming to Dinner is to racism what *Gentleman's Agreement* was to anti-Semitism—ahead of their time but perhaps a little creaky now. Yet the sentiments are still decent ones, and we shouldn't snicker at either film. Given how far human beings still have to go to reach full understanding and acceptance of our differences, the messages in both are still important.

The most troubling aspect of *Guess* is that Poitier must be beyond superman even to be considered acceptable as a dinner guest, let alone a spouse. By the time they get done with the fourth rehearsal of his outstanding distinctions as a World Health Organization doctor and his international fame, you might choke. But it was heartfelt, and it was 1967.

Today the film is seen and cherished primarily as a final vehicle for Tracy and Hepburn. Tracy died that same year. The producers could not get the obligatory insurance for him, as he was that weak. His diminished strength and Hepburn's response to it on screen make for the more believable aspects of the film. You'll note her eyes often well with tears, which we assume has more to do with love for Tracy than emotion for the character she portrayed.

At the time of this movie's release, the liberal good intentions of the director were amply rewarded. Hepburn won an Oscar, as did the original screenplay. There's still plenty of prejudice around, but interracial relationships are no longer such a hot potato (unless you're Trent Lott).

It's also of note for film trivia buffs that this was quite a family affair. The young woman who played Hepburn's daughter was in fact her niece, Katharine Houghton. But Houghton didn't have her aunt's talent, and her career never blossomed. Tracy and Hepburn play very liberal folks until their daughter brings home Poitier, an African American, who is her fiancé. You'll want this if you want the sweep of Hepburn and Tracy from the beginning to this rather poignant end, not because you think the film is a classic. Given the loss of the Hepburn-Tracy romantic real-life and on-screen team just months after filming was over, there is something here for the soft part of your heart.

No extras, except the film dubbed into French.

A Hard Day's Night

CAST: John Lennon, Paul McCartney, George Harrison, Ringo
    Starr, Wilfred Brambell, Norman Rossington
DIRECTOR: Richard Lester
SCREENWRITER: Alun Owen
RELEASED: 1964 (83 minutes)
RATED: Not rated

With only two Beatles left, *A Hard Day's Night* on DVD comes at a bittersweet moment. This was their first and greatest movie. Richard Lester directed a stylishly choreographed romp through their lives, a funny and exhilarating return to a time when we all had more innocence. The inventive "script" is thirty-six hours in the life of the Fab Four.

A Hard Day's Night was responsible for conversions of the unwashed, largely because of the film's humorous spoof on Beatlemania. The Beatles' ability to parody the insanity that surrounded their unprecedented popularity endeared them to an ever-larger audience, creating more victims of Beatlemania. Wilfred Brambell, as McCartney's cranky grandfather, is charmingly impossible. The Beatles sing about a dozen of their most popular songs, including the title song. They run around in mad circles, but it's all been carefully directed and imaginatively photographed. It's a film filled with wit, intelligence, and good-natured irreverence.

EXTRAS

Disc One has an insightful feature entitled "Things They Said Today." It's new material, which is always welcome on DVD supplements. There are also plenty of clips from the making of the film. David Picker proudly talks about how cheaply he was able to sign the band for a three-picture deal. Picker was then head of United Artists. Musical director George Martin is still seething about what he considered an unfair arrangement, despite the overwhelming popularity of the film.

Disc Two might be called "Discmania." Too much, and not enough quality control. You'll have to pick and choose based on your own need to know and see and hear.

Richard Lester's remarks in the feature "Their Production Will Be Second to None" are worth listening to, and there's more of Martin here. There is a funny bit with one of the producers who admits he did the film to get his kids off his back.

"With the Beatles" is an interview feature that is one of the better choices on this disc. Those involved with the making of the film offer their perspectives on the Beatles. We especially liked Lionel Blair's comments about the "dances."

"What You See" isn't rocket science, but it's funny. The conversations with the hair stylist and the director of photography contain amusing anecdotes.

"Busy Working Overtime" shows how to deal with screaming teenagers all the time.

"Listen to the Music Playing in Your Head" is more of Martin, but this is great stuff. He talks about the working habits of the Beatles and the way they put together the single and album releases. Don't miss this one.

"Such a Clean Old Man" offers thoughts about actor Wilfred Brambell, who was only fifty when he was playing a clean old man.

We won't do a laundry list of every single thing on this disc. It would have benefited from some editing and decisions about quality. There are two more that do merit comment.

"Dressing to the Hilt" is a strange interview—talk about filling out a disc with noncontent. Nonetheless, it has a weird appeal. Gordon Millings is the son of the Beatles' tailor. He shows some of the suits the Beatles wore, along with some of the old patterns that were used to make them.

Forget the stupid title of the selection "They and I Have Memories," and just point and click. Klaus Voorman, who was a close friend, recalls the Beatles' youth together and describes exactly what it was like to be a Beatle and to be idolized by millions of girls. This one is one of our favorites on the whole disc. It would have been nice if it could have been longer.

The rationale for the production of this two-disc set appears to be "More is more." Too bad we didn't get fewer options with more meat in them. However, the movie is the bonus and looks and sounds terrific. So, let it be.

Harry Potter and the Sorcerer's Stone

CAST: Daniel Radcliffe, Rupert Grint, Emma Watson, Richard Harris, Maggie Smith, Robbie Coltrane, Fiona Shaw, Harry Melling, Richard Griffiths, Ian Hart, Tom Felton, John Cleese, Alan Rickman, Zoë Wanamaker
DIRECTOR: Chris Columbus
SCREENWRITER: Steven Kloves (based on J. K. Rowling's novel)
RELEASED: 2001 (152 minutes)
RATED: PG

J. K. Rowling's *Harry Potter* is now happily on DVD. You don't need to read the books first to enjoy Harry and his escapades. *Harry Potter* isn't just for kids; it's an adventure movie. In fact, it can frighten the youngest viewers, so use discretion.

The film's special effects are everything the fans of Rowling's books hoped they would be. It's a long movie, clocking in at just over two and a half hours. Staying close to the book's narrative, and loyal to the characters, we are pleased to report that the magic is not diminished by the length.

We first meet Harry, who is enduring a perfectly miserable life with his aunt and uncle who make no attempt to hide their contempt for the lad. He is delivered from this sadness when he is accepted to the British Hogwarts School of Witchcraft and Wizardry. Harry on the screen is somewhat more subdued than the Harry of the book. In the novel his excitement and relief at leaving his home situation almost overwhelm him with joy. Still, you'll find young actor Daniel Radcliffe a more than satisfactory Harry Potter. Harry knows his parents died, but it is only at the school that he learns the identity of his parents. They were powerful and important wizards, and Harry has inherited their mystical gift. He's not only a boy wizard but also a special one at that. His forehead bears the mark of surviving an attack by the evil wizard who killed his parents.

At Hogwarts, Harry makes two friends. First is Hermione Granger (Emma Watson), who is almost too smart and adorable to believe. Harry might possess even more powers, but she's smarter than all of the young wizards put together. Ron Weasley (Rupert Grint), who is all thumbs and seems to have a special knack for getting his spells backward, is Harry's other sidekick. Harry also makes an enemy, Draco Malfoy (Tom Felton).

Hogwarts is overseen and run by headmaster Albus Dumbledore (Richard Harris). Maggie Smith is Professor Minerva McGonagall, the headmistress who assigns newcomers to one of the schools' houses with the help of the talking hat. When not appearing in human guise, she is a cat and moves quickly between these incarnations. Robbie Coltrane is the most lovable gamekeeper Hagrid, who performs many duties other than those of groundskeeper. He quickly befriends Harry and his pals.

Alan Rickman, everyone's favorite villain, is appropriately devilish as Professor Severus Snape. He was the enemy of Harry's parents while they were at Hogwarts and is less than enthusiastic about the younger Potter. There are plenty of other teachers and professors, including the wondrously talented Zoë Wanamaker as Madam Hooch. (She's the daughter of the late Sam Wanamaker, the actor and founder of the Globe in London.) You'll never forget the image of seeing her take off in flight in one of the film's biggest events, the game of Quidditch. It's akin to soccer or basketball but played in the air, with many tricks and obstacles involved. Director Chris Columbus did a magnificent job of bringing this enchanting game to the big screen.

Rowling was obviously inspired by the works of C. S. Lewis and Tolkien, but her novels are more lighthearted than Tolkien's and far less literary than those of Lewis. It doesn't mean that adults won't find this film a treat, especially if you are lucky enough to have the pleasure of the company of a child when watching. If you're an adult, don't expect it to be as satisfying as *The Lord of the Rings*. The novels are not as complex or filled with metaphor as the ones of Tolkien. We're happy to report, however, that a woman has written a series of inventive books about witches and wizards, and she hasn't been burned at the stake. So, sit back and see if you can figure out what's next in the life and times of Harry Potter, boy wizard.

Rowling's books have been an international phenomenon. It does the heart good to see children lined up to buy a book instead of watching the latest television program.

She deserves full marks for writing these tales, which have so enraptured children everywhere.

EXTRAS

The DVD of *Harry Potter* comes with a special features disc that is a bit of wizardry itself. The supplements are really games, with the exception of a sixteen-minute interview with director Columbus and producer David Heyman plus some fairly minimal behind-the-scenes footage. Navigating around the special features *is* a game. You begin your journey with a very cool 3-D, self-guided tour of Hogwarts. You then make your way up Diagon Alley, where you can check out the bank and the wand shop and much more. This is where your adventure begins. You'll have to make your way through the special features and through the school, picking up clues along the way to find the secret in the Mirror of Erised at the end of the game (which, by the way is an egg, but we'll get to that in a minute).

If you don't obtain certain objects and pick up certain clues, you won't be able to continue to the next section to see the other special features. Along your adventure, you will come across "Capturing of the Stone," which is the above-mentioned interview. You also will get to poke around Diagon Alley. And you can go into Harry's classrooms, where you learn how to make potions and get a lesson on spells and charms. In the library, you can look at books and talk to the ghosts of Hogwarts. On the grounds of Hogwarts, you'll get a lesson in the game of Quidditch and a chance to play. And, of course, you get a chance to talk to the talking hat, who will tell you about the four houses of Hogwarts. There are a couple more bonus features, such as "Harry Potter throughout the World," where you can cast spells in different languages. Plus, the DVD-ROM feature allows you to interact with the Web site and download more diversions into your computer.

This DVD was designed for a younger audience, and understandably so. It is, after all, a children's book. But those who are young at heart and read the books and loved the movie will be sure to enjoy this very creative and entertaining DVD.

This time, the Easter eggs are golden ones. You'll find the first one on the movie disc, main menu. At the top right of the screen is an owl in the background; click on the owl, and you will receive a personal invitation to Hogwarts.

The rest of the eggs are on the second disc. When you begin your tour of Hogwarts, you are taken to the common room. You will have the choice to go left or right. Once you are given the choice to go forward, push down on your remote, which will highlight a picture next to the fireplace. Once you have selected it, you move closer to the picture to see the Quidditch field and get more information about the game. Next, while you are in the dinning hall and are facing the teacher's table, you will be given a choice to go left, up, or right; be a proper wizard, and push the down selection instead. Once you select your link, it will take you to the other side of the teacher's table and show the house points scoreboard.

On the main menu, go to Hogwarts grounds and then select Fang's face all the way to the right. This will give you a personal tour of Hagrid's House. Within this egg are two more eggs. Enter the house, and keep going forward until you are in front of the fireplace and select the dragon's egg. Here Hagrid will tell you all about dragons. After you learn about dragons you will still be in front of the fireplace; from there, go left and you will see Hagrid's coat and umbrella. You can select both. They give you interesting information, and you can look through the pockets of Hagrid's coat.

The last egg is the best, and it's what you get when you

win the game. In order to win, there are few things you have to know. First of all, you need to make sure you get your wand while you are in Diagon Alley. After all, what kind of wizard are you if you don't have a wand?

To do this, you will have to find a way to get money from the bank to pay for the wand, and then you have go to the wand shop and select the right one. Oh, and one other thing: in order to enter Diagon Alley, you have to remember the order in which the stones on the wall were pushed in the movie. Then, when you are in the library, be sure to pick up the clue from the screaming book. Select classrooms from the main screen, and then highlight "Transfiguration" but don't select it. Instead, push down. At this point, two owls will fly onto the screen. Select the owls, and you will enter the third-floor corridor. You will have to remember the clues you picked up along the way, and details from the movie. You will be asked a series of questions, catch a flying key, and select the right potion. Once you've done all this, you will be shown the Mirror of Erised with the sorcerer's stone in it. Select the stone, and you've won the game and will be treated to some deleted scenes! Does this all sound like too much for you? Not to worry. Find a young wizard or two in your family or a friend's, and they'll have you navigating Hogwarts in no time at all.

Il Postino

CAST: Massimo Troisi, Philippe Noiret, Maria Grazia Cucinotta, Renato Scarpa, Linda Moretti, Anna Bonaiuto
DIRECTOR: Michael Radford
SCREENWRITERS: Anna Pavignano and Michael Radford
RELEASED: 1994 (108 minutes)
RATED: PG

This movie brought the Nobel Prize poet Pablo Neruda to the world's attention. It also brought the power of love and poetry to everyone who saw it in its original release. *Il Postino* received an Oscar nomination for Best Picture, an almost impossible feat for a foreign film. Luis Enriques Bacalov's original score did win.

Initially, it was difficult to separate the real-life tragedy of the leading man, Massimo Troisi, from the heart-wrenching story of *Il Postino*. Troisi, Italy's much-beloved comedic actor, died of a lingering heart disease the day the film wrapped. Although the death of Troisi will remain the subplot of this movie, enough time has elapsed to lessen its impact on the viewer. Now is the time to see this film again or for the first time. The Collector's Edition DVD has superb extra features.

The plot purports to tell a simple tale. But it is as deceptive in its simplicity as Neruda's poetry or Troisi's life. The story revolves around the exile of Chile's most famous poet and politician, Neruda, and his wife, Matilde. The film opens with a 1950s-style newsreel of Neruda's arrival in Rome and his journey to a remote Italian island. Philippe Noiret looks so uncannily like the poet, it takes a minute to realize the newsreel is a creation of the film.

A relationship develops between a peasant fisherman, Mario Ruoppolo (Troisi), and Neruda (Noiret). Neruda's residence is on the outskirts of the rugged island, and Mario becomes his personal postman. He delivers parcels and letters from adoring fans, mostly women. There is enchantment from the beginning as Mario finds his voice through poetry and through his love for Beatrice, the alluring niece of the tavern owner. Finally, he finds his voice and his death through political activism. The film never slides into sloppy sentimentality, which is a major accomplishment by British director Michael Radford.

There is a wedding but not a "happily ever after" ending. Neruda returns to Chile. Mario never forgets him, but Neruda doesn't maintain the relationship in the manner Mario expected he would. However, his loyalty to Neruda's poetry and political convictions remain solid. The last scenes, played in complete silence by Noiret, are haunting. Neruda's return to the island is marked by redemption and remorse.

EXTRAS

In the commentary by Radford, we get the background story of the making of *Il Postino*. Radford's telling is often more heartbreaking than the film. Troisi purchased the rights to *Burning Passion* by Antonio Skarmeta because he had fallen in love with the character of Mario. Shortly into the filming, he learned he was mortally ill and needed a heart transplant. Radford begged him to stop the production, but he refused. Knowing he would not live to see the film, he proceeded anyway. Radford talks about the last days of Troisi's life and shows scenes in which a double had to be used because of his declining health. There is a moment where the camera catches Troisi hanging between life and death. Radford candidly talks about the selection of the locations and tricks employed to make this film. For example, Noiret acted his part in French. Learning how Radford solved the daunting problems to finish *Il Postino* would be impossible without this bonus feature.

"Poetry, Passion and the Postman: The Poetic Return of Pablo Neruda" is a luscious dessert of a feature bonus. It opens with Sting reading Neruda's famous poem "Naked." Miramax produced this program and pulled out a galaxy of stars—Julia Roberts, Madonna, Glenn Close, Wesley Snipes, Andy Garcia, Ethan Hawke, Samuel L. Jackson, and many more. It is interwoven with scenes from the film and interviews with friends of Neruda. You can see for yourself the astounding resemblance of Noiret to Neruda. A fascinating segment is shot in Neruda's home in Chile. This feature can stand on its own.

It was said that *Il Postino* was about a man who discovers himself through poetry, and so it could be said about Troisi, who gave everything up for his art, and for all of us who have the enduring gift of this film and its accompanying materials.

In the Bedroom

CAST: Sissy Spacek, Tom Wilkinson, Marisa Tomei, Nick Stahl, William Mapother
DIRECTOR: Todd Field
SCREENWRITERS: Robert Fetsinger and Todd Field (adapted from the short story "Killings" by Andre Dubus)
RELEASED: 2001 (130 minutes)
RATED: R

In the Bedroom is the story of the Fowler family. Matt Fowler (Tom Wilkinson) is the town's doctor, but he's also the son of a lobsterman. His son, Frank (Nick Stahl), has finished college with honors and is off to graduate school in September, where he hopes to train to become an architect. Designs of grand buildings drift through his daydreams. His sketches, as well as a telephone call with a famous professor of architecture, suggest Frank may indeed possess genuine talent. Yet both Matt and Frank have an allegiance to their seafaring legacy, which is at the heart of both of these characters. Father and son go out on Frank's boat to check the summer traps. They have a little boy with them.

He's the son of Frank's girlfriend, Natalie Strout (Marisa Tomei). Sissy Spacek plays wife and mother Ruth Fowler. She's the music teacher at the local school and is restrained in both her emotions and her appearance. A cloud of detached disappointment accompanies her every action.

In the Bedroom is an underplayed tragedy that stays with you. It raises questions about the meaning of justice, the endurance of love, and the intractability of social class. Ostensibly a film about the murder of an only son, it goes beyond that to explore the depths of human relationships. Given that so much of the story revolves around a man and a woman in a long-term marriage, the title seems apt. But the title, like the rest of the plot, has layered meanings. *In the Bedroom* is a remarkable directorial debut for Todd Field (last seen as the piano player in Stanley Kubrick's final film *Eyes Wide Shut*). If this is Field's first effort, we can't wait to see more.

The movie was adapted from "Killings," a short story written by the late Andre Dubus. Dubus gave the project his enthusiastic blessing before his death. The original story took place in Massachusetts; Todd Field and cowriter Robert Fetsinger wisely moved it to Maine. It was an equally wise call to change the offputting title to *In the Bedroom.* Maine is as much a state of mind as a geographic location. There isn't the urban rush in the pace of people's lives or in their accents; everything in Maine takes longer to do. Maine also has a certain darkness, making it a perfect setting for this profoundly shocking drama.

Generations of men have made their living harvesting Maine lobsters. But the lives of lobstermen are hard and unforgiving. They rise early and head out to check the traps, with the hope they haven't been tampered with and the prayer they contain lobsters of legal gender and size.

Natalie is exactly the kind of young woman who would

make a boy's mother anxious. At the same time, she's the type who makes fathers a bit envious. Natalie isn't really so disreputable; she's just a woman with too much personal history for a small town. She's thirty-something, and Frank's twenty-something. Natalie doesn't appear to wear much underwear; she has that tousled, just-out-of-bed look. Although Frank attempts to persuade his mother it's only a summer romance, Ruth knows better. Matt might know better, too, but there's substantial dialogue between father and son that hints at Matt's pride over his son's sexy conquest.

Ruth is consumed by her son's relationship. To the townspeople, she looks like a harpy and a snob, until ex-husband Richard Strout's hostility toward Frank and Natalie escalates. Strout (William Mapother) is a total punk; there's rarely been one better portrayed. Discovering Frank with Natalie, Strout punches him, giving him a nasty black eye. As Dr. Fowler patches up his son, he asks, "Did you give it back to him?" Ruth insists they phone the police; both father and son say it will all calm down.

In one of the most searing scenes in the film, the Fowlers finally break down and have a fierce argument. They tell each other every single thing they think about each other. She says it's all his fault; he counters it's all her fault. It's blood on the floor of a different sort. Neither holds back, because in their grief they have lost all their inhibitions. Reminiscent of *Who's Afraid of Virginia Woolf?*, it's more frightening than those scenes of marital disarray, because it's real life. The conclusion seems apparent, but as the film moves forward, there is a very large surprise. Perhaps because of this, it has been incorrectly termed a thriller. It's not that at all. Calling it so cheapens the entangled and richly textured story, which carries this movie through to its "perfect" ending.

EXTRAS

Sadly, there are no extras. But the DVD is worth owning for the performances of Wilkinson, Spacek, and Tomei (all of whom were nominated for Oscars). The film also was nominated for Best Picture and for Best Screenplay.

In the Heat of the Night

CAST: Sidney Poitier, Rod Steiger, Warren Oates, Quentin Dean, Lee Grant, James Patterson, Larry Gates
DIRECTOR: Norman Jewison
SCREENWRITER: Stirling Silliphant (based on the novel by John Ball)
RELEASED: 1967 (109 minutes)
RATED: Not rated

Sidney Poitier first portrayed policeman Virgil Tibbs in this often-effective whodunit. Stirling Silliphant's screenplay is based on the novel by John Ball.

Tibbs is a visitor in a small Mississippi town. The racial tension pulsates in virtually every frame of the film. Initially suspected of murder himself, Poitier's character is then asked to investigate the murder of a wealthy factory owner. As a black man from the North, a well-respected and well-spoken detective, Tibbs encounters resistance and outright prejudice from the townspeople. The Steiger-Poitier confrontations have spark to them, and Steiger won the Oscar for his portrayal of the police chief.

In the Heat of the Night won the Oscar for the Best Picture of 1967, which attests to the power it had for audiences then. Norman Jewison was also nominated for Best Director.

In the Heat of the Night was followed by two sequels

starring Poitier, *They Call Me MISTER Tibbs!* and *The Organization.* Neither one is as good as *In the Heat of the Night.* Quincy Jones's musical score and the singing of Ray Charles are also helpful.

Despite severe space limitations, we feel obliged to make brief mention of the brilliant and varied career of Poitier as actor, director, and writer in both TV and films, and his diverse contributions to activist and humanitarian causes over a period of five decades. Poitier has appeared in more than forty motion pictures. He began as a rising star in the early years of live TV drama in New York City. Poitier is a man of rare natural elegance and eloquence. He is now, and has been for many years, one of the most admired and beloved figures in the American entertainment industry.

EXTRAS

In the Heat of the Night is released through MGM's Home Entertainment Division. The Contemporary Classics line is well produced but doesn't have a great number of extras. On the other hand, the price is right.

The other thing, besides the film, that's quite right about this DVD is the audio commentary. There's Jewison along with Lee Grant and Rod Steiger and cinematographer Haskell Wexler. Unlike some of the newer releases, this audio commentary addresses the movie and does not deteriorate into a self-congratulatory ego-building session. It would have been nice if Poitier had been included, of course. But it's very good to have the talented Grant's perspectives on the making of this film. This is a wise choice for your library and a good buy to boot.

In the Mood for Love

CAST: Tony Leung Chiu-wai, Maggie Cheung Man-yuk, Rebecca
     Pan, Lai Chin, Suit Ping-lam, Chin Tsi-ang
DIRECTOR: Wong Kar-wai
SCREENWRITER: Wong Kar-wai
RELEASED: 2000 (97 minutes)
RATED: Not rated

Spare, elegant, and tragic, *In the Mood for Love* tells the
story of betrayal and love. What makes it captivating is that
the tale is told from the point of view of the man and wife
who are being betrayed, not from the point of view of the
adulterers.

Chow Mo-wan and Su Li-zhen live in crowded Hong
Kong in the 1960s. They live in rooms next door to each
other in one of Hong Kong's typically divided larger apart-
ments. There is no privacy; there is no space for emotion or
feeling to be anything but contained.

They discover in a most unusual manner what is
going on. We won't spoil this, except to say it involves articles of clothing. His wife and her husband are having
an affair. They are the victims of marital disloyalty. They
are put together in this dilemma through circumstances
neither would have chosen. Yet, as they begin to talk to
each other and to role-play what they would do if their
spouses were to confess, their relationship builds. The
colors of the film are subdued, the feeling in the air is of
sadness and rain, and the smoke from a cigarette becomes symbolic.

A deep love develops between them, a love that was
meant to be. But in the middle of this most sophisticated
film, you are left with the homespun phrase ringing in your
head: "But two wrongs don't make a right." They have con-

vinced themselves of the integrity of this position. That's where they find themselves, or where they choose to put themselves. There is agreement that it would be wrong if they became just as awful as their spouses were. Do they really agree? Or do they now feel compelled to play through their parts as the honorable and moral partners in dishonorable marriages?

This could not be done effectively in a flashy way. Hollywood would probably make a mess of it, and even the Europeans would miss the muted but powerful quality of their love. Their plight unfolds in a particularly evocative way, through the lens of an Asian sensibility. Ultimately, the film represents the status of honor in a culture. The longing they share for each other pulsates in every breath they take. You begin to hold your breath, hoping they will change their minds. A few plot threads are left without a place to go in the fabric of the film, and you conjecture what they might mean. This is a subtle winner.

EXTRAS

Criterion has made a superbly finished product. Unusual among foreign releases, this is a two-disc set. The menus are user-friendly, and there's a small surprise in the way they have musically animated the selections.

The first disc contains the movie, but don't jump to the second disc too quickly. There are some excellent supplements on the first one, such as deleted scenes with commentary from the director and a music segment. Most important to watch is a mini-film by the director.

Disc Two provides substantial viewing options. The first feature is a full-length documentary about the making of the movie.

"Toronto Film Festival" is footage that features Leung and Cheung in a question-and-answer session in English.

It's forty-five minutes long and gives a sense of who these actors are and how they approach their craft.

We seldom say this, but this time "The Promotional Material" selection is one to watch, not to avoid. It's filled with posters, a Hong Kong trailer, a French trailer, and something called the "electronic press kit," which is actually an excellent mini-documentary about the movie, about twenty minutes in length.

"Wong Kar-wai Interview" is really two interviews in one feature. The first is from Cannes, and the other is an interview with Wong and two critics. You'll have a fuller sense of what this talented director is all about after listening to him.

The booklet in the package is forty-six pages long and contains the short story that was the inspiration for the film. There's an essay and notes about the production of the DVD.

The entire Criterion volume is special by anyone's yardstick.

Innocence

CAST: Julia Blake, Charles "Bud" Tingwell, Terry Norris, Kristien Van Pellicom, Kenny Aernous, Robert Menzies, Mara Dusseldorp
DIRECTOR: Paul Cox
SCREENWRITER: Paul Cox
RELEASED: 2000 (94 minutes)
RATED: R

Innocence seems an unlikely title for a superb film about very mature love, but therein lies the truth of love. Whenever you find or rediscover your first love, the quality of the time together and the lovemaking is interwoven with feelings of newness, of something totally unique, of Innocence.

Writer-director Paul Cox was born in the Netherlands but has lived in Australia for many years. His films are often quixotic or autobiographical. You can expect the unexpected from Cox. *(A Woman's Tale* dealt with a dying woman, played by the dying actress Sheila Florance.) He steadfastly refuses to make formula movies, Hollywood-style, nor does he make what is now the fairly easily identifiable Aussie-style film. Cox is as daring in his subject choices as the protagonists in *Innocence* are in their actions.

Innocence portrays late love with a grace and sexuality rarely seen on screen. Don't think *On Golden Pond,* think *Splendor in the Grass,* with seventy-year-olds. Sexual love for anyone above thirty is a Hollywood taboo. Remember that *The Bridges of Madison County* was Streep and Eastwood, so it wasn't such a risk. But here we are talking about real people, who find that after a separation of forty years, their love is as strong and as passionate as it had been in their youth.

Innocence begins with the voice of actor Charles Tingwell, who plays Andreas, reading a letter he is sending to his first love, Claire (Julia Blake). He has discovered that by some wild circumstance of fate, they live within a short train ride of each other. As we are introduced to these older lovers, Cox interlaces their youthful love affair. The young lovers are played by Kristien Van Pellicom and Kenny Aernous with a luscious sensuality. Our only complaint is that later in the movie, there's too much of them. It's as though Cox had to excuse himself for making the older lovers so sexual by reminding us that they weren't always old and wrinkled. It wasn't needed; you're already hooked by the story and its grace. In the first part of the film, the scenes of the younger Claire and Andreas are needed to establish the story.

Andreas and Claire were deeply in love, but something went wrong, and they went their separate ways. Andreas went into a marriage that seemed to have been satisfying but left him a widower very early. Claire made one of those reasonable sensible matches and has ended up with a decent, deadly boring husband who barely notices she's alive, let alone that she's still got a fire burning. The meeting between Claire and Andreas was only to be a reunion lunch. Quickly, they understand nothing has changed.

Later, we learn through flashbacks that it was his father who had stopped them from marrying and that Andreas didn't fight for her. She says that her love for him affected her entire life. But she is determined not to make mistakes at this late age that will hurt her husband and her family. Andreas repeatedly calls her at home and hangs up when her husband, John, answers. There's humor in this sequence, for she knows it must be Andreas, the way a teenage girl knows these things. Finally, they connect by phone, and she agrees to see him again, despite her initial resolve. She might as well, because, as she says, "I see you in front of me all the time." And so perhaps they have seen each other in front of their lives all of their lives. When she confesses her adultery to her husband, he thinks she has gone straight off the trolley and calls in their son, a physician.

This love story catches you unaware. Before you know it, you are immersed in the utter rightness of their love. Nothing else could matter; they must be together, if only for these last years. John doesn't go away that easily; after all, they have been married forever. His attempt at martyrdom is short-lived when she reminds him of the affair he had twenty years before. Their marriage isn't a disaster as much as it is a reminder of how easy it is to settle for security or kindness and end up with a hole in your heart at the end of the journey. But John isn't a bad guy, just a clumsy and repressed man who doesn't really have a clue. That is part of what makes this perceptive film so believable and so wrenching.

Blake as Claire has a translucent beauty; her seeming fragility makes her even more glorious in this role. Tingwell isn't handsome and plays Andreas as an opinionated and eccentric old man, unafraid of love, life, or death. He is irresistible as her lover, warts and all. His interaction with a hospital chaplain stands out in an already notable performance. The film doesn't end the way you are led to believe it will, and therefore on first viewing it's a shattering conclusion. But after a few more viewings, a different and transcendent feeling overtakes you, and you are confident in the intelligence of Cox's writing and direction. The R rating is quite unfair, as the movie is tender and involves some nudity and gentle sexual scenes. *Innocence* teaches us that some loves are forever, albeit in the fleeting passages of the last chapters of life. You should own this film. We watch it often, and so will you.

EXTRAS
The DVD includes the original trailer, which is romantically shot and visually satisfying.

Iris

CAST: Judi Dench, Jim Broadbent, Kate Winslet, Hugh Bonneville, Sam West, Penelope Wilton
DIRECTOR: Richard Eyre
SCREENWRITERS: Richard Eyre and Charles Wood (based on the memoirs of John Bayley)
RELEASED: 2001 (93 minutes)
RATED: R

Iris is about two kinds of love, a writer's love of words and the love between two people. It's about the complete loss of the first and the total alteration of the second.

Iris Murdoch, one of Britain's most celebrated thinkers and novelists, developed full-blown Alzheimer's before her death. John Bayley was her lifelong companion and husband. The movie is based on his memoirs of their struggle together with the disease, first published in the *New Yorker* magazine and later in book form. The film has the immense good fortune of having been directed by Richard Eyre, artistic director of the Royal National Theatre in London from 1988 until 1997 and one of the finest theatrical directors in the world. In *Iris,* unerring judgment is evident in both the script and the direction. The film stars Judi Dench and Jim Broadbent as Murdoch and Bayley. Kate Winslet and Hugh Bonneville portray the couple in their youth.

That everything about Alzheimer's is heartbreaking is not a revelation to anyone. There is, however, something especially devastating about the disease when it strikes someone who has lived a cerebral life, a life filled primarily with words and ideas. Murdoch was noted for the tight and complex plots she developed and the absolute precision of her word choices. Bayley, a distinguished scholar in his own right, was at first unable to comprehend that these identifying qualities were leaving her. Her very essence evaporates before his eyes. The movie, like the memoir, is about the tenacity of love; it's about Bayley's stubborn refusal to give up hope. Broadbent plays Bayley with tenderness and good humor; he doesn't make a false move, and therefore the story never turns into sentimental slop. He sometimes becomes frustrated and angry, but mostly he's brokenhearted and remains steadfast in his love.

Dench is a convincing Murdoch. It is hard to imagine

another actress who could so convincingly portray her confusion and pain as she descends further and further into the hell of the illness. Viewers will bring their own experiences and feelings to the story. For us, the most memorable scene is when Murdoch no longer has any recollection that she wrote books.

Eyre's decision to make full use of flashbacks was an important artistic and moral one. It is far too easy to define the person as the disease and no longer as the person, especially one that deteriorates the thinking process. In the effective use of Winslet, we feel the full impact of what is lost to Murdoch. Beyond the ability to create extraordinary works of literature, we observe the loss of other human terrains: sexuality, friendship, judgment. It is an honest and unblinking look at Alzheimer's disease. Yet it is essentially the story of the continuity of love that raises *Iris* to its level of achievement. Broadbent won the Oscar for Best Supporting Actor. Both Dench and Winslet were nominated for Oscars.

EXTRAS

There's a "special message" feature with television sitcom actor David Hyde Pierce of *Frasier*. He talks candidly about Alzheimer's and its ramifications in families, including his own. There's useful information offered about what to do if you suspect you or someone you know may be exhibiting symptoms of the disease. It's a solid public service announcement. Unless you're fond of clips from awards shows, skip the footage from the Alzheimer's Association Gala, which honored the film and its stars for contributing to an understanding of the disease. The Pierce message is much more to the point.

"A Look at Iris" is roughly fifteen minutes of conversation with the cast and Eyre, who talks about his vision for the film, which is quite involving. It's a shame there isn't more commentary or other features, but this does add clarifying information about the artistic process.

Jaws

CAST: Roy Scheider, Richard Dreyfuss, Robert Shaw, Lorraine
  Gray, Murray Hamilton
DIRECTOR: Steven Spielberg
SCREENWRITERS: Peter Benchley and Carl Gottlieb (adapted from
  the novel by Benchley)
RELEASED: 1975 (125 minutes)
RATED: R

Once upon a time, long ago, people swam in the sea unafraid, and Steven Spielberg wasn't a brand name. But that was before Spielberg scared the living wits out of us with his big mean rubber shark, nicknamed "Bruce" by the cast and crew.

Jaws hardly needs a narrative review. It's an idyllic New England tourist island, it's the Fourth of July, and a shark is about to devour a little girl. The mayor (Murray Hamilton) says it's fine in the water, he doesn't want the economy to falter if he closes the beaches, and the tourists flee in shark-fright flight. The righteous police chief (Roy Scheider) knows better, and so does the smart young shark scientist and oceanographer (Richard Dreyfuss). A shark hunter (Robert Shaw) thinks he can fix it all in his little boat. The line everyone remembers is "You're going to need a bigger boat." The image everybody remembers is a shark gobbling up swimmers.

Spielberg's career was never the same after *Jaws*. He became, well, a great cinematic artist. Much as we all still love

Jaws, can we forgive him for ruining the lazy swim on a hot summer's afternoon? *Jaws* is one of the reasons the home swimming-pool industry expanded quickly.

Spielberg took the suspense thriller, married it to the old-fashioned horror movie, and produced a classic. If timing is everything in life and in art, he certainly had that one down. Seeing *Jaws* in its newer anniversary edition, it's remarkable how much of the time you don't see the shark. That's why it's so frightening. It was a lesson learned from the techniques of Hitchcock. When "Bruce" does emerge, it's just as awful as we knew it would be, and that's in the tradition of the best classic horror movies.

Before computer generation, there was Bruce, the great big mechanical shark who had a nasty disposition. Sometimes he wanted to chew peaple, and sometimes he didn't. (Maybe Bruce wasn't getting paid scale.) It doesn't matter what happened then; what we are left with is an enduring Grade A horror-thriller that can still inspire surfside paranoia. The word *Jaws* came into our parlance as quickly as the name Spielberg. We might have been able to live without the fear, but we certainly couldn't live without this man's artful eye.

EXTRAS
It's called the "Anniversary Collector's Edition."

First, let's get the freebie out of the way. It's the prize in the Cracker Jacks box; it's silly, but you know it's there, and you want it. This one is a screen saver for your computer. If you have a CD-ROM drive on your PC, it's all yours.

"The Making of Jaws" is an hour-long documentary. Writer Peter Benchley and Spielberg talk about the problems with the shark as well as a variety of issues. It might be subtitled "Notes from Production Hell." After twenty-five years, everyone has a good time with the memories, but you can be sure that the cast and crew were not so jovial then. It's a very rewarding feature.

There are both outtakes and deleted scenes offered on the menu separately. The outtakes are funny. If you haven't had enough information about sharks, you'll enjoy "Shark World," which gave quite a bit more than we needed to know. There's a better-than-average trivia game entitled "Get Out of the Water."

Jerry Maguire

CAST: Tom Cruise, Cuba Gooding, Jr., Renee Zellweger, Jonathan Lipnicki, Kelly Preston, Bonnie Hunt, Regina King
DIRECTOR: Cameron Crowe
SCREENWRITER: Cameron Crowe
RELEASED: 1996 (139 minutes)
RATED: R

This hit romantic comedy has it all. It's a love story with Hollywood sparkle but enough relationship agony so you feel you're eavesdropping. Before the opening credits have finished, you know Jerry Maguire.

Cameron Crowe's superb direction is aided by a stunning screenplay. (The Special Edition's Disc Two provides the full script, if you have a computer equipped with a CD-ROM drive.) This is a "chick's movie" that guys relate to, or perhaps it's a "guy's movie" that works for women. It's an innovative combination of a sports movie wrapped around a believable love story.

Maguire is a greedy, shallow sports agent with a gorgeously impossible girlfriend, expertly played by Kelly Preston. You'll love hating her. Tom Cruise, as Maguire, has a moral crisis that ends up ruining his career. He re-creates himself; the end result is a human being with a beating heart. However, you're never quite sure he's going to get there.

Unlike *Sleepless in Seattle,* with which it shares two dominant themes, a widowed young person and an adorable kid, *Jerry Maguire* has much more texture. Renee Zellweger, in her first major commercial film, plays Dorothy Boyd, a young widow who lives with her protective and lovingly tough sister, Laurel, played without artifice by the talented Bonnie Hunt. Laurel's angry divorced women's group provides laughs and hoots of recognition for anyone who's been down that particular road.

Some have complained that Boyd's character is just Zellweger playing herself. It doesn't matter. You'd have a heart of granite not to fall in love with her. Jonathan Lipnicki plays her son, Ray. Surprisingly, unlike the usual cute kid, he doesn't mug for the camera. The interaction between mother and son is inspired.

The power of the movie comes from the ensemble cast. Cuba Gooding, Jr., portrays Rod Tidwell, a football player with lots of attitude but not much else. (Gooding received the Oscar for his role.) Regina King plays his intensely loyal wife; their relationship crackles. Gooding, Cruise, and writer Crowe provide viewers with honest dialogue seldom found in standard Hollywood fare. As the movie progresses, Tidwell and Maguire teach each other life's essential truths.

The romance between Zellweger and Cruise has you on edge until the end. Beware: the wedding scene doesn't resolve a thing; it only makes life more complex.

Gooding's line "Show me the money" became a slogan for a time. However, our favorite lines are both from Dorothy Boyd: "First class is what's wrong, honey. It used to be a better meal, now it's a better life." But for romantics of both sexes, the best line of the movie is: "You had me at 'Hello.'"

EXTRAS

These DVDs navigate around the arty concept of Jerry's memo pad. Don't get confused; just read, point, and click.

In the "Director's Cast and Commentary," Crowe, Zellweger, Gooding, and Cruise watch the movie together. It's a beguiling approach. There are many delicious surprises in this segment, particularly Zellweger and Cruise. You also learn inside secrets: what part is played by Crowe's mother, what role Billy Wilder was offered, who was an early boss of Crowe's and what cameo part he plays. For sports fans, Crowe identifies many of the athletes and sports celebrities in the film. Crowe confesses he wanted to make a Billy Wilder–style film, where the movie ends but the characters never really leave your life. And so he has! A few behind-the-scenes clips can be located by clicking "mission statement," then your right arrow.

The deleted scenes are all worth watching. The uncut phone duel is particularly good but contains some fairly rough language.

"Rod Tidwell: My First Commercial" is not to be missed.

"Drew Rosenhaus: Real Sports Agent" seems more like a *Saturday Night Live* sketch, but he's an actual person. However, don't buy the line that he is Jerry Maguire. Crowe says there wasn't one person who was the model for Maguire. Rosenhaus wins the award for the worst tie ever seen anywhere at any time.

In the music video of "Secret Garden," with romantic scenes from the movie rolling by in the background, there's wonderfully sexy Bruce Springsteen upfront. The Boss sings; you sigh.

Key Largo

CAST: Humphrey Bogart, Lauren Bacall, Edward G. Robinson,
   Lionel Barrymore, Claire Trevor, Marc Lawrence, Monte Blue
DIRECTOR: John Huston
SCREENWRITERS: Richard Brooks and John Huston (adapted from
   the play by Maxwell Anderson)
RELEASED: 1948 (101 minutes)
RATED: Not rated

This isn't one of the best films ever made, and we don't pretend that it is. But the cast is extraordinary. Although the plot is contrived, John Huston really drew the best from these fine actors.

You might think of *Key Largo* as a morality tale with weather. There's lots of really bad, wet, scary weather. The story tilts to melodrama, but you're never bored. Don't expect to have the same energy with Bogie and Bacall here that you get in their other films. Yet it's good to have *Key Largo* available on DVD.

Humphrey Bogart plays Frank McCloud, who wanders into a situation with his dead Army buddy's father and widow. Lauren Bacall plays the widow, and Lionel Barrymore portrays her father-in-law. It's Huston at his most atmospheric; he sets the movie on a stormy island off the eastern coast of Florida. Bogart's character becomes involved in the hotel owned by the widow and his buddy's father. Edward G. Robinson stars in his usual gangster role, but this time he's marooned on an island. It is Claire Trevor as his alcoholic moll, a failed singer, who pretty nearly steals the show away from everyone else. (She won the Oscar for her portrayal.)

It's a potent mix of Mafia cruelties and the search for morality and values. As the movie progresses, it becomes a tense and stressful chess game between Robinson's bull-like power and Bogie's awakening integrity.

Cinematographer Karl Freund captured the story's essential claustrophobic qualities of enduring a fierce hurricane in Florida's oppressive climate.

EXTRAS

All you get here is the original trailer and production notes. The transfer isn't perfect, but it's pretty crisp.

Kissing Jessica Stein

CAST: Jennifer Westfeldt, Heather Juergensen, Tovah Feldshuh, Scott Cohen
DIRECTOR: Charles Herman-Wurmfeld
SCREENWRITERS: Jennifer Westfeldt and Heather Juergensen
RELEASED: 2002 (96 minutes)
RATED: R

This is a classy New York romantic comedy. *Kissing Jessica Stein* adds a witty twist to the enduring theme of the search for true love. It's a film about life and love among the artistic urban young who have to maintain themselves by working day jobs they hate. It's a perceptive, droll, and fairly accurate look at Manhattan, depicting the city's attractions and difficulties. Jennifer Westfeldt and Heather Juergensen initially wrote this as a theater piece called *Lispschtick*.

Jessica is determined to find Mr. Right, and the family pressure is enormous. In her path are two obviously wonderful choices, but her blinders are on, until she finally realizes love can be a surprising journey. It's all in the kiss, at least for a time. It's a movie about the fluidity of sensuality and the search for the ultimate Mr. or Ms. Right. It's a more unconventional look at single life in Manhattan. *Kissing Jessica Stein* didn't get a wide release, which is too bad, because it's a worthy film. We've watched it a few times, and it wears well. It's satisfying on many levels.

The opening scene in a synagogue on Yom Kippur is hilarious. Tovah Feldshuh plays Jessica's mother with more dimension than the usual stereotyped Jewish mother in American films. There's a simply wonderful scene with her in a bridal salon. The good humor never lets up throughout this low-budget, high-payoff treat of a movie. The lyrics of a classic Ella Fitzgerald tune are altered to fit the demands of the story line (we won't give it away).

Although *Kissing Jessica Stein* ultimately opts for a more traditional ending, which did disappoint us some, the end isn't a sell-out. There's real integrity in the concluding scenes, which offer satisfying points of view about both gay and straight matters of the heart.

EXTRAS

There's a side-splitting feature about bad dates. It's from the cutting-room floor but filled with scenes that would make an excruciatingly funny short film itself. In fact, most of the deleted material is as funny as anything around in theaters. We particularly liked a boating scene in Central Park. *Kissing Jessica Stein* is an enchantment. Buy it, and you'll own a ready-made laughter kit to use anytime you're lonely or down or want an evening of howls and tears with friends.

K-Pax

CAST: Kevin Spacey, Jeff Bridges, Alfre Woodard, Mary
     McCormack, David Patrick Kelly
DIRECTOR: Ian Softley
SCREENWRITER: Charles Leavitt (based on a novel by Gene
     Brewer)
RELEASED: 2001 (120 minutes)
RATED: PG-13

As if from nowhere, Kevin Spacey appears in New York's
Grand Central Terminal. He calls himself Prot and has arrived from Planet K-Pax. He's interested in us and has visited before. According to Prot, Earth is a "Class BA-3
planet, early stage of evolution, future uncertain."

K-Pax did not receive the attention it deserved when it
was released. K-Pax touches on issues that make some people uneasy. It's an overlooked film of depth and meaning.
To appreciate K-Pax, suspend disbelief.

Who is sane? What is a delusion? What makes us
human? Is there life beyond our planet? Do we really have
the answers to the essential questions of life? Prot ends up
in a psychiatric ward. Jeff Bridges plays Dr. Mark Powell,
who begins as a skeptic but ends up as confused by Prot as
we are. If he's delusional, why doesn't he respond to the
drugs? Why can he see light humans cannot? Why does he
know things about a remote galaxy system that convince
world-class scientists?

Eventually, the story begins to unravel. A man named
Robert Porter from New Mexico endured a grotesque and
violent loss and reacted accordingly. Prot is Porter. Forsak-
ing all other goals and his family, Dr. Powell intends to put
the pieces of Prot's mental jigsaw puzzle back together. As
Prot prepares to depart for K-Pax, Powell confronts him

with his "true" identity. Prot replies, "I will admit the possibility that I'm Robert Porter if you will admit the possibility that I am from K-Pax." This film is about the infinite quality of possibility. Something does happen to Prot on the day of his departure, but you are left to wonder just what.

During his tenure in the psychiatric ward, Prot heals other patients. A common blue jay becomes the elusive "Blue Bird of Happiness." The scenes in the hospital do not authentically replicate medical treatments for serious mental illness, but they offer hope. Prot's relationships with the other patients suggest how little is definitively known about the mystery of the brain. *K-Pax* is not all heavy and sci-fi; much of the movie is humorous. Perhaps K-Pax, and its earthly representative Prot, are metaphors for our time. We live in a world searching for peace among peoples and in our own souls. The movie ends without all the story lines completed or even making sense; it leaves you with enduring questions.

K-Pax crosses film genres. It's murder mystery, sci-fi, comedy, drama, and psychological thriller. Finally, it's a fable of hope.

EXTRAS
It's been suggested that the alternative ending was the director's first choice; it's less ambiguous and therefore not as powerful. Judge for yourself.

"Spotlight on Location" offers interviews with Spacey, Bridges, director Ian Softley, and others. This is our favorite bonus. Softley interviewed psychiatrists and visited mental hospitals. A psychiatrist who served as a consultant discusses the film. We are reminded that Bridges once played an alien in a lovely film called *Starman*. Bridges, Spacey, and Softley all talk about what the film meant to them and why they were compelled to make it.

An alternate series of scenes with scientists filmed at New York's Rose Planetarium provides an insight into the complexity of the director's decision making. This is a generous walk through the cutting-room floor. Not all the scenes are good ones, but they make for exciting viewing. The gem hidden here is one we wish hadn't been deleted. It's the scene between Bridges and his wife, played by Mary McCormack. She is at the piano, and what follows depicts the essence of a marriage. Without its inclusion, we are left hanging regarding the marriage. In the deleted sequence, his wife becomes a more fully developed character than she was in the final edited version.

"The Making of K-Pax/Photographs" is buried at the end of the bonus material and is too easy to overlook. These are still photographs, all taken by Bridges during the making of the film, and constitute his personal scrapbook. They are elegant and ethereal and add much to the experience of viewing.

Lawrence of Arabia

CAST: Peter O'Toole, Alec Guinness, Anthony Quinn, Omar Sharif, Jack Hawkins, Jose Ferrer, Anthony Quayle, Claude Rains, Arthur Kennedy
DIRECTOR: David Lean
SCREENWRITER: Robert Bolt (based on *The Seven Pillars of Wisdom* by T. E. Lawrence)
RELEASED: 1962 (227 minutes)
RATED: PG

Noel Coward is reputed to have said, "If Peter O'Toole had been any prettier, they would have called the movie *Florence of Arabia.*"

O'Toole was indeed beautiful, but so was everything else. Although O'Toole had been in a few earlier films, he was known primarily in Britain as a theater actor. It was David Lean's *Lawrence of Arabia* that really introduced the public to O'Toole. With the release of *Lawrence,* O'Toole's international fame was instantaneous; his subsequent films brought him further acclaim. It isn't so much that O'Toole became T. E. Lawrence as it is that Lawrence became O'Toole. In our minds is etched one image of Lawrence; that image is O'Toole.

Omar Sharif's next Lean movie would be *Doctor Zhivago,* and Sharif is remembered primarily for that part. But his role here as Sherif Ali Ibn el Kharish first brought his stunning visage to the public.

Just who was Lawrence? Both much and little are known. He was originally a British cartographer, who became a legendary hero when he led the Arab revolt against the Ottoman Empire. He was an intellectual, a bit of a mystic, a man of great drives and great sorrows. He was obviously a military genius, yet his strategic victories do not seem to have brought him personal peace or a coherent sense of purpose. He was undoubtedly homosexual, but in 1962 that wasn't a theme comfortably dealt with in any honest way on film. Although Lawrence's layered sexual orientation is not completely ignored in the film, it's well in the background. There's one very memorable scene, however, which is more suggestive than it is declarative.

Although it's overly long and a somewhat self-consciously mammoth production, that's part of what makes it one of the most enduringly popular of all screen spectaculars. There's brilliant acting in places, and always one is aware of Lean's sure hand in the sweep and scope of the drama and the look of the entire film. There's also lots and lots of the truly beautiful O'Toole. His expressive blue eyes dissolve sand into shimmering glass crystals in just one glance.

The American Film Institute ranks it number five on its top 100. In an interview in the extras, Steven Spielberg says of *Lawrence of Arabia* that it is the greatest miracle he has ever viewed on film. He's not wrong. Think of it as a series of exquisitely shot and edited action pieces with tour de force acting by Guinness, Rains, and Ferrer in their supporting roles. If you believe as we do in the mystery of the desert and the magic of cinema, *Lawrence of Arabia* blends them together. The alchemy is pure gold.

Here's what *Lawrence of Arabia* took home from Oscar night in 1962: Best Picture, Best Director, Best Art Direction, Best Cinematography (Freddie Young), Best Editing (Anne V. Coates), Best Musical Score (Maurice Jarre), Best Sound (John Cox).

O'Toole was nominated for Best Actor; the Oscar went to Gregory Peck for *To Kill a Mockingbird*. Sharif was nominated for Best Supporting Actor; Ed Begley won for *Sweet Bird of Youth*. It is worth noting that the editor, Anne V. Coates, remains one of Hollywood's most distinguished and talented film editors. She has received Oscar nominations for her editing work in *Beckett*, *The Elephant Man*, and *In the Line of Fire*.

EXTRAS

Here's what you'll take home when you buy the deluxe two-disc set, *Lawrence of Arabia, Special Edition*.

Although we are obviously big supporters of quality entertainment at home, a caveat is required in this particular case. The ideal place to see the restored version of *Lawrence of Arabia* is in a theater. Quite obviously, even the largest state-of-the-art television set is going to miss much of the spectacle. That said, this new version is your best option, unless you have unspeakably rich friends who have their own full-screen home theaters. If you do run in these circles, make them a gift of the special edition, and invite yourself over.

If you owned the earlier editions, it's time to upgrade, because the new features are worth it. If you own the video, it just won't satisfy you any longer. The Harris/Painten print of 1989 makes it to DVD in such lustrous tones that you can count the grains of sand. (No kidding.) If this is in the AFI's top ten list of films, this DVD transfer is in our top ten of technically perfect DVD releases. What a pleasure it is to watch this flawless restoration in the DVD format.

There are four mini-features: "Wind, Sand and Star: The Making of a Classic," "Maan, Jordan, The Camels Are Cast," "In Search of Lawrence" and "Romance of Arabia." All of these are interesting, but there's a good chance you've seen them before.

The new documentary is "The Making of Lawrence of Arabia," and it's first class. We liked the extras on the equally deluxe edition of *The Bridge on the River Kwai,* but these are even better. The new documentary is more than an hour long and has commentary and remarks by crew and cast. Sadly, we don't have Lean. You do, however, have a very engaging and awestruck Steven Spielberg discussing Lean, which is quite a treat. You'll particularly love Spielberg's anecdotes about attending the premiere of the restored print with Lean at his side.

The menu presentation is delightful and useful. As in *Pearl Harbor,* there is a very informative historical timeline for those who really aren't too sure just what did happen in the Middle East in the Great War. The PC/DVD-ROM capability allows you to participate in some cartography experiments of your own. If you do have this accessory on your PC, don't miss the archival photographs; they're quite amazing. If you don't own a PC with a CD-ROM, cart the DVD set over to a friend who does, and then watch the film together.

Just as in *The Bridge on the River Kwai*'s deluxe edition, there's an original souvenir program in this boxed set as well.

If it sounds as if we're gushing over this DVD release, that's because we are. Lean deserves it. *Lawrence of Arabia* deserves it. And you deserve it.

Neither Lean nor Lawrence had any difficulty imagining his own greatness. Fortunately, this special edition truly does recognize their place in history.

Legally Blonde

CAST: Reese Witherspoon, Luke Wilson, Selma Blair, Matthew Davis, Victor Garber, Jennifer Coolidge, Holland Taylor, Ali Larter

DIRECTOR: Robert Luketic

SCREENWRITERS: Kirsten Smith and Karen McCullah Lutz (based on the novel by Amanda Brown)

RELEASED: 2001 (96 minutes)

RATED: PG-13

How is it that blondes are supposed to be preferred by men, have more fun, and still be the butt of the jokes about "dumb blondes"? Here's a sock in the eye to all of those stereotypes and 1950s riffs on the stupid but adorable blond bimbo. Too bad Marilyn Monroe didn't live to see this; she would have enjoyed it.

Reese Witherspoon is Elle Wood. Her boyfriend, Warner (Matthew Davis), dumps her just when she thinks a ring is on its way to her finger. While Warner had loads of fun with Elle, he now he sees her as an inappropriate choice. He's on his way to great things; he wants to be seen as a serious man. He can't be held back by a politically inappropriate Blondie who likes to get manicures several times a week and bounce around with a ridiculously fluffy little dog on a leash.

Elle is determined to win him back. Her approach is not what you might expect, no soft seduction numbers but a full frontal attack—as in frontal lobe: brain power. Elle morphs herself into Harvard Law School. It's true she gets the aid of a slickster who does a promo video for the applications process. But it's clear. Elle has it all, despite her appearance.

Harvard isn't California, and she's truly the butt of every bad joke. If this weren't so overdone, it would be painful. (Actually, the Halloween party scene is both painful and hilarious.) But the movie has a big payoff, so don't be put off by the seemingly slim story. Presumably made for older teenagers and young adults, this film became a hit with a wide audience.

It's the Cinderella tale with a contemporary spin. Elle uses her brains instead of her charms and beauty. At Harvard, she faces down the snobs and the jokes and ends up triumphant. This film belongs to Witherspoon, but there is excellent ensemble work here. Selma Blair plays the hated rival for Warner's love. As Vivian, she's the kind of smartypants you would like to use as your kitchen floor mop. Victor Garber is convincingly demanding and humorless as Professor Callahan. Luke Wilson's a good choice for the love interest. If you're a Jennifer Coolidge fan, as we are, it's always good to see her on screen, even in minor roles.

EXTRAS

Amanda Brown wrote a novel based on her own life experience at Stanford Law School. Hats off to the screenwriters who did such a good job adapting the original material so that it didn't lose its intimacy or its humorous bite.

A commentary by Witherspoon, director Robert Luketic, and producer Marc Platt is your first feature option. There's much chatter and congratulations to one another, but it's amusing and as lighthearted as the film. In between the "Aren't we the best?" mode, there's a full supply of technical information about how shots were handled, which makes it a decent, if not excellent, selection.

The second feature is yet another commentary. Here it's the crew. There's more information than we were interested in about the costumes and look of the film, but we suspect we're in the minority here. What's really worth your time is the discussion about how the novel was transformed into a popular movie. Since so often the journey from book to movie is nothing but disaster, this is a commentary many in the industry should listen to and take heed of.

You'll get the deleted scenes introduced by the director. There are eight of them, it's an uneven selection, but they do provide a few real laughs.

"Inside Legally Blonde" is a rather standard "making of" segment. The best part of this is Witherspoon, but then that's not a surprise.

"The Hair That Ate Hollywood" is off-the-wall conceptual blonde. This is probably most appreciated by blondes.

Life Is Beautiful

CAST: Roberto Benigni, Nicoletta Braschi, Giorgio Cantarini, Guistino Durano, Sergio Bustric, Horst Bucholz
DIRECTOR: Roberto Benigni
SCREENWRITERS: Roberto Benigni and Vincenzo Cerami
RELEASED: 1998 (122 minutes)
RATED: PG-13

It is almost as difficult to write about *Life Is Beautiful* as it is to watch it.

Roberto Benigni plays Guido, a seemingly hapless Chaplinesque character who refuses to take himself or the world too seriously. He's a waiter; he's clownish; he's a goofy little guy. It's Italy in 1939, but you don't notice that in the beginning. He and his cousin try to find work; Guido wants to own a bookshop. Even though he is of humble background, he falls in love with a beautiful aristocratic woman, Dora (Nicoletta Braschi); he calls her "Principessa."

There is much to laugh at during the first half of the film. Benigni is a comedic genius. Even with the suggestion of the darkness ahead, you don't see what's coming. You're not supposed to see what's coming.

Dora and Guido marry, and the movie fast-forwards into their life. They have a small and adorable son called Giosue. Guido has his bookstore. As the signs of trouble erupt all around him in the Mussolini era, Guido continues with his usual patter and joking manner. It is important to note that you don't understand that Guido is a Jew until the film is well under way. His little boy points out a sign on a store saying "No Jews or dogs allowed here." The boy wants to know why, and Guido makes light of it. Soon enough, Guido and his son are put onto the deportation train, bound for the Nazi concentration camps.

In one of the most memorable moments, his Gentile wife stops the train and gets on with them, obviously thinking that they will all be together and die together if they must. Once they are at the camp, Guido constructs a world of fantasy for the boy. It's a complex business, and too much has been written about it already. But in broad strokes, Guido says that it is really just a game and they must be clever. The first one to win one thousand points will get a real tank.

It's been said that this is a comedy that proves that even in the face of adversity, love conquers all. That's wrong. This isn't a comedy, and it isn't about love conquering all. Love didn't conquer the gas chambers. It is a film that is far more layered and filled with metaphor than many have given it credit for.

The sequence of events in the movie mirror the way things unfolded in Italy. Italian Jews were reluctant to think that the Fascists would organize themselves efficiently enough to round them up. After all, it was Italy, not Germany. The fact that Guido wasn't obviously Jewish is crucial to understanding the story as well.

What Guido does with his comic antics is to save his son from the gas chamber and to provide him with a lesson about living. In the face of the worst and most unimaginable horror, we are human. His great love for his son leads him to attempt to be brave and to appear a fool, rather than a cowering, frightened victim.

Life Is Beautiful enraged some people of all political persuasions and faiths. It wounded many Holocaust survivors emotionally. Benigni was reviled as much as he was praised. It would be inappropriate for us to try to convince the film's detractors of its importance. Everyone is entitled to judge this shattering drama by his or her own experiences and standards.

But *Life Is Beautiful* raises an essential and profoundly thorny question. Who owns the Holocaust? By that we mean, who owns the rights to its interpretation? When Mel Brooks, a Jewish comic, made *The Producers* in 1968, it was considered wildly hilarious and a slap in the face to the Germans and the memory of the Nazis. That was different; Brooks was Jewish, and he was laughing at them. When Brooks and his team later turned *The Producers* into a musical in the late 1990s, it became one of Broadway's most successful musicals. *Life Is Beautiful* is the vision of a non-Jewish Italian. Underneath the anger and the criticism is a lingering accusation. How dare he? Are only Jews allowed to interpret this genocide or to present an audacious look at the Holocaust?

In our opinion, *Life Is Beautiful* is an essential part of the artistic oeuvre of the Shoah. We know everyone won't agree with us, but Benigni dares Jews and non-Jews alike to ask a totally different question. If we can't control what is going to happen to us, can we control how we will choose to respond? The answer to that is yes. It doesn't give the movie away to say that Guido didn't walk out of the camps. Very few did. But the parting scene with his son is a lesson in the hope for the continuity of all humankind.

The story surrounding *Life Is Beautiful* couldn't have happened during the Holocaust. Guido wouldn't have been able to behave as he did in the camps. It isn't based on a real person's story, as Primo Levi's was. *Life Is Beautiful* is an interpretation of opposing hatred and extinction in an absolutely individual way. It's anything but a comedy, despite the many laughs in the early part. It is a tragedy told in a voice not heard before. The seeming impossibility of telling the story of the death camps in this manner is at the core of the film's exquisite truths, however fictional they are.

The film won Oscars for Best Foreign Language Film, Best Actor, and Best Score. Nicoletta Braschi is Benigni's actual wife.

EXTRAS

Once again, we are not supporters of watching films dubbed into English. If you have problems with reading subtitles, there is the dubbing option on this film. In *Life*, the subtitles are particularly well done. We sometimes advise against the English audio track, because you lose a sense of the authenticity of the film. Even if you can't speak the language, you can at least hear its rhythms and cadence. The best dubbing equipment in the world still falls short of being able to synchronize spoken English perfectly to the actors' lips.

The menu offers a series of television spots for the film, the theatrical trailer, and a generous scene selection.

"Making Life Is Beautiful" is a better-than-average segment about the production phase of the film.

Limelight

CAST: Charles Chaplin, Claire Bloom, Buster Keaton, Sydney
    Chaplin, Andre Eglevsky, Melissa Hayden, Nigel Bruce,
    Norman Lloyd
DIRECTOR: Charles Chaplin
SCREENWRITER: Charles Chaplin (based on an unfinished novel)
RELEASED: 1952 (141 minutes)
RATED: Not rated

Limelight is a sentimental story and certainly Charlie Chaplin's most revealing and self-indulgent film. To carry on about the movie's sentimentality is akin to complaining bitterly that the singing in an opera was beautiful but you didn't understand the words.

Sentiment and excessive emotion are what this film is supposed to be about. Chaplin plays Calvero, a music hall entertainer far past his prime. He can't make people laugh anymore; he has lost his only power, the power to entertain. He finds a ballerina, the young and gorgeous Claire Bloom, virtually starving in the street. She believes she is permanently paralyzed and sees no reason to go on living. Calvero rescues Bloom's Thereza.

Limelight is an important film in many ways, not least in the teaming of Buster Keaton and Chaplin. There's an all-too-brief sequence that finally unites the two greatest comics of the Silent Era. It's enormously funny and also sad to see them so aged. The true sadness is that despite the greatness of Chaplin's talent, his generosity toward Keaton was miserly. Chaplin cut most of Keaton out of the film. That is the true tragedy of *Limelight*. Keaton was always lavish in his praise of the brilliance of Chaplin, Chaplin largely silent on the subject of Keaton's.

One sees the recurring theme of *City Lights* in *Limelight*. Once again, Chaplin must rescue the desperate girl from herself and her sorrows. However, this Chaplin was too old to keep the girl he saved and was doomed to watch her drift away from him. One is swept away by the vulnerability of Bloom's character and by the pure sweetness of her performance. The ending is indeed a duet, but a tragic one for Chaplin's character, Calvero.

Because of the extremist right-wing politics in American life in 1952, *Limelight* received much less attention than it deserved. During this period, Chaplin was considered politically subversive and was essentially hounded into exile. He lived for many years in Switzerland. He was then married to playwright Eugene O'Neill's daughter, Oona. They produced many children, including actress Geraldine Chaplin (see *Doctor Zhivago*). *Limelight*'s release in the 1950s was limited. In 1973, very belatedly, Chaplin's score received the Oscar. *Limelight* was rereleased in wide distribution. (The musical score was written in collaboration with Ray Rasch and Larry Russell.)

EXTRAS

Limelight's supplements are marginally better than those contained in the *City Lights* disc. There are a few minutes of footage deleted from the film by Chaplin after its release. There's a wacky six minutes of the original flea circus routine. It's footage that was shot in 1919. You can also view Chaplin's manuscript on which *Limelight* was based.

In 1916, Chaplin signed a contract with the Mutual Studio Company. The deal was for $670,000 and made him the biggest star in Hollywood. Now, amazingly, Image Entertainment has brought these films to DVD, with digital wizardry worthy of Harry Potter's friends. (They were on 35mm negatives.) The Chaplin Mutuals include many of his short films such as *The Immigrant*, *The Cure*, *Easy Street*, *The Count*, *The Vagabond*, *The Fireman*, *The Pawn Shop*, and *The Floorwalker*.

There are twelve films in all, and there's no other way to view these Chaplin masterpieces in such a satisfactory manner. His work at the Mutual Studio Company comprises three discs; you can buy them separately or in a set.

The Lion in Winter

CAST: Peter O'Toole, Katharine Hepburn, Anthony Hopkins, Timothy Dalton, John Castle, Nigel Terry, Jane Merrow
DIRECTOR: Anthony Harvey
SCREENWRITER: James Goldman (based on his play)
RELEASED: 1968 (135 minutes)
RATED: PG

When you finally do decide to go to that remote desert island for good, take this DVD with you. *The Lion in Winter* is on our personal top ten list.

Anthony Harvey's major motion picture debut as a director is a staggering achievement. The setting is England at Christmas. The year is 1183. Henry II and his wife,

Eleanor of Aquitaine, bring the family together for a royal celebration of the season. It's not filled with Christmas cheer and presents under the tree. Henry and the Queen battle over the succession to the throne. They favor different sons. The intrigue and resulting conspiracies unfold in a manner that will have you on the edge of your chair.

The Lion in Winter is simply one of the very best historical/royal dramas ever filmed. This is due to the firepower of the lead actors, Peter O'Toole as Henry II and Katharine Hepburn as Eleanor. Their screen chemistry is thrilling, and their love/hate relationship is played with a faultless pacing of the dialogue. Harvey, previously known for his work as Stanley Kubrick's editor *(Lolita, Dr. Strangelove)*, put as much importance on the spoken part of the story as on the costumes and pageantry. That is one of the many reasons this classic just doesn't age. Many of the later lavish historical dramas have been far more involved with costumes and sets. Here we want to follow the story and not gasp at the scenery.

We won't give away the story, so younger people who haven't had the opportunity to see this wondrous film will be surprised by the unfolding narrative. We will tell you that Henry II wants his youngest son, John, to become his heir. (Nigel Terry took this part.) Eleanor wants her eldest son, Richard the Lionheart, to succeed Henry. Papa thinks that Richard is too temperamental and perhaps even a bit off-balance. You'll roar like a lion yourself if you don't know that Anthony Hopkins portrays Richard of the hot temper. This was obviously his first "dress" rehearsal for Hannibal Lecter. It was Anthony Hopkins's debut film. Harvey picked stage actors for the supporting roles of the sons. Hopkins was in a play in London's National Theater, then under the leadership of Laurence Olivier.

Besides the film debut for Hopkins, the other first-timers, fresh from the theater, were Timothy Dalton, Nigel Terry, and John Castle. Timothy Dalton delivered a fine performance as the child king of France.

The Lion in Winter stands the test of time because of the strength of the story written by James Goldman. It was a successful play before it came to the screen. It also endures because of the perceptive astute judgment calls made by director Harvey. He was honored with an Oscar nomination for direction, although he lost to Sir Carol Reed for *Oliver!*—a film that also took the Oscar over *Lion* for Best Picture. Harvey won the Directors Guild Award, however. O'Toole was nominated for his role, and the Academy weirdly awarded the Oscar to Cliff Robertson for *Charly,* a touching but ultimately forgettable formula-driven vehicle. But Hepburn, as Eleanor of Aquitaine, took the Oscar; it was her third of what would be a total of four Oscars. She shared it with Barbra Streisand for *Funny Girl;* the Academy had tied their votes. They might have done the same for O'Toole.

In the end, it is the magnificence of Hepburn and O'Toole, cast together in roles deserving of their power and range, that makes this an unforgettable experience.

EXTRAS

The Lion in Winter is a film that we would recommend if it had only a trailer, or even if it didn't have that and came in a paper bag. But that's not the case. The full audio track commentary by Harvey is at the top of the "best of breed" category for these features. It's as insightful and enjoyable as any we've heard.

As we mentioned, Harvey had distinguished himself as a film editor before he was given the chance to direct this film. He had made one small, very low-budget film that O'Toole had seen and admired. He wanted Harvey for this job, and he wanted Hepburn as Eleanor. O'Toole flew to Hollywood to persuade Hepburn. This was a difficult time for Hepburn, as she was still in mourning over the loss of Spencer Tracy. In the commentary, Harvey talks about how the challenge of this role helped Hepburn through the darkest passage of her personal life.

You'll see why Harvey was such a noted film editor; his comments about his own film have a razor's edge of clean detail. He's fond of actors as well, which comes through clearly. He toyed with the idea of becoming an actor but jovially says that he would have had to compete with Albert Finney and didn't think he'd come out the winner.

This remarkable historical film based on real events was shot in twelve weeks, a feat now unthinkable. Along the way in the audio track, you will hear Harvey's many amusing and detailed anecdotes about the cast and the production. It is rare that we return again to a director's commentary, although we often return to see a favorite film again. This is a commentary you will want to hear more than once.

Harvey and writer James Goldman teamed up again in 1971 to make *They Might Be Giants*. This is a tragically overlooked film that is worth owning now that there's a superb special edition released by Anchor Bay. The story is about a distinguished judge who goes off the deep end when his wife dies. He thinks he's fine; it's just that he's realized he's actually Sherlock Holmes but is upset because he is never able to track down that evil Moriarity. Others think he's a paranoid lunatic. His brother, who has his own agenda, wants him sent off to the L.Bin immediately.

In order to have him declared insane, a psychiatrist is brought on the case. One rather large problem emerges; the doctor's name is Watson. It's Mildred Watson, but any Watson will suffice for our deranged Judge Playfair.

Soon the doctor and the judge are pursuing Moriarity together, fighting windmills, which is also a subplot. They fall in love, of course. The film has quite a large cult following. Now it's on DVD in a very good transfer, again with Harvey commenting on the audio. It's a film that should have been a big box-office hit, but the releasing studio neglected it.

Here's the secret if you've never heard of this film. Judge Justin Playfair is George C. Scott in a role unlike any other he ever had the opportunity to play. Dr. Mildred Watson is none other than Joanne Woodward. It's rated PG and runs about an hour and a half. This is one that you can delight unsuspecting guests with every time. We know you won't be disappointed in this offbeat film.

Lord of the Rings: The Fellowship of the Ring

CAST: Elijah Wood, Ian McKellen, Viggo Mortensen, Sean Astin, Ian Holm, Liv Tyler, Christopher Lee, Cate Blanchett, Billy Boyd, Dominic Monaghan, Orlando Bloom, Hugo Weaving, Sean Bean
DIRECTOR: Peter Jackson
SCREENWRITERS: Frances Walsh, Phililppa Boyens, and Peter Jackson (based on the work of J. R. R. Tolkien)
RELEASED: 2001 (178 minutes)
RATED: PG-13

In a modern world where the forces of dark and evil seem to be more resonant than ever, *The Lord of the Rings* has a particular beauty and relevance. The first of the trilogy, *The Fellowship of the Ring*, opened in theaters in December 2001. J. R. R. Tolkien spent fourteen years writing the Ring cycle. He couldn't know the world we face today, yet it feels like surreal prophecy-vision.

You don't need to be familiar with the books to become an immediate participant in the action of the movie. The narrated prologue covers a great deal of material and takes you right into the center of Hobbiton and forward to the quest for the return of the ring. It's a ring of evil long slumbering but now awakened. An unlikely crowd of hobbits and elves and dwarves and leaders of men form the Fellowship. Their mission is to destroy evil by returning the ring to the fiery land of its origins so that all may live in peace.

This is a technological masterpiece, which enables Tolkien's unbelievable world to become visual. Without the vast advances in computer-generated special effects and a $300-million budget, it couldn't have been done. The hobbits are still central to the story, and without Frodo, the hero hobbit, nothing could happen. But the action is more than that, and our age deserves this version. And by the way, so does the genius of Tolkien's work.

EXTRAS:

"Welcome to Middle Earth: Houghton Mifflin In-Store Special" is an unexpected pleasure. A short interview with Rayner Unwin, the son of the original publisher of Tolkien, talks of his lifelong relationship with Tolkien. He also reads his "reader report" of *The Hobbit*, written when he was a small boy at his publisher father's request. Unwin also shares his discussions with his father about publishing *The Lord of the Rings*, which he told his father was a work of genius that would probably lose about a "thousand pounds sterling." Unwin died shortly after the filming of this sequence; it's a lucky accident of fate to have this literary history preserved. This feature also includes behind-the-scenes interviews with artists, actors, and the current publisher of Tolkien.

"Quest for the Ring: Fox TV Special" and "A Passage to

Middle Earth: Sci-Fi Channel" are excellent detailed looks at the making of the film. Forty-eight thousand new pieces of weaponry were actually manufactured for this film. The sword-making itself is worth it. Interviews in both with Ian McKellen, the Wizard Gandalf, are engaging and emotionally satisfying. You have to be willing to hear some of the same things from the interviewed actors, director, and other participants. But the features are different enough to warrant watching. The Sci-Fi Channel was involved in the technical development and design of the film.

"Lordoftherings.net Featurettes" are viewed online and run about three minutes each, containing some of the same material as viewed on your TV screen. Particularly appealing are "Finding Hobbiton," "Hobbiton Comes Alive," and "Believing the World of Bree." For Enya fans, there is an evocative "May It Be" musical sequence.

In the Special Edition DVD, all the special features are on two bonus discs, totaling almost four hours of bonus material.

Disc One, "From Book to Vision," starts off with an introduction by director Peter Jackson describing the disc and how to navigate through it. Despite the hype, the MTV awards segment isn't that thrilling, but you should see it. Go to scenes, ending chapter 27, and select the ring icon.

"J. R. R. Tolkien: Creator of Middle Earth" contains a biography of Tolkien and the developmental process of creating his books. It includes lots of interesting background information, including other books that Tolkien has written.

"From Book to Script" goes through the thought process of making the book into a screenplay. You hear clips from the cast about their thoughts on the book and how the writers and producers broke down the book by sections, dissecting each part to make it into a feasible screenplay that would cover the story and yet not be ten hours long. After watching this section, you appreciate *LOTR* even more. Some of us, after seeing the film for the first time, loved it but were a little disappointed that some things were left out. Once you understand the decision-making process, you have a new respect for their decisions and the magical movie.

"Visualizing the Story" tells us how given scenes in the movie were developed and the processes required to attain the precisely right visual effect. We see the digital technology of Pre-Viz, which animates a scene on the computer for everything from set design, to camera location, to choreography on fight scenes. There are also storyboards for the scenes and a split screen view of both. More often than not, the storyboard feature of a DVD is boring. This is not the case here, where a narration of developing the ideas step by step while there's a script reading from the director over the top allows you a glimpse at the early stages of film development.

You can't even begin to imagine the amount of work and detail that went into this movie until you see "Designing and Building Middle Earth." The WETA workshop was responsible for creating all the special effects, from the sets, to the makeup and all of the armor and weaponry of each civilization in Middle Earth. Every sword, every shield, every helmet was handcrafted and unique to the person carrying it.

The costume design is detailed for all the characters, from hobbits to elves to the men of Gondor. The designer faced daunting challenges to create these costumes and remain as true to the Tolkien descriptions as possible. In the Design Gallery are hundreds of sketches for each character and the set. These are presented in a slide-show fashion, or you can flip through at your own pace, depending on your level of interest.

Trace the paths of Frodo and of Gandalf from Hobbiton to Rivendale on the map of Middle Earth. This is a great feature, especially if you have never read the book. In the book, you are given the same map and detailed descriptions of where they are going at all times. In the movie, you don't have time for that, so this feature allows you to get even deeper into the story by following the characters around Middle Earth. You can chart the path to Mordor.

In "New Zealand as Middle Earth," you follow Jackson around New Zealand as he looks for filming locations for each scene. The sketch artists took the landscape and created a living civilization on it. Jackson then took these drawings and built the civilizations on the landscape. It's a beautiful extra feature because you get to see almost all of New Zealand from the ground and from the sky.

Disc Two, "From Vision to Reality," is introduced by Elijah Wood.

"The Fellowship Cast" section contains interviews with the cast members, who share their experience of life on the set in New Zealand, where the filming lasted for two years. These clips are cut with behind-the-scenes footage of the cast on and off the sets.

"A Day in the Life of a Hobbit" focuses on the hobbit cast, from makeup to filming to unguarded off-camera fun. Each hobbit cast member talks about experiences making the film and the relationships that developed. There's plenty of footage of cast members together. This section is very entertaining.

"Cameras in Middle Earth" shows how the cameras were placed around the sets, how many cameras were used, and the special ways the cameras were used to get certain visual effects. There's an illuminating sequence about the size difference between humans and hobbits.

Lots of photos were taken on set during the two years of filming. You can see these in a slide show or by browsing at your own pace.

"Visual Effects" shows models, miniatures, and the WETA Workshop. Take your own journey through the developmental process of creating many of the special effects, from original drawings to the models and to the final product.

In "Post Production: Putting It All Together," the editors discuss the difficulties they had bringing vast amounts of raw footage together to make the final cuts. One scene in the movie is shown from every camera angle. There's fascinating raw footage from six different cameras that were filming during this scene compared to the final cut.

The "Digital Grading" section shows how they used digital technology to bring the colors of Middle Earth to a new level and to help create that fantasy world. You'll see how they took the film and used computers to change its color and brightness. This enabled them to make it brighter in some spots, darker in others, and to create the magical effect of the elves.

The "Sound and Music" section shows how they created the sounds for the different characters in Middle Earth. In addition, a portion of the developmental process of the musical score behind the film is included. There's an interview with Howard Shore, the composer for the film. He discusses how he created music for Middle Earth with Jackson.

"The Road Goes Ever On" follows the cast and crew around to the world premieres of the film. You get some reflective thoughts from the cast, as well as their thoughts on attending the premieres.

The special features of this disc are incomparable to any other. The design is done beautifully. The information contained with the special features is endlessly fascinating. You don't ever get tired of what cast and crew have to say; you want to hear more. You gain a deeper level of appreciation for this movie after seeing all the work that went into it and all the challenges. You almost feel as if you were there with them every step of the way.

In addition, the special edition DVD has thirty minutes of extra footage in the film that was not in the original theatrical release. That alone is worth the purchase.

Manhattan

CAST: Woody Allen, Diane Keaton, Meryl Streep, Michael Murphy, Mariel Hemingway, Wallace Shawn
DIRECTOR: Woody Allen
SCREENWRITERS: Woody Allen and Marshall Brickman
RELEASED: 1979 (96 minutes)
RATED: R

Scores of professional critics and legions of movie lovers have embraced this as one of the top 150 films of the twentieth century. In fact, it is a cinematic sonnet to a vibrant New York. From the opening titles, you have a sense of bittersweet loss for a New York now changed forever. The letters of the word *Manhattan*, each fashioned as a recognizable building—the Chrysler, the Empire State, the Citicorp Center, and, of course, the now destroyed World Trade Center towers. But this film is far from an antiquated look at the city. If anything, we need this movie even more now.

Woody Allen's voice opens the film, and he sets the pace from the beginning. It is a voice of the energy, love, confusion, and, yes, self-involvement that are so crucial to any authentic definition of life in New York City. Allen can't quite decide what he wants to say about Manhattan, so he keeps it all in rather than editing it out. In one of the takes, he says he adores Manhattan. This is a different point of view from in the earlier *Annie Hall.* In that film, Diane Keaton, as Annie, declares that New York is a dying city.

Manhattan is still a number one New York category pick. At the end of the opening montage, which is involving and inventive, Allen says this about the lead character, Isaac Davis: "New York was his town and always would be."

Manhattan is a lyrical valentine to the city. The soundtrack completes the fantasy of love and loss with some of the most glorious melodies George Gershwin ever wrote, including "Rhapsody in Blue" and "Embraceable You." The soundtrack complements the poignant love scenes among cerebral urban dwellers who seem to get it all wrong in love but can't let go of the fantasy.

The love stories embedded in the film are a metaphor for the New Yorker's own passionate yet ambivalent relationship with the city itself. Manhattan is a human entity, and the feelings one has about the city often mirror real life. One day, you're in love with it all from the bottom of the island to the very top. The next day, you could turn your back on the whole place and never see it again . . . or think you could, for about twenty minutes. Allen's genius is that he seamlessly interweaves the backdrop of Manhattan into the lives of the characters. This is high cinema art, without being at all arty. Unlike previous films or later films, Allen is at his most comfortable here as both director and actor. He doesn't mug for the camera or try to be too cute; here is the New York of the 1970s many of us actually lived in and through.

Allen portrays forty-two-year-old Isaac Davis, generic

Jewish intellectual and comedy writer. The scenes in which he woos a seventeen-year-old, played by Mariel Hemingway (granddaughter of Ernest), are quite wrenching. As art has that cheeky way of imitating life, this might be hard going for some viewers, given Allen's not-so-private personal life. But if you find yourself wincing during these scenes with a high school girl, remember that art exists in its own world.

Diane Keaton returns in this film as Woody's more age-appropriate girlfriend, but she feels the sands shifting under her feet as he falls under the spell of the seemingly naive but quite sophisticated Hemingway. Meryl Streep is magnificent in a tiny but significant role as Allen's ex-wife who wants to write a tell-all book about their failed marriage. If you don't blink, you will even see Mia Farrow. All of this can be a bit harrowing if you recall the many turns and twists of Allen's personal odyssey, but it's best not to let your brain go there.

The script is superb and has a near-perfect batting average of self-deprecating remarks and wisecracks that perfectly fit the personalities of Allen's pals. There is the usual anti-mother jibe, this one when he calls his mother "a castrating Zionist." A far funnier line is that the brain is the most overrated organ. It is hilarious because you know on the face of it that it is the thing he believes the least. And the classic: "People should mate for life, like pigeons and Catholics."

Bella Abzug plays herself, a fierce and fiery one-of-a-kind politician determined to change a world that stubbornly refused to listen.

By the time *Manhattan* came out in 1979, Allen, director, writer, actor, musician, had already been involved with thirteen films, but *Manhattan* was his most accomplished. In many ways, it remains so, if for no other reason than that the male character is actually a fully developed, if besieged, human male. Allen's more than thirty films, many award-winning, now span five decades. He is clearly at the top rank of American filmmakers. *Manhattan* was nominated for two Academy Awards, one for the screenplay and an oddly mis-placed one for Hemingway. Also of note is that this was the first of Allen's films to be made in black and white.

EXTRAS

The extra features are minimal, but the payoff is quite high. The original trailer was magnificently shot by Gordon Willis with magisterial skyline vistas. If you are a displaced New Yorker or just want to be a New Yorker, you can watch this for a quick urban hit. Another feature allows you to view New York logos, which is diverting. It's especially use-ful if you are trying to waste time so that you can appear late to a dinner party you know can't possibly be as gratify-ing as this film. The DVD also offers scene selections in the standard format.

The Matrix

CAST: Keanu Reeves, Laurence Fishburne, Carrie-Anne Moss, Hugo Weaving, Gloria Foster, Joe Pantoliano, Marcus Chong, Julian Arahanga, Matt Doran, Belinda McClory, Anthony Ray Parker, Paul Goddard, Robert Taylor, David Aston
DIRECTORS: Andy Wachowski and Larry Wachowski
SCREENWRITERS: Andy Wachowski and Larry Wachowski
RELEASED: 1999 (136 minutes)
RATED: R

The Matrix is a film filled with special effects that will take your breath away. It was a watershed in the industry's special effects world. It's all about action sequences embellished with incredible computer-generated wizardry.

The Matrix might not be your cup of tea, but if you want to see something that truly blows you away in this genre, don't pass it up. It's a futuristic vehicle where machines have intelligence and have taken over the thinking world. Humans live in an alternative reality, unaware of their state of slavery to the machines. In addition to the rather classic sci-fi story, there are mystical elements, complete with an oracle.

Neo (Keanu Reeves) is the computer-hacker code name of Thomas A. Anderson, an anonymous software programmer working in his cubicle somewhere in a large city. Throughout his computer career, Neo has heard of this strange thing called the Matrix. It's whispered about here and there, and although he doesn't know what it is, he understands it's a major deal. Determined to find out, he takes a journey down a strange path following a White Rabbit (yes, it's true), but he won't end up in Wonderland with Alice. Instead, he meets Morpheus (Laurence Fishburne), named for the Greek god of dreams. Morpheus tells Neo that he can show him the Matrix, but he must eat either the red or the blue pill first to decide if he wants to go on pursuing it. One will make you grow smaller; one will make you grow bigger.

In this brave and fearless new world, humans built machines with artificial intelligence many years ago. These machines then revolted and conquered the human race. Humans are grown in huge fields, then plugged into their operating systems to be used as batteries. The machines have created an artificial environment to keep humans alive. When plugged into a mainframe system, they are in a virtual reality, which makes them feel they are living normal lives.

None of it's real. The reality is that the world has been

destroyed, and the computers have completely taken over. Morpheus and his small crew are among the few lucky ones who managed to escape this false reality and are trying to find a way to defeat the machines and bring back human civilization. It has been prophesied that there will be the One who comes and has the power to defeat the machines and restore humankind. Morpheus feels that Neo is that One. Their battles take place in the Matrix, the virtual reality world that everyone seems to be living in, against computer programs in the form of federal agents.

Fast action sequences are slowed down to make each second last about a minute. A new technology called Bullet Time yields 3-D views of action sequences. Some are so stunning, it's hard to describe. People run along walls, leap across buildings, dodge bullets, and the like. With the expert help of Hong Kong filmmaker and Kung Fu master Yuen Wo Ping, *The Matrix* dazzles the viewer.

Although individual performances aren't paced properly and are either underplayed or overplayed, it doesn't lessen the film's impact. The plot has holes that can be confusing. But, again, it won't diminish your thrill. *The Matrix* won four Oscars: Best Editing, Best Effects/Sound Effects Editing, Best Effects/Visual, and Best Sound.

EXTRAS

Bonus material on the original release includes mini-bios on the cast and crew. There is also a bio on the Wachowski brothers. When you select this option, you are taken to another screen, where you can view the bio or select the red pill. The red pill is a hidden bonus feature, the first DVD egg. In this feature, you see storyboards and film clips done with a techno-music background that plays along with the storyboards perfectly.

"The Dream World" is a commentary about how the

special effects were created and implemented. There's a lively discussion sequence about the editing process. Zach Staenberg was Senior Editor.

"Making of *The Matrix*" is a rewarding documentary that gives lots of information. The crew went through a four-month training period with Kung-Fu master Yuen Wo Ping learning how to do the fight scenes. There are behind-the-scenes images as well as interviews. On the first screen is the other red pill, the other egg. This will take you to a behind-the-scenes look at Bullet Time, the special effects technique developed for this movie.

One option plays the movie with only the musical component. Don Davis discusses how he created the music for this film and for certain sequences during the times when it's silent.

With "Follow the White Rabbit," you can watch the movie, and a white rabbit or a telephone will appear on the screen. When it does, if you hit enter, you will be taken behind the scenes to see how they developed that scene. The movie then picks up back where the symbol first appeared, and you can watch the final cut of the sequence.

"Go Further" is behind-the-scene footage of the making of the video game that will be coming out soon. This is a short segment, mainly with shots of car chase rehearsals and fight scenes, and then a short commentary from the producers of the game.

Animatrix is a series of short films created by famous Japanese animation artists. These short films will be accessible on the Web site in the future. They will consist of side stories from the film, such as what happened before the machines created the Matrix.

"Whatisthematrix.com" is a promotional feature for the Web site. The director and writers of the film talk about what they did and why it is different from the standard movie Web site.

"The Dance of Master Yuen Wo Ping's Blocking Tapes" is a funny feature. It looks like one of those old Kung Fu movies. The footage is from rehearsal when Yuen Wo Ping's fighting team worked through the fight sequences to develop camera angles, blocking, and so forth.

"The True Followers" should have been left out; if it's a joke, it falls flat. These are interviews with extreme fans of the Web site and *The Matrix* itself. They talk about how the *Matrix* experience changed their lives and created a new circle of friends for them.

In "Bathroom Fight and Wet Wall," two of the more difficult scenes to shoot during the filming are given a behind-the-scenes treatment, as well as insight from the cast members. It's not very long and is an interesting clip.

EGGS

The first egg is on the first menu screen of the special features. Click the cursor to the right, and a lady in a red dress will appear behind Morpheus. Hit enter, and you will be given a behind-the-scenes look at this character in the movie.

The second egg is on the second menu screen of the special features. If you go to the right again, Neo changes position. Hit enter, and you will be given a behind-the-scenes look at Reeves in the movie, as well as footage of the other cast and crew discussing his work.

Monsoon Wedding

CAST: Naseeruddin Shah, Lilete Dubey, Shefali Shetty, Vasundhara
    Das, Parvin Dabas, Vijay Raaz, Tilotama Shome
DIRECTOR: Mira Nair
SCREENWRITER: Sabrina Dhawan
RELEASED: 2001 (113 minutes)
RATED: R

At one point in her life, director Mira Nair had a family
nickname. She was called Toofani, which means "whirlwind." That is the best way to describe her latest film, *Monsoon Wedding*. It is a whirlwind of color, feeling, confusion,
class, and people. Ultimately, it is a warmly entertaining
and embracing whirlwind.

If you are coming to this with the expectation of *My Big
Fat Greek Wedding* but located in India, you're going to
have a problem. This is a far more subtle film, where the
payoff is not in smart quips and broad laughs. Nair, in her
early forties, has been working in film since she was twenty.
It has been a joy to watch the development and risk-taking
of this fine artist. *Monsoon Wedding* in some ways is her
most challenging film to date, not because of the subject
matter but because of the techniques she employs.

There are sixty-eight people floating in and out of your
line of sight, although you'll swear there are three hundred.
It's a series of stories arranged around the theme of a big
wedding, but to say that is to dismiss the enormity of what
Nair has pulled off. The characters speak three languages,
moving from Hindi to Punjabi to English with the same
fluidity with which they live their lives. (The movie is primarily in English; there are subtitles provided when
needed.)

The Verma family is about to marry off their daughter

in lavish Indian style. It's a traditionally arranged marriage; the bride and groom are strangers to each other. (He's living abroad and has come home to India to marry.) It's set in today's India. Aditi (Vasundhara Das) is a not-so-innocent bride; she has been having a long-term affair with a married television celebrity. It's unclear why she has accepted this turn of events. It's to Nair's credit that everything isn't tied up in neatly stacked and pretty wedding boxes for you. Perhaps Aditi has decided it's time to marry. Or did she believe a proposed marriage would make her married lover suddenly divorce and become available as a spouse for her? We never learn, and that's good.

What matters is the way Nair weaves diverse stories and people into one deft story. The point isn't what is going to happen next but to be in each moment of the film. In every frame, you feel Nair's familiarity with her native country, as well as her love of its textures, colors, and contradictions.

It's an impressionistic film that isn't pretentious; that's not an easy task. One subplot involves the manic wedding planner P. K. Dubey (Vijay Raaz). An unexpected romance develops between him and the family's maid. Dubey provides comic relief throughout. Although he is from a lower caste, the wedding is Dubey's show; he's in charge. Constantly on his cell phone with caterers, decorators, and the like, Dubey flies from one spot to the next in an explosion of orders and commands. He screams incessantly that he needs more money from the bride's father. He's the universal wedding planner.

In the midst of all of this, as the wedding hour advances, Aditi vacillates between excitement and denial. In many ways, she represents any modern young woman in a traditional culture who tries to find her own path without losing all of her family's traditions.

There are many touching scenes in the film. We were

especially moved by the honesty with which Aditi and her intended, Hemant Rai (Parvin Dabas), achieve an understanding that incorporates both the new and the old India. The darker theme of sexual abuse is handled strongly but without a tinge of preachy social commentary. It seems that one of the wedding guests, an uncle who lives abroad, has a long history of pedophilia inside the family. A female cousin who was abused by him confronts him when she sees his next unaware victim. What will Aditi's father do? He is a man whose belief in family loyalty is so strong that it all but imprisons him. He's also a man who wants to impress his richer relative. His moral and ethical dilemma is resolved dramatically but not at all melodramatically.

There is a wedding in the end. You've not seen one like it before, unless this is your cultural heritage, or you've been lucky enough to be a guest at such a glorious event. The groom arrives in splendor on his white horse. If it seems realistic to you, it is. Nair based many of the wedding scenes on her own first marriage.

Come to this film as a guest. Let the images, the floating colors of the wedding tent, the disjointed conversations, the family squabbles, the tensions, all the sensations of being in India flow through you. If you can do that, you'll come away from *Monsoon Wedding* enchanted and enriched. It deserves to be seen more than once.

Nair is a gifted director, whose full depth and artistic dimensions we have only begun to see, despite previously interesting and creditable work. Mira Nair grows with each film she makes. We hope to be watching her unique, edgy, ever-changing take on life for a long time to come. If you're interested in Nair's life, we suggest you read John Lahr's excellent profile of her in the December 9, 2002, issue of *The New Yorker* magazine. It's entitled, aptly enough, "Whirlwind."

EXTRAS

Since this is a new movie, the transfer is perfect. We saw *Monsoon Wedding* in the theater as well as on DVD. We did not feel cheated seeing it on the smaller screen. The colors that are so crucial to the atmosphere are exactly as they were in its original release. The beauty of the DVD is that you can move back and forth if you lose a thread of the many stories and subplots.

Nair's commentary is critical to an understanding of her stamina, discipline, and craft. No wonder she was once called Whirlwind; she's a force of nature. She made the film with a tiny budget of $1.2 million and did it all in thirty days, in monsoon season. The film won the Golden Lion in Venice at the 2001 festival. In the commentary, Nair explains her system for pulling an enormous cast together, which begins with a group yoga session every morning.

Monsoon Wedding is an especially intimate look at the lives of women in modern India. Nair has tremendous insight into their lives and the choices they make. She reveals her thoughts in a lively and animated way. Nair is very deeply connected to this film, for obvious reasons. The thrill of this audio track is that she lets us into her world and her feelings.

There's a standard trailer, which isn't worth much. The IFC behind-the-scenes "special" is an odd description for something that lasts less than ten minutes. The true bonus is the Nair commentary, which should add immeasurably to your enjoyment of *Monsoon*.

If you're a Nair fan, or are becoming one, her 1988 film *Salaam Bombay!* is also available on DVD. So is the visually evocative and tremendously erotic *Kama Sutra* (1996). These are both films of merit. (When you've got *Kama Sutra* safely home, take it out of the plain brown wrapper, click subtitles, and make a delicious belly button glow. You will have a tiny morsel of the actual book. Our advice: Buy the book.) Sadly, Nair's quite wonderful *Mississippi Masala* from 1991 is not yet on DVD. In 2002, she skillfully directed *Hysterical Blindness* for HBO. It stars Uma Thurman, Gena Rowlands, Ben Gazzara, and Juliette Lewis and is the story of a working-class New Jersey neighborhood in the mid-1980s. Rowlands plays Thurman's mother. Gazarra is Rowlands's love interest. It's more than a good effort, it's a worthy movie. Grab it now that it is on DVD. You'll want to see it for the ensemble acting, as well as for yet another creative expression in the Nair oeuvre.

Monster's Ball

CAST: Halle Berry, Billy Bob Thornton, Peter Boyle, Heath Ledger, Sean Combs, Coronji Calhoun
DIRECTOR: Marc Forster
SCREENWRITERS: Milo Addica and Will Rokos
RELEASED: 2001 (111 minutes)
RATED: R

Monster's Ball is a prison euphemism for the condemned's last night. Lawrence Musgrove (Sean Combs) is a black man in a Georgia penitentiary who is about to be electrocuted. His ex-wife, Leticia (Halle Berry) brings their son, Tyrell (Coronji Calhoun), to say goodbye. This sparely acted scene is the clue to the rest of the film. The family's meeting is low-key and honest; there are no dramatic claims of innocence or injustice. Musgrove tells his son that what's good in him is in his son, but not what's bad. Tyrell is a grotesquely obese little boy whose emotional pain is evident in each lumbering step he takes.

Back at home, Leticia's rage and discontent with her wretched life spill over on Tyrell when she discovers his hidden stash of candy bars. The instant she leaves, he stuffs himself again. Tyrell is a metaphor for the emptiness of a life lived without hope, or even a door marked "This way out." After the execution, Tyrell's prized possessions become the portraits his father drew during his years on death row. Many of the drawings are quite good, including those of his two executioners, Hank and Sonny Grotowski, sketched during the last hours of his life. (Those portraits, however, are given to the men, not to Tyrell, a factor that becomes crucial to the plot.) Tyrell proudly hangs his father's various drawings around the house. Leticia works the late shift in a diner, where she seems half-asleep and half-dead. An eviction notice nailed to the screen door of her home indicates there's more sorrow coming her way. The effectiveness of the film is that you can't possibly imagine what's next.

The execution is portrayed with a sickening exactitude. Sonny Grotowski is clearly not cut out for his prison job. Hank is unrelenting in his contempt for his son. The setup for the actual execution takes no shortcuts; you are witness to every detail in the preparation of the prisoner for his death. You are also in a front-row seat when the switch is flipped. After Lawrence Musgrove is dead, Hank comes after his son with a vengeance for "fucking up" the man's last walk. (Sonny lost control and vomited on the walk to the death chamber.) Other guards try to come to Sonny's aid when it appears Hank might bludgeon his own son to death. Hank lays off but makes it clear he's in charge; he's both Sonny's father and the warden. Sonny will later show that no one in the Grotowski family is in charge of their lives or their feelings.

At home, there's also "Papa" Grotowski, called Buck,

who needs constant oxygen but is still fueled with a full tank of racial hatred. He whiles his days away watching television and working on his scrapbook. Each time a black man is executed, Buck proudly pastes the newspaper clipping in his book. Apparently, he's keeping score. Peter Boyle delivers a riveting performance as an unredeemed Southerner who hates even small black children. We learn of his sexual attraction to black women, however, through a conversation he has with Leticia. His words are as chilling as they are repulsive. (You'll be hard-pressed to recognize Boyle as the father from the popular sitcom *Everybody Loves Raymond*.)

Hank turns up at the diner where Leticia is a waitress; she pulls the graveyard shift. In the beginning, he doesn't know who she is, and she doesn't know who he is. Hank's bigotry is never as vocal as his father's, but his feelings are clear in his disapproval of his son's friendship with the local black children. Hank cuts his son no slack, although it is hard to determine exactly what it is about Sonny that makes Hank such an unloving father. Their life revolves around the world of the prison, poisoned family relations, and racial prejudice. Buck is retired from the prison, Hank is the current warden, and presumably Sonny will be launched into the family career. The aftermath of the execution of Lawrence Musgrove changes the lives of the Grotowski family as much as it does the Musgroves'.

We won't tell you what goes on among Sonny, Hank, and Buck because to do so would ruin one of the most meaningful family scenes in the film. Suffice it to say it's not happy, and it's surely not pretty. Following the hideous action Sonny takes, Hank resigns his post at the prison. As always, Billy Bob Thornton's nonverbal expressiveness can be as riveting as his spoken lines. Watch his eyes as he burns his uniform in his front yard in total silence.

How Leticia and Hank come together involves another tragedy that verges on melodrama but fortunately pulls out quickly. (There's no question that parts of the story are contrived.) Yet the payoff is enormous, even with some heavy-handed manipulation of characters and story. The impact of *Monster's Ball* doesn't deteriorate. The love scenes between Berry and Thornton are evocatively woven into the fabric of the story. As the film progresses, the textures of the lives of Hank and Leticia are highlighted in memorable sequences. After she's been evicted, Leticia sits outside her former home, her things strewn around her. Yet in Berry's portrayal, there's no sense of victimization. Instead, you see a depth of elegance despite her dire circumstances and a determination to move on, however tentatively or unpredictably.

The surprise of *Monster's Ball* is that it keeps going on, just the way life goes on. Sometimes the most horrific things imaginable are followed by unanticipated human sweetness, just as unimaginable. At very different moments in the story, Hank and Leticia discover who they are to each other in relationship to the dead man. The true triumph of this film is that they do not reveal their knowledge to each other. It's one of the major reasons you will have a hard time forgetting these characters.

EXTRAS

If possible, purchase the newer "Signature Edition." It's a slightly longer version of the film.

There are two audio commentaries, and director Marc Forster is heard on both. You listen to him with Thornton and Berry and again with Roberto Schaefer, the cinematographer, who did a magnificent job. Schaefer's remarks are quite technical, but we found they add greatly to an understanding of the complexity of the filming process. We enjoyed listening to Berry and Thornton chatting about their experiences together.

Skip the "deleted scenes" feature. These are boring and pointless clips that should have been swept up with the other scraps from the cutting-room floor.

There are several new interesting extras in the revised, expanded "Signature Series" for Lions Gate, released in the winter of 2003. Our favorite is an informative commentary from producer Lee Daniels, an experienced young studio production veteran getting his pivotal break with this, his first producer credit. Daniels notes that he reads three shooting scripts each day. He candidly comments on how he reacted to the *Monster's Ball* screenplay from Academy Award nominees Milo Addica and Will Rokos, with its powerful themes including racism, interracial love, prison brutality, poverty in the South, and the highly charged question of the death penalty in contemporary American society.

The scenes leading up to the execution were filmed inside the infamous Angola prison in Louisiana. You won't soon forget Heath Ledger and others talking about different aspects of shooting the film with the actual electric chair looming in the background.

Daniels notes, for the record, that the much-publicized "love scene" between Berry and Thornton resulted from a clear understanding that the actors were free to do whatever they wanted during the sequence. However, footage would not be released in final theatrical release without the formal permission of the two charismatic stars.

Mostly Martha

CAST: Martin Gedeck, Maxime Foerste, Sergio Castellitto, August
    Zirner, Sibylle Canonica, Katja Studt, Antonio Wannek, Idil Uner
DIRECTOR: Sandra Nettlebeck
SCREENWRITER: Sandra Nettlebeck
RELEASED: 2001 (107 minutes)
RATED: PG

Martha is the second-best chef in Hamburg. You wouldn't
suspect that from what you see coming out of her kitchen.
Like most chefs in busy chic restaurants, her days are
chaotic, but her personal life isn't. At home alone, she sits
down to a meticulously prepared meal. She makes a half-
hearted attempt to find a new male neighbor interesting
but ends up offering to cook for him. Mostly, Martha just
wants to cook for people, paying customers and others,
even her psychiatrist.

Her relationship with her analyst is a mess of a seduction, a sort of cross-transference, and Freudian confusion.
She cooks for him; he says that they agreed she wouldn't do
it any longer, but he eats what she makes. When she's not
watching him eat the luncheon she's prepared for him, she's
on the analytic couch talking about how to kill a lobster
humanely. She talks endlessly about food but not about her
life. There's nothing sexy in her relationship with her
shrink. There's nothing sexy about Martha. She's a
buttoned-up obsessive-compulsive who has a bit of a problem controlling her impulses in one area.

Beware the customer who doesn't like Martha's food.
She's likely to tell them off or tip the table over. When she
is overwhelmed by everything in the restaurant or the
kitchen, she retreats to the walk-in freezer to cool off.

She's also a freak about an orderly and neat kitchen.

There's something you have to love about Martha. The owner of the restaurant decides that the kitchen needs a little something new and hires Mario, an assistant chef. She hates him; he seems indifferent at first. But Martha's life is altered forever when her sister is killed and she ends up as the guardian of her young niece, who doesn't like Martha or her food. She loves Mario and his food, however. Eventually, this leads where you knew it would, but not without some romantic suspense. There's a kissing scene that's one of the best of its kind. (We collect kisses on films, and this is one of our top kissing scenes.)

The love story in this movie is as much about the texture of food in our lives as about the need to connect to others. It's a story about letting go and getting on with things, whether you're a child in mourning for her mother or an adult who hasn't figured out how to make a life work. It's not a splashy movie, nor is it one with the poignancy of *Babette's Feast,* but it's a good food and love flick. We liked it because the pace isn't as slickly orchestrated as most American romantic comedies. It lumbers along sometimes and doesn't always make perfect sense, which we find refreshing. This is an impressive debut film for director/screenwriter Sandra Nettlebeck. As in a few other European films, you'll need to watch all the way through the credits to find out what really happens.

EXTRAS

There are no extras. Just remember to order what Martha wants you to when you hit the neighborhood bistro after the film's finished or when you're ordering in, or there could be trouble . . .

Moulin Rouge

CAST: Nicole Kidman, Ewan McGregor, John Leguizamo, Jim
   Broadbent, Richard Roxburgh, Kylie Minogue, Christine Anu
DIRECTOR: Baz Luhrmann
SCREENWRITERS: Baz Luhrmann and Craig Pearce
RELEASED: 2001 (126 minutes)
RATED: PG-13

It makes no sense. It's wild; it's silly; it's campy; it's goofy;
it's virtually without a proper plot; it's positively ridiculous.
It's Luhrmann-land. Don't miss it!

   This isn't the historic tale of Toulouse-Lautrec and his
debauched friends told in a sequential, plot-driven manner.
It's a riot of color, music, and dance, loosely (very loosely)
strung together by a story that's been told before. It's part
parody and part invention. Suffice it to say, we don't think
there's ever been a musical like this. Your eyes boggle at the
amount they need to take in during even one camera shot.
It deserves repeated viewings because there's so much going
on you can't possibly take it all in the first time. It's a joyous
and daring confection. It takes more than guts to make
something like this; it takes a director whose brain is moving as fast as the can-can. Luhrmann's diverse talents are
formidable. He recently directed a smash hit Broadway
musical of Puccini's *La Bohème*.

   The story (such as it is) revolves around a dancer/courtesan
called Satine, who, like all fading swans of the Belle
Époque, is afflicted with consumption. It's a secret we're
told almost from the beginning. We know, but she doesn't.
She's fallen in love with an impoverished writer called
Christian. At first, she mistakes him for the rich Duke of
Worcester. She believes the Duke will take her away from
the tawdry Moulin Rouge and give her the opportunity to

become a real actress. Realizing her error, she falls in love with Christian anyway. He writes a thinly veiled version of their love story as a new musical for Satine using the Duke's money for the production. But the Duke wants more than a smile from our little Satine. Everyone in this cast bursts into song at almost any moment; Luhrmann set the score with pop tunes from the past. It's giggle time. But once you're beyond the sensation that you're in the middle of an overproduced Coca-Cola commercial, it's quite fabulous. Put away your need for intellectual stimulation and tightly constructed plots; just go with this.

Satine lives inside an elephant inside the Moulin Rouge inside a Paris that seems to be encapsulated inside a giant glass bubble. A very pale Kidman plays Satine. She gives the role enough vitality, despite her pale demeanor, that you feel something akin to real emotion when she collapses. Kidman is a fine actress whose depth and range are beginning to be more fully understood. She's a transcendent beauty, the way the original movie star beauties were.

McGregor plays the lovesick Christian, who only wants Satine, at any price. He will risk continued poverty and even death to have her as his own; they play well together. Jim Broadbent, as the impresario Zidler, commands the entire spectacle—as in, "Spectacular/Spectacular," the title of their new musical. There's a campy rendition from the *Sound of Music,* which is musical time travel that under anyone else's direction could be grotesque slapstick. John Leguizamo is a lovable version of Toulouse-Lautrec. Richard Roxburgh plays the unhappy role of the mean and vile Duke but pulls it off with grand style and a certain devilish relish.

In the first exciting moments, we're told that life is only about "truth, beauty, and love, but most especially love." Despite the relentless melodrama of it all, including too much annoying and unnecessary farce, maybe this film really is about watching a creative energy like Luhrmann's burst forth unbridled.

EXTRAS

There's audio commentary on the first disc with designer Catherine Martin and cinematographer Don McAlpine. They tell the tricks of the trade. Find out what color was used to enhance that already porcelain skin of Kidman's. We liked this audio track because so much information was given about how the various scenes were shot. With so many cast and crew and a myriad of special shots, it was illuminating, if somewhat exhausting, to hear it explained. The second commentary, also on the first disc, is Luhrmann and Craig Pearce (who cowrote the script). They are amusing, and it's less formal than the first commentary.

Disc Two has the best feature in the package, "Making of Moulin Rouge." If there is madness to Luhrmann's genius, you'll hear it from his own lips. The Rouge makes more sense artistically when you hear Luhrmann's vision clarified. There's a standard set of interviews with the actors entitled "The Stars." Do watch "The Story Is About . . . ," which gives more of the Luhrmann-Pearce collaboration. If only we had this sort of footage from Rodgers and Hammerstein's collaborations. (By the way, the word is that they are BOTH turning over in their graves every single time this DVD is played anywhere in the world. But don't let that haunt you and ruin your pleasure.) We think those are the best features, but you also might be interested in watching the deleted scenes, the music, and the dance features.

If you're into cracking the eggshells, you can have a few guffaws with *Moulin Rouge*. The secret here is to catch the red windmill as it turns or a red or green fairy mid-flight.

There's been much discussion about the myriad of hidden material on the disc. There are about twenty eggs, depending on how you count. But they are of vastly differing quality. We won't take you through them all, just the most amusing ones. All are on Disc Two.

MOULIN ROUGE ICON

1. Select "The Cutting Room" from the main menu. When you see the red windmill, select enter. You will see a big deleted scene of "Your Song."

2. Go to the second frame of the main menu. Select "Marketing" and then "Photo Gallery" to Mary Ellen Mark, turn right, select red windmill, see Leguizamo in a rehearsal take.

3. Stay on second frame of main menu, proceed to "The Design" and then the suboption "Set Design." Highlight "The Gothic Tower." Keep going with the remote, and your windmill returns. All of this for a fleeting glimpse of the ravishing Kidman in "civilian clothes."

4. Our favorite egg, under the sign of the windmill, is also found in "The Design" menu. Press remote in downward direction to "Costume Design," again downward until "The Bohemians" will take you to the windmill. When you highlight the windmill, you get the male cast during "Can-can."

GREEN FAIRY ICON

1. On second frame of main menu, choose "The Dance." After this selection, "The Dance" will be in red letters; select again. You will see to the left the words "A word from Baz." Go right on remote, to green fairy, presto! Baz Luhrmann on tango.

2. On second menu frame, "The Design" to "Costume Design." Select "A Courtesan's Wardrobe," where a green fairy will fly into the screen after four clicks of the remote. Blooper of Kidman with McGregor.

3. Our absolute favorite egg is Toulouse-Lautrec dressed in his musical instrument costume. It's not a long take, but it's very funny. Here's the key to finding it: main menu, select "The Stars," after a collage of Kidman and McGregor, select "More," you'll see "John Leguizamo as Toulouse-Lautrec." Select it, and a green fairy appears.

RED FAIRY ICON

Some people claim this egg as their favorite. It could be because we all love Broadbent so much. Or it might be that it's the easiest to find. Select "More" on main menu, click remote in downward direction to "Back." Red fairy comes into view; select, and you get Broadbent dancing the can-can.

My Big Fat Greek Wedding

CAST: Nia Vardalos, Michael Constatine, John Corbett, Lainie Kazan, Gia Carides, Louis Mandylor, Bruce Gray, Joey Fatone, Fiona Reid, Christina Eleusiniotis
DIRECTOR: Joel Zwick
SCREENWRITER: Nia Vardalos (based on her one-woman play)
RELEASED: 2002 (96 minutes)
RATED: PG

It all began in a small way, with actress Nia Vardalos from Chicago's Second City improvisational group. She wrote an autobiographical one-woman play about her extended

Greek family. Rita Wilson went to see it and was captivated. She is also of Greek lineage and is married to Tom
Hanks. Hanks was smitten as well, and, together with partner Gary Goetzman, the three agreed it would make a good
romantic comedy. They worked to complete the film in
record time, twenty-seven days, with a bare-bones budget
of $5 million.

The rest of the story is more of a fantasy than the love
story they shot. With a meager budget, there wasn't an opportunity for a major advertising campaign. *Wedding*
opened in a few select cities. Quickly, people began to talk
about it, and the snowball of communication turned into
an avalanche of support. It could be called "The Little
Wedding Movie with the Big Fat Box-Office Gross."

The studio didn't create the hype; the audiences did.
We went to see it more out of curiosity than anything else.
Why were we getting so many calls from friends telling us
we had to see go to see it immediately? We went in the
middle of the afternoon; the film already had been around
for some weeks in the town we were visiting. A male friend
of ours was exiting the theater from the earlier showing as
we were going in and we were eager to hear what he
thought about it. (He's a scholar and not at all frivolous.)
We came close to asking him what he was doing there,
when he said it was the third time he had seen it. He
wanted to bring his friends who hadn't been yet. (No, he
isn't Greek; he's High Church Episcopal, not unlike the
groom's parents.)

Such is the unlikely journey of this movie that just
doesn't stop delighting its audiences. At the time of the release of the DVD in February 2003, the film had grossed
more than 225 million. This put it at the top of the heap,
making it the highest-grossing romantic comedy to date.

The story is based on the real life of Vardalos and her

marriage to a non-Greek. It could be an Italian family, a Jewish family, an Irish family, or any family group that has a strong connection with its original ethnic roots and culture accompanying an American identity. *My Big Fat Greek Wedding* is so alive the people virtually jump off the screen with energy and emotion. The characters are so real you feel you've known them your whole life. In the case of Michael Constatine and Lainie Kazan, we practically have. Constatine plays Nia's father, and Kazan plays her mother. It's a sheer delight for those of us who are followers of *Sex and the City* to find our friend John Corbett loved and adored instead of dumped and rejected by Sarah Jessica Parker, as he was in the television series. Corbettt plays Vardalos's Prince Charming who has that fatal flaw.

As the film opens, you are introduced to Toula Portokalos and her Greek family. You can tell she's not measuring up to the family's standards for women. As Vardalos says, to be a successful Greek woman, you must marry a Greek man, produce babies, "and feed everyone until you die." Toula never felt as if she really fit in anywhere. Her ethnic identity isolated her at school. And yet she was not all that excited about being Greek. Her father insists on finding the Greek root for all words. He starts all conversations with a definition of the essence of being Greek. He also insists Windex can fix anything and cure most ailments.

Toula just doesn't fit the Greek plan for womanhood. Her family is concerned; they're afraid she's mentally unbalanced. Toula loves her mother but doesn't want to end up with the same kind of life her mother has led. Instead, Toula shuffles around the family's diner, looking depressed and waiting on the customers. She's reliable and painfully plain. You can't imagine how she'll emerge from the cocoon, because she seems to put so much effort into looking as exciting as a brown bag.

As the movie moves forward, we witness her image of failure entrenched in the entire family. She's thirty; she's unmarried, without a prospect in sight for even a date, let alone a husband and a family life. She drifts through her life, half-asleep; her routines in the restaurant go on; the family feels pity and confusion. Her older sister, however, is the pride of the family because she married a nice Greek boy and made three Greek babies and, of course, is feeding everyone until the day she dies.

Toula is no fool; she knows she must take charger of her life. In fact, she's desperate to do something with herself and with her mind. Constatine plays her father with a loving, exasperating stubbornness. He wants her to work in the restaurant until she meets a nice Greek boy. With the sympathy and support of her mother, she manages to attend college to take a few courses. As for so many children of immigrants, a new world opens for Toula. As she gains an education, she also gains confidence in her self.

She begins to wear makeup, fixes her hair, buys new clothes, and trades in her aggressively unattractive glasses for contacts. With the help of her mother and aunt, her father reluctantly relents and allows her to work in her aunt's travel agency. One of the film's few truly poignant moments is watching the women conspire for the sake of Toula. They must work within the system they are locked into, but they do so with wisdom and strategic skill. Whose idea was the Trojan horse?

Mr. Right has dined in the restaurant before, but Toula had blended into the pattern of the floor, and he never noticed her. She had certainly noticed him. While sitting in the agency one day, he walks by and spots the newly glamorous Toula. The slapstick visual gags in this segment are worthy of any of the best comedies. Toula's whole life has changed, but this is just the start.

The mystery man played by Corbett is Ian Miller, a young professor, altogether perfect with the exception that he isn't Greek. While one might complain that Corbett's character is too flawless, his "Greeklessness" is such major a deficiency you forgive Vardalos and director Joel Zwick for making the rest of him so velvet. The clash of the cultures begins, but the young lovers won't be stopped. It's not only the Greeks they have to deal with but his family as well. His family makes the dinner scene in *Ordinary People* look like an ethnic gathering. They'll arrange the wedding at their country club (where Toula's family undoubtedly wouldn't be allowed access, except as waiters). His mother bakes a bundt cake; the Greeks throw flowers in the middle of it.

Ian is an only child, from an upper-class reserved family. Toula tries to warn him that his parents might not be ready for thirty cousins. He goes along with all of it without so much as a grimace. (Except for the moment when her male family members say they'll kill him if he hurts her.) They make fun of him and give him the wrong Greek expressions to use. It all works out, of course. The preparation for the wedding is as riotously funny as it is absurdly over-the-top. The wedding ceremony itself, however, is done with enough grace that it isn't offensive. It's a big, fat, good time. Don't overanalyze it. There's no hidden message.

EXTRAS

There's only one extra on the DVD other than the cast biographies and the amenity of being able to switch easily from widescreen to full-screen format.

That one extra ought to be named "My Big Fat Audio Commentary about the Little Movie That Could." It might also be called "My Big Fat Mouth That I Can't Seem to Shut." We're harsh, but this is not an audio you'll want to return to again, unless you're related to the cast, are in the cast, or are really trying to kill time.

The movie was a delightful surprise. This extra is Greek food with only the grease; they left out the spice. If you watch it before you see the charming film, the wrath of all the Greek gods should descend on you for exercising poor judgment despite being warned. This audio is nothing more than a self-congratulatory love-in. Everyone is so surprised, so stunned, so boring about being so surprised, so stunned . . . and, p.s., rich!

Here are the few high points:

Kazan enjoyed portraying an anxious Greek mother and says it's not different from an anxious Jewish mother.

Corbett says in a touchingly wrongheaded moment that he really loved the romantic sequences with his costar Vardalos because she looks so much like Ava Gardner.

We were comforted to learn that Hanks is just a regular kind of guy.

We don't think you want to know about the pimple or zit and the camera shots. If you do, you'll need to watch and listen on your own.

Here's our last word. Buy this DVD for the movie. If you care about your friends, tell them about the commentary. Don't spoil this delicious movie with this leaden, ego-driven drivel.

My Fair Lady

CAST: Rex Harrison, Audrey Hepburn, Stanley Holloway, Wilifrid
Hyde-White, Gladys Cooper, Jeremy Brett, Theodore Bikel,
Mona Washbourne, Isobel Elsom, John Holland
DIRECTOR: George Cukor
SCREENWRITER: Alan Jay Lerner (based on the musical by Lerner
and Frederick Loewe, adapted from George Bernard Shaw's
Pygmalion)
RELEASED: 1964 (170 minutes)
RATED: Not rated

Alan Jay Lerner and Frederick Loewe's delightful Broadway
stage musical, based on George Bernard Shaw's 1913 play
Pygmalion, was gloriously transferred to the screen by director George Cukor. Bravura performances lend the film
more substance than many other musicals and give a tim-
less appeal. Professor Henry Higgins energetically endeav-
ors to transform a Cockney girl, Eliza Doolittle (Audrey
Hepburn) into an upper-class London lady. The role of
Higgins was tailor-made for Rex Harrison, who played it
on both stage and screen. Some of the songs include "I
Could Have Danced All Night," "Get Me to the Church
on Time," and "The Rain in Spain." However, do remember that it is Marni Nixon's voice coming out of Hepburn's
mouth.

To win a bet with Colonel Pickering, another linguist,
Higgins claims he can transform the street urchin into a
lady in record time. Not just any English lady but a lady
who could be welcomed into the top ranks of snobby London society. The scene at the grand reception where Eliza
demonstrates she is a proper lady is one of cinema's most
memorable. She dances and sings when she returns to the
home of Higgins. Although it's Hepburn and Harrison

who star, the entire cast is extraordinary. There's not one false casting decision in this one.

The gossip behind *My Fair Lady* lingers. It's about the two competing Elizas. Julie Andrews had played Eliza on stage both in London and on Broadway, opposite Harrison. Her performance was widely acclaimed. But Jack Warner just couldn't envision Andrews in the movie. He instead gave it to Hepburn but wouldn't let her sing. Hepburn's elegance appealed to Warner. Maybe he didn't want her to do much more than model all those divine Cecil Beaton clothes. She did far more than that. His decision will always remain an open question in film history. But we have no complaints about Hepburn. No vocal questions were ever raised about Harrison, who was a suave, resourceful actor. He could not sing, either, but what he could do was talk his songs with an absolutely perfect sense of timing and heartfelt emotion.

My Fair Lady ran away with the Oscars. The *Lady* took eight: Best Actor: Rex Harrison; Best Art Direction/Set: Gene Allen, Cecil Beaton, George James Hopkins; Best Cinematography: Harry Stradling, Sr.; Best Costume Design: Cecil Beaton; Best Director: George Cukor; Best Musical Score (adaptation): Andre Previn; Best Picture: Jack Warner; Best Sound: George Groves.

EXTRAS

The Warner Home Premiere Collection brings rewards to your home. The distinguished team of Robert A. Harris and James C. Katz restored the film. Some of you might have seen the new print when it was briefly rereleased. It is this fantastic print that's on the DVD. So we begin with a first-class print for one of the most lavish and enchanting musicals ever produced.

The audio commentary is the best of the bonus stuff.

It's the restorers along with the head of the art department at the time, Gene Allen, and also Marni Nixon. Hepburn singing "Wouldn't It Be Lovely" and "Show Me" have been preserved. Hepburn never pretended to be a vocal legend, but in these two songs her limited range would have been acceptable, especially in the former song. There is quite a bit of chat about the making of the film that is enjoyable.

The so-called documentary is very short and was made at the time of the film's release; it's really a promotional piece and should be regarded as such.

You want to own this for the *Lady's* perfection and for the opportunity to hear a few bars of Hepburn herself. It's an excellent edition. We always prefer a DVD package that contains a flawlessly restored classic, even if there are limited extras.

Network

CAST: Peter Finch, Faye Dunaway, William Holden, Robert Duvall, Wesley Addy, Ned Beatty, William Prince, Beatrice Straight, Marlene Warfield
DIRECTOR: Sidney Lumet
SCREENWRITER: Paddy Chayefsky
RELEASED: 1976 (120 minutes)
RATED: R

It's funny how some films that seemed so important at the time of their release quickly fade. Others we thought would fade quickly age well. *Network* belongs to an entirely different subset of movies. It's one that has aged all too well.

Network is the story of a news anchorman, Howard Beale, who is fired because his ratings fall. He then proceeds to go completely bonkers before our very eyes and in so doing becomes a kind of pop-culture Messiah. It was a dark and farcical film in 1976; it seems a little close to the bone these days. We hope Paddy Chayefsky's television set is turned off in his heavenly apartment; he would find too much resonance in today's media industry. With the essential death of anything that even pretends to be a serious news program on the major networks, the movie now has a prophetic feel to it.

Faye Dunaway is far more frightening as Diana Christiansen, the evil program "suit," than she ever was as Bonnie in *Bonnie and Clyde*. William Holden plays her lover and toady, Max Schumacher, a pathetically complicated news executive. Chayefsky's script is a lacerating satire of the television industry. He had paid his dues and wanted this film to be taken as a scathing indictment of the manipulative aspects of the media. Sidney Lumet also paid his dues in full. He was a top director of live TV drama in the early 1950s and since has gone on to direct a huge number of very good feature films during a remarkable and distinguished career. *Network* is also a dark look at the American mass public—and this film was made before the phrase *dumbing down* became a regular part of the vernacular.

Peter Finch's last role is certainly one that he is remembered for, perhaps as much as for his brilliant portrayal of the homosexual doctor in *Sunday, Bloody Sunday*. As he plunges toward complete insanity while uttering total nonsense, his Nielsen ratings soar. "I'm a human being, and God damn it, my life has some value. I want you to get up now. I want all of you to get up right now and go to the window, open it and stick your head out and yell, 'I'm mad as hell, and I'm not going to take it anymore.'"

Beale's on-screen lunacy became America's mantra. It was hard to go anywhere at the time of the movie's release

and not hear this sentence incorporated into normal conversations. Well, guess what? We are still "taking it," and
there are more rubbishy "news" shows on network and
cable TV than ever before.

What is far more interesting about the film from today's
perspective is the behavior of the Dunaway character. Ec-
static with the change in the ratings, she dubs Beale the
"Mad Prophet of the Airwaves." If you pay much attention
to the drivel put out by the networks' programmers during
"Sweeps Month," you'll think twice about how farcical this
film really is. Some of the more recent stunts employed by
supposed "news" executives on some cable networks also re-
flect Chayefsky's prescience.

Finch's and Dunaway's robust, over-the-top performances earned them Oscars. Beatrice Straight, who played
doormat wife to Holden's Max Schumacher, won Best Supporting Actress. It remains one of the most powerful depic-
tions of a betrayed wife captured on film. Holden was
nominated as well. The film has more than its share of hys-
terically funny scenes. But it's more food for thought than
we ever believed it would be.

You want to see *Network* and to own it because the star
performances are of such quality. Sadly, you won't get new
chances to see the work of Finch or Holden. Besides
Straight, Oscars also went to Finch, Dunaway, and Chayefsky. Lumet was nominated for Best Director, but that
award went to John Avildsen for *Rocky*.

EXTRAS

The 1998 release from MGM is no longer available, but try
to get it on eBay or through a used disc/video dealer.
There's a small treasure that's mildly interesting about the
history of the Nielsens. We aren't believers in the hunt for
"Easter eggs," but as the quality of the transfer is more or

less the same on both the 1998 and the Warner 2000 release, you might as well get the 2000 entry.

If you can't track it down, don't fret; it's not such a bonus. You actually can look up the history of the Nielsen ratings in any encyclopedia. The 2000 release has a very stupid and pointless trivia feature.

If you do end up finding the original, click the special features option, and the screen will show a TV. Hit the button on the screen TV, and you will get to this brief history lesson. The people who dream up these hidden treasures and call them Easter eggs obviously have never experienced an actual Easter egg hunt. That's it; we've had it. We're as mad as hell about all the hype surrounding DVD Easter eggs, and we're not going to take it anymore.

North by Northwest

CAST: Cary Grant, Eva Marie Saint, James Mason, Jessie Royce
   Landis, Leo G. Carroll, Philip Ober, Josephine Hutchinson,
   Martin Landau
DIRECTOR: Alfred Hitchcock
SCREENWRITER: Ernest Lehman
RELEASED: 1959 (136 minutes)
RATED: Not Rated

This beloved action classic is really a series of imaginative set pieces—a crop-dusting attack, a disrupted auction, a chase on a cross-country locomotive, and a scramble on the face of Mount Rushmore. It all highlights one of Hitchcock's most romantic, stylish, and suspenseful thrillers.

Cary Grant plays an unsuspecting Madison Avenue advertising executive who somehow gets mistaken for a spy. He becomes embroiled in a sinister espionage plot and finds himself scrambling all over (including Mount Rushmore) to stay alive. It's too loose a plot to be taken very seriously, but it always has been a favorite that is part suspense and part frolic.

Eva Marie Saint costars as a beautiful double (or triple) agent with whom Grant falls in love. Grant and James Mason are matchless as hero and villain, respectively. It's Hitchcock at his most playfully perverse—intellectually perverse, that is.

EXTRAS

The picture is clear and well defined, which is the first time we've seen a good version of this film in a long time. Remember those late-night television runs with the commercials and the grainy speckles? You won't have that here.

Surprisingly, there are two really top-notch features. The commentary with scriptwriter Ernest Lehman is a treasure. He talks about his relationship with Hitch and how they came to do this picture. Having him available at the time of the release of this DVD makes such a difference. There's also a new documentary about the making of the film that Saint narrates and hosts. (Some of Lehman's material from the commentary is repeated here.) Martin Landau has a funny moment doing an imitation of Hitchcock, which comes close but still is no cigar. There was only one Hitch.

We were amused and pleased by the spiffy animated menu that isn't suspenseful to use at all.

One Flew over the Cuckoo's Nest

CAST: Jack Nicholson, Louise Fletcher, William Redfield, Will
   Sampson, Brad Dourif, Marya Small, Delos V. Smith, Jr.,
   Scatman Crothers, Danny DeVito, Michael Berryman, Peter
   Brocco, William Duell, Sydney Lassick, Christopher Lloyd,
   Louise Moritz, Dean R. Brooks
DIRECTOR: Milos Forman
SCREENWRITERS: Lawrence Hauben and Bo Goldman (adapted
   from the Ken Kesey novel and the play by Dale Wasserman)
RELEASED: 1975 (129 minutes)
RATED: R

One Flew over the Cuckoo's Nest is a film with the values and
attitudes of the 1960s that was produced in the dead center
of the 1970s. That's no surprise, because the novel on which
it was based was written in 1962 and was a bestseller. Ken
Kesey was the embodiment of the 1960s anti-establishment,
anti-authoritarian American cultural revolution. He was one
of a band of eccentric commentator-reformers who called
themselves the Merry Pranksters. It's no surprise the book
represented so clearly what everyone was shouting about in
1962.

The miracle of *Cuckoo* is that more than a decade after
that, it still hit a chord with Americans. In fact, the film
resonated with an even larger and more diverse audience
than the book had. It also introduced a new phrase into
common usage, "Nurse Ratched," not unlike the way
Joseph Heller's *"Catch-22"* entered our communal consciousness. Nurse Ratched meant then, as it does now, anybody with a bit of power who wants to exercise it against
others in nefarious and cruel ways. The Nurse Ratched of
Kesey's book was a more complicated character than she
was in the movie.

In a nutshell (why can't we avoid such puns?), the movie is about a man who thought he could beat the system and instead was ultimately destroyed by it. Randle Patrick McMurphy (Jack Nicholson) is a troublemaker. He was probably a juvenile delinquent. He's not a dangerous criminal, but he's not a member of the Chamber of Commerce, either. He manages to land himself in the slammer.

He's too smart to be in the slammer, so he figures a way out. He acts insane enough to get transferred to a mental institution. McMurphy figures that hanging out there has to be better than jail. Nicholson is so perfect for the part that if you didn't know the film's history, you might suspect Kesey wrote it for him. Once he gets to the mental institution, he is confronted with a number of surprising revelations. He's not free there, either, and a bad, bad, baddie is in charge, Nurse Mildred Ratched. (Rhymes with *wretched*, *hatchet*; you get the picture.) Louise Fletcher plays the role with such authenticity that she's never really dodged the rap for it.

Undaunted by the system and Ratched, McMurphy sets about to organize the inmates. You shouldn't think this is an American version of the gentle French film *King of Hearts*. Try as he might, the inmates in this asylum will not ultimately triumph and take over the mental ward or the surrounding town. Much of the film, however, is uproariously funny. At first, it seems that McMurphy will succeed in undermining the tyranny of Nurse Ratched. McMurphy's presence and antics give hope to the otherwise spiritless patients. He also wreaks havoc; that's what people who are put together like McMurphy are supposed to do. And people who are put together like Nurse Ratched are supposed to crush people like McMurphy.

In *Cuckoo's Nest*, Nurse Ratched represents the world, and McMurphy represents individual people. At the betting window on the ticket "You versus the World," we've been warned to bet the world. The ending is tragic and shattering. Along the way, the interaction among the actors is refreshingly, tangibly real. We are compelled not to sympathize with them but to identify with them. We don't cry for them but with them.

That was the dirty little secret of Kesey's marvelous book. It appeared to be about a particular time in American sociopolitical history, but it was far more than that. It was the reason the Douglas family kept the dream of the film alive until it became reality (more on that below).

Cuckoo's Nest was impeccably directed by Milos Forman, whose previous work gave little reason to believe he could command this material as well as he did. Yet anyone who knew his personal history (his parents were killed by the Nazis) might have guessed that he would be able to direct the film in the assured, risky manner he did. His one major work up until that time was the oddly penetrating *Fireman's Ball*, which is what drew the producers to Forman.

One Flew over the Cuckoo's Nest dissolves preconceived boundaries between sanity and insanity. It is one of those rare movies that both broadly entertains and subtly changes us.

One Flew over the Cuckoo's Nest is the only movie since *It Happened One Night* (1934) to win the five major Academy Awards. It took away Oscars for Best Picture, Best Director, Best Screenplay, Best Actress, and Best Actor. *Cuckoo's Nest* had touched a raw nerve. That nerve was in all of us.

The influential *New York Times* critic Vincent Canby wrote about *One Flew over the Cuckoo's Nest* when it opened in Manhattan: "Even granting the artist his license, America is much too big and various to be satisfactorily reduced

to the dimensions of one mental ward in a movie like this."
We've got to wonder if he eventually felt like one of the editors who rejected the *Kon-Tiki* manuscript.

EXTRAS

The first thing you should do if you have the miserable 1998 DVD is send it to Nurse Ratched; only Ratched deserves such a hideous version of *Cuckoo*.

The history of the film's time in development hell is almost as torturous as what happens to the patients in Ratched's care. Kirk Douglas bought the option to the novel shortly after its publication. Douglas was McMurphy in the Broadway play adapted by Dale Wasserman. But Douglas couldn't get a green light from any studio, for reasons that remain murky. His son Michael took over the project and pulled it together more than a decade later.

The Warner Brothers special edition has two discs and almost does justice to the film and its history. The commentary track has Forman and producers Michael Douglas and Saul Zaentz. (Zaentz is the Berkeley, California patron saint of Fantasy Films who also produced *Amadeus* in collaboration with Forman, which garnered another Oscar.) Douglas is a wealth of information about the process of bringing *Cuckoo's Nest* to the screen. His intelligence and wisdom as an artist come through here. Forman, a natural storyteller, is riveting in his descriptions about the method he used with his cast. Our only complaint is, where's Jack?

The second disc is a little light on content. However, the "making of" documentary is excellent. There's more in-depth coverage of the Douglas family's involvement in this feature. Two problems with the documentary are most unfortunate, however; neither Kesey nor Nicholson is in it. Kesey's no-show is predictable, because the screenplay changes the point of view from that of Chief Bromden to

McMurphy. It was an artistic decision that Kesey couldn't come to terms with. The documentary is newly produced for this release, although there are clips from the previously produced "Completely Cuckoo." Despite the absence of the star and the author, this is an excellent companion to the film. No shortcuts were taken to make *Cuckoo's Nest* seem real. It was shot in a state mental institution in the Pacific Northwest, and the hospital's actual psychiatrist played the role of Dr. Spivey.

Watch the eight deleted scenes for further confirmation of the clarity of Forman's vision for this film. None of them moves the story forward in any meaningful way. Those scenes belong just where Forman put them, in the waste bin.

Pearl Harbor: The Director's Cut

CAST: Alec Baldwin, Cuba Gooding, Jr., Jon Voight, Ben Affleck, Josh Hartnett, Kate Beckinsale
DIRECTOR: Michael Bay
SCREENWRITER: Randall Wallace
RELEASED: 2001 (183 minutes)
RATED: PG-13

More than with any other movie in recent memory, your response to *Pearl Harbor* will be profoundly affected by when you first watched it. This highly publicized film was released in May 2001 to capitalize on the sixtieth anniversary of the Japanese sneak attack. The film took a deservedly critical bashing in most reviews because of its contrived love story. It's too predictable to be exciting. Two American pilots (Ben Affleck and Josh Hartnett) become involved with the same woman, a nurse played by Kate Beckinsale. The film is a mixture of the unfolding horrors of the war in Europe and the tragedy of the attack on Pearl Harbor and the war in the Pacific. Unfortunately, the love story is not strong enough to hold the film together in the tradition of the great war love stories.

However, the "day of infamy," December 7, 1941, has a companion date, September 11, 2001. Viewing *Pearl Harbor* now has a different feeling and meaning than it had before the attacks on the World Trade Center and the Pentagon. Despite the film's flaws, this four-disc set has much to recommend it and is worth your time and money if the subject matter interests you.

The film is spread out over the first two discs, with an intermission. The attack sequence lasts for forty minutes and utilizes the newest computer and digital technologies, by now quite familiar to audiences. We cannot, however, put out of our minds the historical event, which slaughtered more than three thousand people, military personnel and civilians alike.

Be forewarned that the Japanese bombardment footage is not for the faint of heart. It is extremely graphic, showing dismembered bodies and hundreds of victims floating in a harbor ablaze with burning oil. In the midst of this carnage, there is one visually beautiful and erotic love scene shot in a parachute-packing hangar.

EXTRAS

The features on the additional discs provide information about diplomatic and intelligence failures leading up to the Japanese attack. This is harrowing viewing, as there are similarities to the present time. As the nation worries about missed intelligence opportunities before September 11, 2001, *Pearl Harbor* has special resonance. How and why did we fail to connect the dots on these two most tragic days in our history?

In addition to the film, an audio commentary by director Michael Bay and film historian Jeanine Basinger is worth a glimpse. Basinger is Bay's former college teacher, and the supplement is marred by her overly deferential manner. Bay had a budget of more than $135 million. Notably, he presents disturbing data gathered during audience research for the film; for example, a large number of today's twenty-year-olds believe JFK was president during the attack on Pearl Harbor.

"Production Diary: Baja Gimbal" appears on Disc Three. The production staff used the same facility in Baja, Mexico, where much of *Titanic* was filmed. Here we view a model, called a gimbal, of the set they digitally created, enabling them to roll over and sink huge Navy battleships.

The air raid over Tokyo on April 18, 1942, led by heroic pilot Jimmy Doolittle is, ironically, poorly portrayed in the film. But the History Channel's documentary, "Thirty Seconds over Tokyo," is stirring. There's commentary by veterans who survived this death-defying assignment.

"Unsung Heroes of Pearl Harbor" is also worth your time. A naval historian shows the haunting site where many ships in the fleet lie in their watery graves.

"Boot Camp" introduces a Marine drill sergeant, straight from central casting: "I'm not smart enough to figure out all this crap by myself."

On Disc Four, "When Cultures Collide" is a well-conceived timeline that is also visually pleasing. It traces our country's relationship with Japan from Admiral Perry (circa 1840) to the attack. This informative feature has comments about Presidents Polk, Taft, and Teddy Roosevelt. Narrator David Ogden Stiers reminds us that there was talk about war with Japan before 1900. There is newsreel footage from the time when Americans were told, "Japanese are naturally poor airmen."

Disc Four also contains interactive PC war games for those who haven't had enough bloodshed.

The packaging of the four-disc set is well designed and contains booklets and other surprises.

Pretty Woman

CAST: Richard Gere, Julia Roberts, Ralph Bellamy, Jason Alexander, Laura San Giacomo, Hector Elizondo
DIRECTOR: Garry Marshall
SCREENWRITER: J. F. Lawton
RELEASED: 1990 (125 minutes)
RATED: R

Julia Roberts became Hollywood's debutante by playing a Sunset Boulevard hooker. They call the movie a Cinderella tale, but who is Cinderella—the prostitute Roberts plays or Roberts herself? This movie was her formal presentation to cinema society, and it made her a superstar. It isn't an important movie, a serious movie, or a work of art. It's a movie movie. In other words, it's a Hollywood movie with a Hollywood ending using a tried-and-true Hollywood romantic script. It's a variation of a thousand other love comedies. What made it such a huge box-office winner and a perennial favorite for millions of fans is that it works. The script works; the acting works; the story works. It makes us feel good. We love the characters, and we're happy with the ending.

You might say it's just good, old-fashioned, clean fun in an R-rated wrapper, about prostitution, money, greed, and getting a better life. In other words, it's Disney's version of an R film. Richard Gere plays corporate raider Edward Lewis. He buys companies, takes them apart, puts them back together again, and makes millions. The casualties are the people who worked for the companies; he doesn't care. It's his metier. Roberts plays Viv Ward, a streetwalker who came to Los Angeles with a boyfriend and ended up turning tricks to pay the rent. Her metier is sex for money. In the oft-quoted line from the movie, Gere says to Roberts, "We both screw people for money."

That levels the playing field. Trying to find his way through the maze of Los Angeles Gere asks for help from Roberts. She doesn't do anything for free, even give directions. For a fee, she drives him to the hotel. He's in town to make some deals and ruin some lives. But he needs to look like a distinguished businessman with a proper girlfriend. He offers her $3,000 for a week of escorting him around, no sex required. She can't believe it, laughing as she goes under the water in a luxurious bubble bath in his hotel suite.

Pretty Woman enabled Roberts to show her talent as an actress with comic flair, not just a beautiful body, lots of hair, and those big, luscious lips. Her timing in *Pretty Woman* was perfect. She's regained that lately. Viv needs to spruce up, so she goes off to the dreamland of Rodeo Drive's boutiques. The salespeople aren't idiots; they know a hooker when they see one. They won't do business with her, and she returns to the hotel shattered. Edward takes the matter into his able hands, and they return to the stores. His money talks, and suddenly everyone is solicitous to Viv.

Take *Pretty Woman* on its own terms and enjoy it. Gere has never played a romantic role with more grace or humor. Roberts's big debut film reminds us why she gets the big bucks now. Art and life again, or, shall we say, movies and careers again. The film is filled with solidly satisfying performances from the other cast members. Ralph Bellamy is

Jim Morse, the older business tycoon. Should Edward destroy him or accept him as the father he always wanted? Laura San Giacomo, always superb, plays Viv's roommate with a wisdom and assurance that is endearing. Hector Elizondo is Barney, the hotel manager who mentors Viv in the finer details of dining and living. The interactions between them sparkle.

This is the one on your shelf for the Friday night of the week from hell—sheer fantasy, diversion, and good-looking people.

EXTRAS

The 10th Anniversary Special Edition isn't what it's cracked up to be, but the quality of the transfer is, in fact, better than the original release. What the special edition does have is the director's cut, restoring a substantial number of deleted scenes.

Garry Marshall's commentary is witty and quick. He doesn't take himself or the movie too seriously but enjoys himself along with the viewer. Roberts was not yet twenty-one years old when the film was made. She was shy about love scenes. Marshall's rendition of what happened when they got ready to shoot the first nude scene with Gere is exceedingly entertaining. (We won't spoil this.) He also confesses a practical joke he played that accidentally ended up making the film better. There's a Natalie Cole segment, if you are a fan of her musical style.

If you already own *Pretty Woman,* you don't need to go buy the newer one. If you don't yet own it, buy the anniversary version.

The Producers

CAST: Zero Mostel, Gene Wilder, Kenneth Mars, Estelle Winwood,
     Renee Taylor, Christopher Hewett, Dick Shawn, Lee Meredith
DIRECTOR: Mel Brooks
SCREENWRITER: Mel Brooks
RELEASED: 1968 (88 minutes)
RATED: PG

Before there was a Broadway musical sensation, there was a small movie that didn't open to rave reviews, or even very good ones, but slowly gathered steam at the box office. Eventually, *The Producers* developed an extremely loyal following. Before Nathan Lane and Matthew Broderick appeared as Max and Leo, there were Zero Mostel and Gene Wilder. But before it all, there was the "2000 Year Old Man" himself, Mel Brooks.

The Producers was Mel Brooks's feature debut, which earned him the Oscar for Best Screenplay. The movie is wildly uneven but contains many magnificent, hilarious scenes. Mostel, in his best screen role by far, plays a bankrupt producer named Max Bialystock. He hatches a foolproof plot to get rich with the help of his quivering milquetoast accountant, Leo Bloom, played to perfection by Wilder. They will find the worst play ever written, sell more than 100 percent of the show's shares to gullible old ladies, and clean up. The play isn't a flop; their plan to swindle the investors turns out to be the flop.

Thanks to the success of the Broadway musical, everybody now knows that the play within the movie is called "Springtime for Hitler." It was the highlight of the film. Dick Shawn as Hitler is a total riot, once you forgive yourself for laughing at the lunacy of the entire concept. Many of the scenes are fragmented broad humor, but the hilarious bits add up to something pretty wonderful. Apart from inspiring one of Broadway's classic winners, the film has maintained a loyal cult following for over thirty years. Brooks's directorial skills became keener and more sophisticated in his later films, but his raucous, outrageous sense of humor is never in better evidence than in *The Producers*.

It's all but impossible to watch Mostel and not feel an aching sadness for the lost opportunities of his career and our enjoyment. Blacklisted in the 1950s and into the early 1960s, unable to get work except in the theater, he retreated to his artist's studio, where he produced paintings as broad in range and color as his acting gifts. His enormous comedic genius was never fully utilized in other films.

After the huge Broadway success of *The Producers*, MGM decided to capitalize on the market and release a high-quality DVD of one of the funniest and most inventive comedies ever made.

EXTRAS

The "Special Edition" of *The Producers* was released in December 2002. It contains a number of features. This is a one-disc set, so remember to turn over the disc after you've enjoyed the film.

Fortunately, the main feature, "The Making of *The Producers,*" was made before Wilder's death. You'll find other cast and crew in this documentary as well. But Wilder's remarks about Mostel are priceless. He confesses that Leo Bloom's frightened expression, which captured the essence of the character, wasn't mere acting. He was afraid and intimidated by Mostel at the beginning of the production.

Brooks confronts the criticisms he has received about the concept of *The Producers*. For Brooks, humor is the best weapon against hatred, and ridicule should be fired off against evil. He puts it as only he can: "Laugh Hitler into oblivion."

The segment entitled "Playhouse Outtake" is very brief but contains the alternative ending to the film, so don't miss it.

There's a photo gallery, sketches, and a blink-your-eyes-and-it's-over appearance of director Paul Mazursky, who reads what Peter Sellers said when *The Producers* was released. The usual advertising rubbish is, of course, included. However, there's a short trailer for the Broadway musical's cast album that is enjoyable.

On the first side are a few audio-only mini-interviews, easy to find by clicking on numbers and letters that resemble a theater ticket.

Pulp Fiction

CAST: John Travolta, Bruce Willis, Samuel L. Jackson, Harvey Keitel,
    Uma Thurman, Christopher Walken, Maria de Medeiros,
    Amanda Plummer, Rosanna Arquette, Quentin Tarantino, Tim
    Roth, Eric Stoltz, Ving Rhames
DIRECTOR: Quentin Tarantino
SCREENWRITER: Quentin Tarantino (with Roger Avary)
RELEASED: 1994 (154 minutes)
RATED: R

Pulp Fiction resuscitated John Travolta's career. Tarantino's previous film was *Reservoir Dogs*. It is assuredly one of the most influential films of the 1990s, and its release was a genuine event. It was exceedingly controversial at the time of its release. Despite being nominated for Oscars in five major categories, it didn't win. It's less startling by now but no less compelling. Travolta, Uma Thurman, Samuel L. Jackson, and Bruce Willis all turn in star-class performances. Christopher Walken has only one extended scene in the film, but he's unforgettable.

It's a convoluted plot that starts out with Travolta and Jackson, as small-time hoods, on their way to a rubout ordered by their boss (Ving Rhames). There are many departures and diversions, and it is far too messy a screenplay to have deserved the acclaim it received. Nonetheless, this $8 million film is a Hollywood legend and showcases Quentin Tarantino's peculiar gift. Tarantino once worked in a video store, and his film is full of references to films and celebrities, good and bad. The script isn't cohesive, but it is jolting, until it sort of disappoints and poops out at the end. Take note, Bette Davis, wherever you are; this one really is a bumpy ride.

The low-budget winner made back its investment and went on and on, grossing more than $100 million in U.S. theaters. It had a warm reception overseas and won Tarantino the Palme d'Or at Cannes. If you've not seen it, you need to be prepared for excessive violence and lots of foul language. Tarantino's 1997 *Jackie Brown* is a comedic departure from *Pulp Fiction*. We'll see what's next for him in the many decades ahead. He may surprise us by going in completely different directions.

EXTRAS

The first DVD of *Pulp Fiction* was released in 1998 and was quite poor. The enhanced and expanded edition is a vast improvement. It's a two-disc set, with the film on the first disc. There's also an interactive trivia subtitle quiz that is amusing.

Disc Two contains substantial bonus materials.

"The Facts" is an interview feature with Tarantino, Roger Avary, and most of the cast. If you've never heard Tarantino's personal saga before, this is the segment for you. (These are not new interviews, however.)

"Siskel and Ebert: Tarantino Generation" is a fifteen-minute clip from the time of the film's release. The feature focuses exclusively on the seemingly instant fame of Tarantino.

Featurettes include production design, Independent Spirit Awards, and the Palme d'Or acceptance speech. These are all pretty much what you would expect. There are buried gems here and there but nothing too spectacular.

We save the best for last, the Charlie Rose interview taken directly from Rose's show at the time of the theatrical release of *Pulp*. Rose handles Tarantino deftly, and it is here that you begin to understand the man and his work. The two-disc set is worth it for the Rose interview alone, unless you habitually tape Rose's show and already have it on your shelf. Nonetheless, the quality of this *Pulp Fiction* over the earlier edition is so much better that it is still worth it.

Raging Bull

CAST: Robert De Niro, Cathy Moriarty, Joe Pesci, Frank Vincent, Nicholas Colasanto, Theresa Saldana, Frank Adonis, Mario Gallo

DIRECTOR: Martin Scorsese

SCREENWRITERS: Paul Schrader and Mardik Martin (based on the book by Jake La Motta with Joseph Carter and Peter Savage)

RELEASED: 1980 (129 minutes)

RATED: R

The rise and fall of middleweight boxing champion Jake La Motta is the story of one of the finest films about professional boxing ever made. Director Martin Scorsese incisively explores the violent and destructive nature of La Motta, both in and out of the ring.

Raging Bull details La Motta's two failed marriages, his

brief reign as a champion prizefighter, his falling in with gangsters, and his years in decline as a third-rate nightclub comic. Robert De Niro's Oscar-winning performance is more riveting than any of his other sociopathic roles (*Mean Streets, Taxi Driver*). Cathy Moriarty gives solid support as his second wife, Vickie, and Joe Pesci as his nice-guy brother, Joey.

There are some minor flaws in period detail and editing, but they are eclipsed by otherwise superb production design and brilliant black-and-white cinematography (by Michael Chapman). Unlike *Rocky* and its sequels, *Raging Bull* is unafraid to show the ugly side of the boxing profession and the people in it.

Thelma Schoonmaker also won an Oscar for film editing. The movie was nominated for Best Picture, and nominations went to Pesci for supporting actor, Moriarty for supporting actress, and Chapman for cinematography. Scorsese was nominated for Best Director but lost to Robert Redford for *Ordinary People*. Many observant critics consider *Raging Bull* to be one of cinema's greatest accomplishments.

EXTRAS

There's an excellent transfer so that the overall impact and sense of the film are enhanced on DVD. Other than that, it's you, La Motta, and Scorsese. You wanted something more? If you're building a library by great directors, be sure to add this to the sizable Scorsese shelf.

Rambling Rose

CAST: Laura Dern, Diane Ladd, Robert Duvall, Lukas Haas, John
　　　Heard, Kevin Conway
DIRECTOR: Martha Coolidge
SCREENWRITER: Calder Willingham (adapted from his book)
RELEASED: 1991 (140 minutes)
RATED: R

Southerners are renowned for their storytelling ability. It's
no mere geographical accident that so much writing talent
has come from our Southern region—Tennessee Williams,
William Faulkner, Eudora Welty, Flannery O'Connor, and
on and on.

The Southern narrative voice is particularly well suited
to the screen, perhaps because the stories often involve
complicated and intense family situations with deep secrets. One of our favorites is a 1991 release that didn't get
the audience it deserved, despite the Oscar nominations of
both Laura Dern for Best Actress and Diane Ladd for Best
Supporting Actress. It's *Rambling Rose,* which was directed
by a talented Yankee woman, Martha Coolidge (born in
New Haven, Connecticut, as it happens), who also should
be more appreciated.

Rambling Rose is the story of a "loose woman" who lived
in the 1930s in the Deep South (small-town Georgia).
There is truth to the story because it is based on the memories of writer Calder Willingham, who brought his original
autobiographical novel into screenplay format for this
Southern surprise. Although the book and the script have
the softness of memory, this isn't a film dripping nostalgic
sentimentality.

Many avid moviegoers missed Rose the first time she
ambled around; you might have as well. That is easily

remedied with a "Pioneer Special Edition" DVD that's been around since 1999 but was not accompanied by any buzz. This seems to be a recurring theme for this overlooked jewel.

Let's begin with the cast: Robert Duvall, Dern, Ladd. That alone should have your attention. Duvall plays "Daddy," and Ladd plays "Mother." The boy from *Witness,* Lukas Haas, is their son, Buddy. Dern is Rose. John Heard plays Willcox Hillyer, better described as Buddy all grown up. The character of Buddy is based on Willingham.

Rose appears at the Hillyer house to work as a maid or to stay as a guest. The line is blurry. She has had her share of encounters with men. At only nineteen, she has more history than is appropriate, particularly in the South of the 1930s. She's a Rose, not a proper Southern belle; nobody knows quite what to do with her. She's beautiful, charming, and so sexy and seductive that the men of the households she works in pass her on to others quickly. They find their moral consciences aren't up to the long-term task of rejecting Rose. Her presence ends up causing more than a mild disturbance in the domestic harmony of the Hillyer home.

Duvall plays the part of a Southern gentleman who will resist the temptation, so help him God. It isn't that he finds it easy, but he'll resist her, even when she wants nothing as much as she wants to be loved. The scenes with young Buddy suggest the tragic aspect of Rose and the hormonal rush of a teenage boy. Although a scene in Buddy's bed is a strong one, Coolidge handles the hot subject with an appropriately delicate hand.

Rose causes trouble in town. She bites a policeman. Things come to a screeching halt, but we won't tell you the reason. This is a story that deserves to be reserved for first viewers. Let's just say that the memory of *Rambling Rose* and her troubles will linger in your memory, and you'll return for repeated viewings and to share with friends who have yet to meet her.

The premise of the film is that Rose had such an influence and effect on Buddy that even as a middle-aged man, he can't shake her from his mind or his heart. He comes home to his family's house and remembers her as vividly as he did as a young teenager. Dern is the reason this story doesn't turn into *Fried Green Tomatoes with Sex*. We disliked the flashback technique in that film, but it works well here.

Ladd and Dern are, of course, mother and daughter. (Dern's father is actor Bruce Dern.) Knowing the relationship doesn't spoil the movie, but it does make some of the more daring scenes especially meaningful. This project was Dern's dream. She went through a smaller version of what Duvall went through to produce *The Apostle*. Duvall's performance here is as arresting as his bigger, showy parts in blockbuster hits. Ladd and Dern, who have teamed before but never quite like this, are a wonder together. The word *wonder* describes the whole film.

In 1975, Coolidge made *Not a Pretty Picture*, a film about rape that put her on the map as a director to watch. (We hope the time will come when directors are directors, and their gender, if female, won't always be used as a descriptive modifier.) Following that, Coolidge made some films that probably paid her bills but didn't display her talents. She has done some excellent work for television, however, including directing a segment of the series *If These Walls Could Talk*. In 1999, she directed *Introducing Dorothy Dandridge*, which brought Halle Berry to the television screen. We hope that Coolidge comes back into full focus and is given the scripts she deserves to direct. She is highly esteemed by her colleagues; in 2002, she became the president of the Directors Guild of America. She is the first woman ever to hold this post.

EXTRAS

We start at the end. There's an alternative ending. You can watch the movie with the theatrical release ending or the alternative. We advise watching it as it was released and then seeing the other. However, if you loved the film and hated the ending, try it with a new ending, and then go back and review the original. We find Coolidge's commentary about why she opted for the original ending interesting, if not completely convincing.

The deleted scenes are more bloopers than deletions but, as always, a nice addition to any DVD. The production extras here are a cut above the usual. There's extensive coverage of storyboard material, script changes, costumes, locations, and sets and a behind-the-scenes feature with Coolidge.

There is an excellent full audio commentary with Coolidge. We suspect you'll come away with the same respect for this director that we have.

Rear Window

CAST: James Stewart, Grace Kelly, Thelma Ritter, Raymond Burr, Wendell Corey, Judith Evelyn, Ros Bagdasarian, Georgine Darcy, Sara Berner, Frank Cady
DIRECTOR: Alfred Hitchcock
SCREENWRITER: John Michael Hayes (from a short story by Cornell Woolrich, "It Had to be Murder")
RELEASED: 1954 (115 minutes)
RATED: PG

Rear Window is one of Alfred Hitchcock's greatest films. It is certainly our favorite for sheer purity of entertainment.

James Stewart plays an action photographer immobilized in his apartment by a broken leg. He idles away his days by spying on his neighbors through the telephoto lens of a camera. Naturally, he sees what he shouldn't—or does he?

Hitchcock gives his most fascinating and disturbing definition of what it means to watch a "silent film" of other people's lives. He integrates the themes and emotions of *Rear Window* into a plot that will keep you riveted. In one of his finest performances, Stewart epitomizes the Hitchcock hero.

Grace Kelly is luminous, as always. As Stewart's girlfriend and co-conspirator, she helps build the suspense. Accolades must go as well to John Michael Hayes's script, adapted from Cornell Woolrich's short story.

Hitchcock's work remains timeless. It doesn't matter when you discover his work, you'll stay a devoted fan. He probably wouldn't think that much about the option for the DVD director's cut; he always knew what he was doing, sometimes on the first take.

EXTRAS

Once again, it is the team of Robert A. Harris and James Katz, film archivists and restoration experts, who have saved another classic from the abyss. These two are going to cinema heaven, that's for sure; they might achieve saint status while still here on earth. As with other old classics, the existing prints of *Rear Window* were virtually in tatters.

You can read the script on your computer if you have DVD-ROM capacity and follow along, although we think that might ruin the thrills.

What really counts in the bonus section is the documentary entitled "Rear Window Ethics: Remembering and Restoring a Hitchcock Classic." It includes a great Hitch story that writer Hayes tells, which is a simile. The rest of the documentary offers conversations with Peter Bogdanovich and some surviving crew members, as well as Georgine Darcy, who was "Miss Torso," the ballet dancer, through Stewart's lens. The real surprise is a bit of audio interview of Hitchcock from Bogdanovich. Bogdanovich is, as always, illuminating. Don't forget the segment with the restorers Harris and Katz.

Road to Perdition

CAST: Tom Hanks, Paul Newman, Jennifer Jason Leigh, Tyler
    Hoechlin, Jude Law, Stanley Tucci, Anthony LaPaglia, Liam
    Aiken, Daniel Craig, Ciaran Hinds
DIRECTOR: Sam Mendes
SCREENWRITER: David Self (based on the novel by Max Allan
    Collins and Richard Piers Rayner)
RELEASED: 2002 (119 minutes)
RATED: R

Perdition: "Loss of the soul . . . eternal damnation . . . hell."
As in, on the road to . . .

On the way to the loss of his own soul, Irish gangster Michael Sullivan (Tom Hanks) enables his son Michael Jr. (Tyler Hoechlin) to find his own and the way to a different life. This is the unique team of director Sam Mendes and cinematographer Conrad L. Hall *(American Beauty)* in what was to be Hall's last film. It is a fitting epilogue to the career of one of the greatest cinematographers.

In the lighting and photography of *Perdition,* the contrast between darkness and life is best exhibited. Paul Newman wonderfully portrays the boss gangster, John Rooney, a complex man whose only human weakness is about his fatherhood. It is also the strength of Sullivan's otherwise murderous personality. Mendes has made a film more about the connection of fathers and sons than about the life of gangsters and their victims. He has directed a masterpiece that will last as a classic and perhaps already is one.

Perdition is a relentlessly violent story yet not a violent film. If that sounds impossible, watch it and then argue with us. The murders and death are not done in theatrical *Godfather* style. The reality of the cycle of murder over turf, revenge, and justice is as moralistic as in any other classic tragedy.

Mostly, *Perdition* is about a man's attempt to free his son from the life he himself has led. There are moments when you believe that they will both be able to make a new life in a new place, together. But the place they are headed is a town called Perdition, and that ought to give you clue enough.

Perdition is filled with suspense and emotion. It is understated, sadly brilliant, and haunting. Hanks and Newman are extraordinary. Everyone plays a muted role here, to spectacular effect.

EXTRAS

If you enjoyed the movie, you will appreciate the commentary. Even if this movie is not on your top ten, but you liked *American Beauty* and admire the work of young British director Mendes, you'll have the opportunity to hear his commentary. He is a director of immense, wide-ranging talent. He walks you through his decision-making process for each scene of *Road to Perdition*. It is particularly illuminating to listen to him discuss the characters, and their relationship with the world around them.

You can watch the deleted scenes with or without the commentary from Mendes. We advise viewing with the commentary on. Mendes explains why he chose to leave them out of the film. Again, you'll get a real feel for his work. Mendes pays great attention to details, resulting in a high payoff in his finished product. These scenes are great to watch by themselves.

HBO always does a great job of presenting films to us in their "making of" series. The cast and crew talk about their experiences making the movie and working with the other actors in the film. Mendes and producers Richard Zanuck and Dean Zanuck reveal their thoughts on cast selection and the creative process of the film. The behind-the-scenes shots are excellent. Hall is discussed at length. His precision and attention to detail created some of the best cinematography ever. It's a deserved tribute to a great artist.

The CD soundtrack is only an advertisement for the soundtrack of the movie.

As usual, the production notes are hard to read from the screen because the text coloring blends in with the background.

In one of the better photo galleries on DVD, these are stills from the movie and are beautiful photos. The color and lighting make them absolutely gorgeous. Don't miss this small gem.

The Rodgers and Hammerstein Collection

Here's a DVD birthday cake to celebrate the one-hundredth birthday of Richard Rodgers, a genuine musical genius. It's a boxed set that works for the whole family and invited guests as well. The collection contains musicals Rodgers wrote with his equally talented lyricist Oscar Hammerstein. The films are *The Sound of Music, South Pacific, The King and I, Oklahoma, Carousel,* and *State Fair.*

Two of them, *The Sound of Music* and *The King and I* are based on real people and events. Many of Rodgers's most popular tunes are included and are, of course, superbly sung. The production values of the discs are first-rate. Here's the rundown on three of the best.

The Sound of Music

CAST: Julie Andrews, Christopher Plummer, Eleanor Parker, Richard Haydn, Peggy Wood, Charmian Carr, Heather Menzies, Nicolas Hammond
DIRECTOR: Robert Wise
SCREENWRITER: Ernest Lehman (adapted from the stage musical by Richard Rodgers and Oscar Hammerstein)
RELEASED: 1965 (174 minutes)
RATED: G

Dismissed by serious critics as sugary slop, *The Sound of Music* is actually a better film than most will give it credit for. One of Rodgers and Hammerstein's weaker Broadway shows, ironically, it became one of the better film versions of their work, despite the disapproval of the elite. Most of the world loved it and made it one of the biggest-grossing movie musicals ever. *The Sound of Music* saved 20th Century Fox from filing for bankruptcy.

It's the true story of Maria Von Trapp, a young novice in a convent, who comes to the home of Captain Von Trapp to become the governess to the widower's many children. They fall in love, and she forsakes her final vows to become his wife. Together, the entire family is able to flee from the Nazis. The danger of developing diabetes from repeated exposure is somewhat reduced given that the backdrop to the story is 1930s Salzburg, and everyone knows what came next in Austria, Germany, and the rest of Europe. There's no question it's very sentimental. However, the film still provides gratifying moments from the musical score, which includes "Climb Every Mountain" and "My Favorite Things." The songs, perhaps more than the story, have become part of American cultural history. The gifted classical actor Christopher Plummer plays a stilted Von Trapp, although he is still a dream to watch. It's been said he quipped that he had starred in *The Sound of Mucus*. There's a great deal of goo here, but the movie's qualities appeal to young and old. The opening sequence with the title song, photographed in the Alps, remains a cinematic treat.

EXTRAS

Disc Two features an excellent documentary called from "From Fact to Phenomenon," which is the best of the numerous extras and supplements in this entire collection. Director Robert Wise was initially worried about whether Julie Andrews was "photogenic enough." He changed his mind after attending a prerelease screening of *Mary Poppins*. There's an interesting interview with surviving Von Trapp family members who tell of their invitation to sing on a radio show for Hitler's birthday celebration. When they said no, they had to flee Austria immediately. Plummer says he spent four days with the screenwriter "trying to get the schmaltz out."

The King and I

CAST: Yul Brynner, Deborah Kerr, Rita Moreno, Martin Benson, Terry Saunders, Rex Thompson, Alan Mowbray
DIRECTOR: Walter Lang
SCREENWRITER: Ernest Lehman (adapted from the stage musical by Richard Rodgers and Oscar Hammerstein)
RELEASED: 1956 (133 minutes)
RATED: G

You'll see why the electrifying Yul Brynner won an Academy Award playing the quarrelsome king. The musical is based on the life of a British woman, played by Deborah Kerr, who travels to far-off Siam (Thailand) in the 1860s to teach the children of the royal court. (Kerr's singing voice was dubbed by inveterate "voice-over queen" Marni Nixon.) The cultural clash is inevitable and culminates in one of movie history's most beautifully choreographed seductions, "Shall We Dance?" All remains proper and, we must add, terribly colonial, but the songs are the show.

Fortunately, the United States has become a far more culturally diverse society than it was in 1956 when this film was released. Enjoy *The King and I,* but put your politically correct spectacles away. Classic songs include "Getting to Know You," "I Whistle a Happy Tune," "Shall We Dance?" and "Hello Young Lovers." The DVD transfer has simply enhanced the luscious colors of the sets and costumes.

EXTRAS

There's a theatrical trailer which is pretty standard. A "singalong" is goofy but entertaining. You can play a trivial trivia quiz about the king, or a better bet is to watch the film again. In the "News Oscar" item, Brynner accepts his award with the comment that he won't give it back, even if the Academy made a mistake. Although the supplements are slim, the film is still satisfying. If Brynner were alive, one can only imagine the comments he might have made about his years of playing this role onstage.

South Pacific

CAST: Rossano Brazzi, Mitzi Gaynor, John Kerr, Ray Walston, Juanita Hall, France Nuyen, Russ Brown, Ken Clark, Floyd Simmons, Candace Lee, Warren Hsieh
DIRECTOR: Joshua Logan
SCREENWRITER: Paul Osborn (adapted from the musical by Richard Rodgers and Oscar Hammerstein, based on the book *Tales of the South Pacific* by James A. Michener)
RELEASED: 1958 (171 minutes)
RATED: Not rated

This Rodgers and Hammerstein musical has more relevance today than any of the other classics in the set because there are some serious issues dealt with in the story. Where the recent *Pearl Harbor* was a war story with a slight love story overlay, *South Pacific* is a love story with a World War II overlay. It deals openly with tolerance of cultural diversity, which marked it as a story ahead of its time, as well as timeless. It's based on the Pulitzer Prize–winning book by James Michener, *Tales of the South Pacific*. The love story, set amidst the Pacific theater of operations during World War II, involves an American Navy nurse, Nellie Forbush, and an elegant French planter, Emile de Becque, played by Mitzi Gaynor and Rossano Brazzi. The more radical love story is that of young naval officer Lieutenant Cable (John Kerr) and a young native woman, Liat, memorably acted by France Nuyen. The only acceptable way to end their love in 1958 was to kill off Lieutenant Cable.

South Pacific was a huge hit on Broadway, starring Mary Martin and Italian opera star Ezio Pinza. This movie adaptation won an Academy Award and contains some of the most spectacular songs in the history of film musicals, including "There Is Nothing Like a Dame," "Some Enchanted Evening," and "This Nearly Was Mine." Hammerstein had prophetic advice in his lyrics for "You've Got to Be Carefully Taught."

EXTRAS

The historic footage of opening night is a hoot. One is reminded that there actually was a time in this grand old country when women past fifty had their own faces and not surgically altered ones (even in Hollywood). Movie lore insists Elizabeth Taylor was considered for the lead role of Nellie Forbush but clutched during the audition for Rodgers.

Roman Holiday

CAST: Audrey Hepburn, Gregory Peck, Eddie Albert, Hartley Power
DIRECTOR: William Wyler
SCREENWRITER: Ian McLellan Hunter (story by Dalton Trumbo)
RELEASED: 1953 (119 minutes)
RATED: Not rated

Roman Holiday is as much a celebration of the Eternal City as it is a tale of a love that cannot be fulfilled. It was a first in a number of ways. It was completely shot on location in Italy, the first time this was done by an American director and production company. It also brought Audrey Hepburn her first Oscar, in what was essentially her first time around the track. Gregory Peck was slated for lead billing; the credits were to read "Introducing Audrey Hepburn." During production, Peck called the studio and told them she was the real star. He understood immediately that Hepburn would become America's sweetheart.

Peck plays Joe Bradley, an American correspondent for the fictional *American News Service*. While he's living the life of an expatriate, a dream story literally falls into his lap. He's to cover the "mysterious" disappearance of a young princess named Ann from a small, unspecified European country. She's on her first diplomatic visit to Rome. He keeps her under wraps, puts her in his pajamas, and takes her on a whirlwind tour of Rome, as a free person. For this brief interlude, she tastes what it would be like to be able to do anything she would like to do, without royal obligations and protocol. Peck falls hopelessly in love with her, with the aching knowledge that it can never be. It's all very chaste by today's standards but still unbearably romantic. In the unforgettable scene at the "Mouth of Truth," although you know what's coming, you still can't help laughing, even if it's the hundredth time you've seen it. Peck and Hepburn fill the screen with elegantly glamorous performances in the high style of the 1940s and '50s. Eddie Albert is Peck's sidekick, playing photographer Irving Radovich. While the love story between Hepburn and Peck is the main attraction, the scenes with Albert are high comedy.

After the princess has returned to her royal life, the ending scene depicts her first press conference. As she meets the press for questions, you see how concerned she is about what might happen. Will Bradley and Radovich exploit her time with them and run a story about her disappearance, complete with photographs? By this time, however, we're all aware that Bradley would never hurt his very own princess. His remarks to her are as elegant as the real-life Peck always was.

She descends from the royal stage, refuses to be escorted by her entourage, and personally greets the members of the press. As she approaches Bradley, she meets his eyes with a clear message of a love returned, so discreetly that only he knows. Bradley's eyes tear up as she leaves. He waits in the empty reception hall, just in case she might reconsider, become a commoner, and stay with him forever. Of course, she doesn't, and that's what keeps us coming back to this film again and again. Perhaps he's still waiting for her. We know we're still waiting for both of them.

EXTRAS

Paramount did a fantastic and complete restoration of the film. It's virtually grain-free. There were between four hundred and five hundred pieces of dirt per frame. All of this was cleaned up with the miracle of modern digital technologies. A generous number of extra features includes one about the restoration process itself.

The Edith Head documentary is well worth your time. (See our notes for *Sunset Boulevard*; it's the same feature.)

"Remembering *Roman Holiday*" includes interviews with Albert, Wyler's daughter Catherine, Albert's son Edward, and longtime producer A. C. Lyles. There's plenty of archival material—photographs and clips. One of the surprises is a screen test done with the young Hepburn, who talks about her days as a student dancer and young performer. There's also the mature Hepburn at Lincoln Center, toasting Peck at a 1992 tribute to him.

It is important to note that for many years, Dalton Trumbo's writing credit was left off this movie. Trumbo, who wrote the screenplay, was blacklisted, and therefore his name didn't appear. He was "fronted," as so many were during those terrible days. It took four decades to have his name rightfully restored to the credits.

When the movie was released, the tabloids in London were filled with the doomed love affair of Princess Margaret and Peter Townsend. Like the fictional Princess Ann, Princess Margaret chose the life of duty. She allowed Townsend to leave her life. Unlike the real-life Hepburn, the real-life Margaret never did recover from that decision. The scandal in London involving the royal family served as quite a publicity campaign, however unintended, for *Roman Holiday.*

The Royal Tenenbaums

CAST: Gene Hackman, Anjelica Huston, Ben Stiller, Gwyneth Paltrow, Danny Glover, Luke Wilson, Owen Wilson, Bill Murray, Alec Baldwin
DIRECTOR: Wes Anderson
SCREENWRITERS: Wes Anderson and Owen Wilson
RELEASED: 2001 (103 minutes)
RATED: R

From the fertile and zany minds of Wes Anderson and Owen Wilson comes *The Royal Tenenbaums.* It's not about royalty but about a dysfunctional family. Royal is the first name of the father, played to aggravating perfection by Gene Hackman. This dad is selfish, cruel, dishonest, and unloving. Ultimately, he becomes a human being struggling with his failures. It is in Hackman's performance that the entertainment and the integrity of the film rest.

Anderson, who also directed the acclaimed *Rushmore,* is an acquired taste. But if you are going to acquire a taste, try this one. He tells the tale of an urban family living the life of luxury and achievement. Presumably set in Manhattan, nothing in the city seems quite the way it's supposed to be; it's a surreal look. That's the point of Anderson's vision, which is offbeat and a bit Gothic. Hackman, as Royal, is shady and disreputable, even in his glory days. When he leaves the family, things more or less fall apart, despite the heroic efforts of Anjelica Huston, who plays Royal's wife and mother to his three kids. Her performance is too reminiscent of Morticia Addams to take totally seriously until late in the film, another Anderson sleight-of-hand.

Is this real or not? Is this dark humor or a cartoon strip come to life? The confusion works, because your interest never wanes. Gwyneth Paltrow, with a deadpan expression, her eyes ringed in black, might be another refugee from the Addams family. She's the adopted daughter. Ben Stiller plays an angry and anguished son. In between, there's a lot to keep you busy: an inappropriate love interest between Margot (Paltrow) and her sibling Richie; a diverting romance between the mother, Etheline (Huston) and her accountant Henry Sherman (Danny Glover); mice that look like tiny Dalmatian dogs; a flashback to Margot finding her birth parents; a pet falcon; an attempted suicide . . . and plenty more.

A note to Bill Murray fans: as Raleigh St. Clair, he's depressed, low-key, and vulnerable. Don't be deceived by his character. Clue: what he does for a living.

The movie presents itself as chapters in a book about the Tenenbaums, narrated by Alec Baldwin. After a brief prologue about the early life of the rich, wacky family, the book takes the movie forward more than twenty years. Here's where the engine of dysfunction drives the family's activities and interactions. Royal comes back broke and dying. Well, he comes back broke, that's for sure. But dying or not, this slickster dad again is determined to make things right. The movie is never sentimental, because Anderson's style is too postmodern for that. But it does get to you; there's a special poignancy in the scenes between Hackman and Stiller, Hackman and Huston, and Hackman and Glover. It isn't "happily ever after." It's "life goes on." The surreal becomes both real and rewarding.

EXTRAS

There's an excellent commentary with Anderson on the first disc.

On Disc Two, begin with the main menu and select "Criterion Collection." You'll hear the ever-adorable Stiller's take on the film.

For the "Scrapbook," click on the paintings on the wall for a look behind the scenes at the making of the film. Find the mouse, and you get a candid Murray.

"With the Filmmaker" is probably the most rewarding supplement, produced for the Independent Film Channel Series by distinguished documentary filmmaker Albert Maysles. It shows the creation of the sets inside the house in some detail. It's also worth watching for the shots of the falcon trainer and his falcon (no computer-generated bird here). You also can view some interesting takes with the actors, including Hackman. 300 different sets had to be made.

"Deleted Scenes" shows Anderson's one big editing mistake. The romantic dinner scene between Glover and Huston with a flaming dessert should have been in the film.

Watch all of the interviews. Select by portraits. It's great stuff from the actors.

The Secret of Roan Inish

CAST: Jeni Courtney, Mick Lally, Eileen Colgan, Richard Sheridan, Susan Lynch
DIRECTOR: John Sayles
SCREENWRITER: John Sayles (based on the book by Rosalie K. Fry, *The Secret of Ron Mor Skerry*)
RELEASED: 1994 (103 minutes)
RATED: PG

This is a departure for John Sayles *(The Return of the Secaucus Seven, Matewan, City of Hope)* but shows his strength as a storyteller. *The Secret of Roan Inish* is an Irish folktale about selkies. A selkie is more or less the Irish version of a mermaid but far more interesting. *The Secret of Roan Inish* is filled with rich magic realism, which makes it a wonderful fairy tale for adults as well as children.

Although the subject matter is perfect for family viewing, you don't need to rent a child to enjoy the secrets revealed. Fiona is a little girl whose head is filled with the fantasies of her culture's oral history whose practicality and determination far outweigh her dreamy interludes with Irish tales. In Fiona's family tree is an important figure, a selkie, part woman and part seal. This selkie was captured by a local fisherman who loved her dearly. They married, had beautiful children, and presumably were to live happily ever after. But this selkie longed for the sea more than anything. One day, she found her true self again. She discovered the dry and scaly sealskin her husband had hidden away many years before when she became fully human. She slips it on and returns to the sea. The scene where she discovers her sealskin is shot with such tenderness and intimacy that myth quickly becomes possibility.

If you've ever looked into the eyes of a seal, you know

the story of the selkie isn't such a stretch to believe. Fiona carries the story of her selkie ancestor with her as fact, not fantasy. Fiona's family is filled with dark-haired relatives routinely referred to as a genetic link to their ancestral selkie.

The story moves away from this mode quickly enough to establish credibility with the viewer. The movie also deals with the dreary state of the economy in Ireland for small fishermen and others who make a living from the sea.

Fiona's life is anything but a fairy tale; her mother is dead, and her father regularly drowns his sorrows at the pub. She is shipped off to live with her grandparents, where her strength and independent spirit evolve further. Her grandparents live on the coast, just across from the island of Roan Inish, where the entire clan once lived, happily and more prosperously. As if a selkie ancestor weren't enough to fill a child's imagination, now she discovers she had a brother, Jamie. While unattended for a moment, he was carried out to sea in his tiny cradle and lost forever. He has been mourned ever since.

From the moment she learns of her vanished brother, Fiona is determined to go to the island of Roan Inish. She believes she sees things, but she's dismissed by her grandparents. The modern world is closing in on her grandparents, who fear eviction and relocation. In the ever-expanding quest of the global rich to buy a country house for each month of the year, the dialogue about the wealthy people who want their cottage property rings quite true. Sayles has managed to work a miracle with *Roan Inish* by incorporating a story of people in the contemporary world with an ancient story about a different time and way of life. The fact that they work together so seamlessly is a great testimony to Sayles's gift. He's as talented a writer as he is a director; it's a pleasure to see those talents combined here so artfully.

With the help of her cousin, Fiona reclaims the family island. They find a tiny footprint in the sand and know it must belong to the missing Jamie. He is frightened by the children when he encounters them. He jumps into his cradle, where he is quickly escorted out to sea by his protective seal family. The family moves from its many tribulations to an ultimate victory, largely thanks to Fiona's resilience and good judgment.

EXTRAS

The commentary by Sayles is as engaging as the film. He talks about the making of the film in a manner that instantly lets you know that his affection for this story remains undiminished. There are many humorous lines about the perils of filming in the sometimes unforgiving Irish climate.

The Secret of Roan Inish is one of the few fables with animals that doesn't become a candidate for Disney animation. The quality of the relationship among the people, the sea, and the creatures is a triumph because of the work of Sayles and Haskell Wexler, his cinematographer.

Shadowlands

CAST: Anthony Hopkins, Debra Winger, Roddy Maude-Roxby, Edward Hardwicke, John Wood, Peter Firth, Julian Fellowes, Julian Firth, Michael Denison, Tim McMullan, Matthew Delamere

DIRECTOR: Richard Attenborough
SCREENWRITER: William Nicholson (from his play)
RELEASED: 1993 (133 minutes)
RATED: PG

Most people come to know the writer and philosopher C. S. Lewis in one of two ways. First and foremost, he is revered as the author of the *Narnia* books, which have enchanted children for many years (*The Lion, the Witch and the Wardrobe,* among others). Or he is known for his popularly theological commentary on God's relationship to the world and to individuals. But through the play and the subsequent movie *Shadowlands,* his less well-known private life is revealed.

Shadowlands is based on a memoir by Douglas Gresham, who was the stepson of Lewis. The book is entitled *Lenten Lands,* and it's how we first came to the story of Lewis and his late-life marriage to Joy Gresham. In the back of our minds was the faintest memory that Lewis married a woman who was a convert to Christianity. When the play opened on Broadway with Jane Alexander and Nigel Hawthorne, we were first in line to buy tickets. With Hawthorne as Lewis, it was as though Lewis himself walked through the wardrobe door and onto the stage. We weren't as convinced by Alexander's performance. It's true she's a great stage actress, but she was too refined. She fit rather perfectly into the world of the stuffy and proper British academic don and his equally stuffy and confused brother, Warnie.

Cut to the film version. We can think of no other actress who could have played Joy Gresham with more authenticity and conviction than Debra Winger. This time it was Joy Gresham Lewis who had come back to life, in the person of Winger. Lewis and Gresham had a correspondence about theological issues. He had serious correspondences with lots of people. When she came to England, she asked to see him, and he invited her to tea. She walked into a proper English tearoom and said in a loud, nasal voice,

"Anybody here named Lewis?" You imagine that is just what she did. With a jumpy start and an uncertain middle, Gresham and Lewis came to be very much in love and deeply attached to each other.

Joy Gresham turned the bachelor home of Lewis and Warnie upside down. She set Lewis spinning with the notion of real love, not only spiritual love. She was outspoken, serious, uninhibited. He was proper and inward, shy and awkward with women and with people in general. Although Anthony Hopkins isn't quite as convincing as Hawthorne was, the movie ultimately succeeds where the play failed because of Winger's performance.

We know that Winger knows how to die well. We watched her do it in *Terms of Endearment*. She's really the star of *Shadowlands;* showing a depth and understanding of the complexity of coming into the late life of Lewis, a man both famous and repressed. She puts a lump in your throat. It doesn't end well; she dies. But it ends triumphantly because in their brief time together, they expanded each other's understanding of things mortal and spiritual. There's a difference between a manipulative weeper and *Shadowlands:* this is a real-life heartache. *Shadowlands* is a treasure for anyone who knows anything of the life of Lewis or his books. It's also for anyone who wants to see wondrous performances by two exceedingly able actors, Hopkins and Winger. Mostly, it's a real love story of a kind that is rarely captured on film.

EXTRAS

There's a behind-the-scenes feature with the director, Richard Attenborough, as well as with Hopkins, Winger, and writer William Nicholson. But for us, the bonus was the opportunity to see and hear Douglas Gresham talk about his mother and Lewis. *Lenten Lands* is out of print, but perhaps you can find it at a used-book dealer or online. It's worth the time to track it down and read it.

Shakespeare in Love

CAST: Gwyneth Paltrow, Joseph Fiennes, Judi Dench, Geoffrey Rush
DIRECTOR: John Madden
SCREENWRITERS: Marc Norman and Tom Stoppard
RELEASED: 1998 (113 minutes)
RATED: R

British playwright Tom Stoppard and screenwriter Marc Norman have created a captivating romantic story. Set in 1593 in London, this movie weaves fiction and history. Why does it all work so well? As they say in the film about the magic of theater, "It's a mystery." What isn't a mystery is why this film won seven Oscars. It is an edible delight of love, life, and lust.

Joseph Fiennes plays young Will Shakespeare with passionate tenderness. Director John Madden says Shakespeare was just like other fledgling playwrights, then and now, "broke, horny, and hungry for an idea." Will has an idea for a new play that he's going to call *Romeo and Ethel, the Pirate's Daughter*. With a little help from his friends, the play takes shape before our eyes. Gwyneth Paltrow is Viola, the object of Shakespeare's consuming, if impossible, love. She adores the theater so much that she disguises herself as a boy, since women were banned from the stage.

Viola says, "Love is like a riot in the heart." So is this film, which moves with grace between the offstage romance of Will and Viola and the stage romance of Romeo and Juliet. The view is so fresh you feel as though you are seeing

Romeo and Juliet for the first time. Utilizing Shakespeare's own device of mistaken gender identity, the trick is played on Will himself. This is a play within a play within a movie, a love story for all audiences.

The all-star cast includes Oscar winner Geoffrey Rush *(Shine)*, who plays a harassed theater owner, and Judi Dench as an unforgettable Elizabeth I. Talented British stage actor Anthony Sher has a cameo part as the "psychiatrist" who treats Shakespeare for his writer's block, which is caused by something quite personal. The problem is cured by Viola without the aid of Viagra. Ben Affleck plays Ned Alleyn, who was an actor of the time. You'll learn in a bonus feature interview with Affleck that Alleyn was the Tom Cruise of the period.

How authentic is the story? It is best said by Viola: " 'Tis not life, Will, it is a stolen season." Steal a few hours, and fall in love, along with Shakespeare, for the first time or once again. Be sure to watch through to the very end, past the credit crawl, and then do brush up on your Shakespeare.

EXTRAS

The "Collector's Series" offers many bonus hours well worth the extra price and your time.

"Shakespeare in Love and on Film" and "Commentary with Cast and Crew" are the bonus gems. You get an easy historical overview of Shakespeare's world as well as some wonderful movie gossip. How long did it take for this film to get out of development? Try ten years! You will learn how Miramax ended up with the project. Dench reveals an amusing detail about the identity of her ladies in waiting. Costume designer and Oscar winner Sandy Powell talks about the job of making the costumes work as "real clothes people put on every morning." Additionally, she shows the first sketches and drawings for the queen's magnificent "peacock dress." (Don't bother with the costume feature itself; it doesn't deliver the goods.)

There's a bit of historical footage of some of Shakespeare's other plays made into films. Most notably, you can glimpse Laurence Olivier and Kenneth Branagh. Don't miss Billy Crystal as the gravedigger in Mel Gibson's *Hamlet*.

Madden had an entire Elizabethan city built, which included period theaters that closely matched the original Rose and Curtain. The commentary on this is both informative and entertaining.

A scene-by-scene look from the director's point of view separates true movie buffs from pretenders. If you are an aspiring actor, director, or film scholar, it's a free, valuable short course on the art of film.

The deleted scenes are well worth selecting. You'll find the original ending, which was corny. (We won't spoil the surprise.) Observing the decision to change the conclusion provides satisfying viewing.

"Shakespeare Facts" are on-screen facts about the life of Shakespeare plus biographies of actual people of the time who are portrayed in the film.

Shrek

CAST: (Voices) Mike Myers, Eddie Murphy, Cameron Diaz, John Lithgow
DIRECTORS: Andrew Adamson and Vicky Jenson
SCREENWRITERS: Ted Elliot and Terry Rossio (based on the book by William Steig)
RELEASE: 2001 (90 minutes)
RATED: PG

Shrek is likely to become just as beloved as *The Grinch Who Stole Christmas*. This inspired animation was the biggest box-office hit of 2001. Both kids and adults filled the theaters.

Based on William Steig's 1990 book, *Shrek* is about an ogre who is "tickled to be so repulsive." But he isn't; he's lovable and doesn't frighten anyone. We are tickled to be in his company and in his swamp. He wants his privacy but is constantly invaded by most of the known fairy-tale world. Steig's book didn't have a true villain, but the movie does. He's Lord Farquaad, and, thanks to John Lithgow, he has a convincingly menacing voice. His evil knows no bounds! He tortures the Gingerbread Man by dipping him in milk.

Shrek's sidekick is Donkey, who talks, and does he ever, with the brilliant vocal timing of Eddie Murphy. Shrek's voice is donated by Mike Myers, and they are the stars of the movie, with a vast supporting cast of wisecracking animals and other timeless characters. When Shrek saves Donkey, he says, "Freaks got to stay together. Every monster needs a sidekick." They must free Princess Fiona from a unique dragon in exchange for peace and quiet in Shrek's swamp. The journey is a riotous ride, and the ending is a traditional fairy-tale one turned more than slightly around.

Shrek works on so many levels because of the adept writing. Children will take it on its own terms; adults will understand a variety of subtle and not so subtle cultural and Hollywood jokes. One inside joke is the obvious appearance of Disney characters out of their copyright chains, including the Three Blind Mice, Tinkerbell, the Big Bad Wolf, and Pinocchio. It's been suggested that this is Dreamworks partner Jeffrey Katzenberg's bit of revenge. His departure from Disney and highly publicized fight with Michael Eisner were hardly material for an animated romp through the enchanted forest. If aimed at his former employers, it seems all in fun.

Even in the new world of animation, with such sophisticated releases as the *Toy Story* films, *Shrek* was the most advanced animation seen at the time of its release.

While the word *shrek* has been defined as feeling fear or being a wreck, this ogre is too adorable to do anything but make you love him and cheer for him, every little mean, green step of his way. *Shrek* deserves a great batch of extras, and the two-disc set delivers eleven whole hours of family fun.

EXTRAS

On Disc One, some of the special features are enjoyable primarily for children. Click on the Donkey, and he will take you to a scene-by-scene breakdown menu. You will also hear Baby Bear's memorable line, "This menu is too small." Another click will turn the Donkey into Tinkerbell and into the DWK Information Booth, where you can find Shrek's Music Room and the Game Swamp. The Game Swamp is loaded with interactive games; the Gingerbread Man, Ask the Magic Mirror, and Rescue the Princess are the best here.

On both discs, the Gingerbread Man is a silly little gimmick kids love. Hit "Special Features," and with the main menu highlighted, select upward to the Gingerbread Man's buttons, press the enter button, and a "fun Shrek fact" emerges. (Some call this an egg.)

HBO's "The First Look: The Making of *Shrek*" is a promotional feature that is far better than most, with footage of Myers, Murphy, and Diaz.

"Shrek in the Swamp Karaoke Dance" is an endearingly wacky rendition of popular hits.

Disc Two contains the director's commentary. This feature is for adults and includes extensive remarks about the making of the movie from the directors and producer. Much of it is amusing, and all of it is informative.

"The Tech of Shrek" is for those who love to know the technical details of how a movie like this can be made at all. There is super footage of the animators at work.

"Technical Goofs" is only three minutes but worth every second. It's animation gone wrong, some of it quite suggestive, and absolutely hilarious.

Singin' in the Rain

CAST: Gene Kelly, Donald O'Connor, Debbie Reynolds, Jean
    Hagen, Millard Mitchell, Cyd Charisse, Rita Moreno, Douglas
    Fowley, Madge Blake
DIRECTORS: Gene Kelly and Stanley Donen
SCREENWRITERS: Betty Comden and Adolph Green
RELEASED: 1952 (103 minutes)
RATED: G

There's not much of a plot, and what there is doesn't really grab you, yet this remains one of the all-time favorite American musicals. It's been called the greatest musical Hollywood ever produced. It's set in Hollywood just at the transition from silent films to the talkies. Gene Kelly plays a silent-screen legend named Don Lockwood. Jean Hagen is his leading lady, Lina Lamont. The adoring public can't wait to see and hear their favorite sweethearts talk to them from the silver screen.

However, lovely Lina has a big liability: she has a jarring Bronx accent. It is on this flimsy skeleton of a story filled in with charming romantic interludes that we have been given some of the most innovative song-and-dance numbers ever filmed.

The real story behind this movie is Arthur Freed (who once was known as Arthur Grossman). Freed was *the* American musical comedy machine in Hollywood, which started churning them out with Judy Garland in *The Wizard of Oz*. Name a musical you loved as a kid, or love now, or have come to love, and it's likely to be an Arthur Freed production. The list includes everything from *Wizard of Oz* through *Bells Are Ringing*. In between, he made *Meet Me in St. Louis, Easter Parade, Annie Get Your Gun, Gigi, An American in Paris*. And those are just the highlights.

Freed wasn't just a producer but a lyricist as well. Like its counterpart from today, *Moulin Rouge, Singin' in the Rain* is filled with songs from other movies and other shows. With Stanley Donen's sense of structure and Kelly's choreographic genius, the result is musical comedy as we dreamed it could be. *Singin' in the Rain* was produced toward the end of the Freed production line, so everything he learned is packed into this film.

Kelly's dancing in the rain has been shown on just about every clip reel of Americans' favorites that we can think of. However, nothing takes the place of seeing him do this number within the context of the film itself. Debbie Reynolds was really still a "deb" when the film was made; she was barely twenty. As Kathy, she is hired to dub Lina's high-pitched whine. You've got to know that Kelly's character, Lockwood, is going to fall head-over-heels in love with her.

Luckily, that doesn't happen before there's lots of heels clicking and toes tapping. Cyd Charisse, whose dancing has always seemed so effortless that it's almost ethereal, appears in a dream sequence with Kelly. It's one miracle of entertainment after another, from the ridiculous but still amusing "Moses Supposes" duet of Donald O'Connor and Kelly to the gymnastic antics of O'Connor in "Make 'Em Laugh."

Singin' in the Rain still makes us laugh. You'll cry with joy, however, when you see the 50th Anniversary Edition.

EXTRAS

Extras hardly describes what you're in store for in this two-disc Warner Brothers set.

Disc One includes a feature-length audio with the surviving stars and writers, including Reynolds, O'Connor, Charisse, Donen, Betty Comden, and Adolph Green. They've also wisely included Baz Luhrmann; you begin to understand more about *Moulin Rouge* when you hear him appreciate and comment on *Singin' in the Rain*. Don't be put off by all these folks on the audio track; it's a party, and you're invited.

Disc Two features documentaries about the making of musicals. In 1996, "Musicals Great Musicals: The Arthur Freed Unit at MGM" aired on cable television. If you missed it then, don't worry. The entire documentary is here on the disc (it's almost an hour and a half in length), and you won't want to let it go when it's over. Fortunately, you don't have to. Just play it again. You'll see clips from the beginning of the Freed productions in 1929 until the end of his musical comedy career in 1960. (He felt he needed to go on and make "regular" motion pictures after that and failed miserably. However, we still think that the B movie *Light in the Piazza* in 1962 had some lovely moments in it. There are at least ten other Americans who agree with us.)

The other documentary on the second disc was made for the anniversary edition and is called "What a Glorious Feeling: The Making of *Singin' in the Rain*." Reynolds more or less hosts the show, and you'll hear from just about everyone that you heard in the audio but with a somewhat different perspective.

A truly satisfying feature is the song excerpt option, where you can find those tunes in their original settings. There's also Reynolds singing to a billboard with Kelly's picture on it, "You Are My Lucky Star," but they took out that version. Too bad, but it's great to have it now.

We could go on and on, because there are even more things to say about the features, but we hope you're going to watch them all.

Sleepless in Seattle

CAST: Tom Hanks, Meg Ryan, Bill Pullman, Ross Malinger, Rosie O'Donnell, Gaby Hoffman, Victor Garber, Rita Wilson, Barbara Garrick, Rob Reiner, David Hyde Pierce
DIRECTOR: Nora Ephron
SCREENWRITERS: Nora Ephron, Jeff Arch, and David S. Ward
RELEASED: 1993 (101 minutes)
RATED: PG

Sleepless in Seattle belongs in the genre "airplane movie." See our entry for *You've Got Mail* for our instructional manual on how best to use an airplane movie.

If you don't know the plot, here goes. Sam Baldwin is a handsome and sad man who has lost his wife. He moves to Seattle because he is so depressed. (Don't people move *away* from Seattle when they are depressed because of all that rain?) In Seattle, he and his eight-year-old son live on a houseboat, where Sam can continue to mope around and continue to be a successful architect. His dead wife does stop in from time to time to tell him she still loves him.

The guy is in bad shape. His son, Jonah, takes things

into his own hands. One of the best things about this film is Ross Malinger as Jonah. Rosie O'Donnell also is terrific as Becky.

The kid calls a radio shrink and tells his father's story on the air. Then Sam ends up on national tell-all radio with his story. Far away in the East, Annie Reed is driving to spend the holidays with her parents. She hears the man on the radio. She's already engaged to someone else. She pulls off the interstate and stops in a diner, where all the waitresses are also listening to the sad man in Seattle. This is a genuinely hilarious scene. Annie knows it immediately; it's love at first sound bite. Is there anything as sexy as a depressed, widowed architect?

Her friend Becky encourages her to follow this dream to its rightful conclusion. If this sounds ridiculous, it is. Why was this film so popular, and why do we recommend it as one of your top "airplane movie" selections? It's simple: the comic timing and pacing of Nora Ephron at her best is hard to beat for sheer escapist entertainment. Her script is just as good here as *When Harry Met Sally*. Ephron gives these characters a bit more time to develop. Sam's grief is completely believable because of that, as well as Hanks's natural acting gifts. Annie seems just goofy enough to go for a dream but sensible enough to ask herself what she's doing. Mostly, Ephron is comfortable with parody and knows how to use it. And this time around, she's not so in love with her own dialogue.

At the time of its release, it was called the quintessential chick flick. We didn't realize small chickens went to the movies. However, if that means it's only a women's film, that's not fair, because it isn't true. There's more than enough unisex humor here to go around. (The film really speaks to baby boomers. Ephron hit an entire generation's neurotic love nerve.)

An Affair to Remember (with Cary Grant and Deborah Kerr) plays on a television set somewhere in the background of *Sleepless* at all the appropriate moments. It's actually fairly campy. What sets this apart from the other variations on the theme is Ephron's sense of humor. She has an almost unerring touch when it comes to combining what's in the headlines about men, women, and sex with a movie's theme.

Sleepless is a romantic movie. It should carry the tagline, "And they lived happily ever after," because it is a fairy tale for grown-ups. The twist that makes the film so much fun is that it's an adult story about falling in love with the right person, not the wrong one. It's about trying to pick up the pieces after personal tragedy. Yet it's the little kids who are given the roles that make the plot move forward. Without their intervention, Sam would continue to drip sorrow and raindrops. Worse than that, Annie would marry a guy whose nose constantly drips from his allergies to everything. In case you haven't seen it or have forgotten, we'll stop the plot summary. But it's Jonah and his pal Jessica who cleverly and deviously conspire to make it all possible.

Sleepless delivers precisely what is promised. You won't have a sugar overload at the end. You'll just be happier than you were before you put the disc in the player.

EXTRAS

In 1999, Columbia TriStar brought out its special edition, which has audio commentary with Ephron and her equally talented sister and collaborator, Delia. For us, that's the delight of this edition.

There's a short feature called "Love in the Movies," which is not what you think. It is actually a social commentary on the unrealistic expectations movies just like this one put on real people. There's something ironic in this selection that made us chuckle.

Finally, there's the music video with Celine Dion, "When I Fall in Love."

Some Like It Hot

CAST: Tony Curtis, Jack Lemmon, Marilyn Monroe, Joe E. Brown,
    George Raft, Pat O'Brien, Nehemiah Persoff
DIRECTOR: Billy Wilder
SCREENWRITERS: Billy Wilder and I. A. L. Diamond (adapted from
    Fanfares of Love by Robert Thoeren and M. Logan)
RELEASED: 1959 (119 minutes)
RATED: PG

If you were allowed to choose only one comedy to take with you to that proverbial desert island, this one is it. It's that good. The American Film Institute rated it number one on its list of the Best Hollywood comedies. *Some Like It Hot* comes as close as you can get to absolutely flawlessly timed and paced comedy. It is even better viewing now than when it was released in 1959. That's because we've become a more tolerant and open society sexually. We can sit back and enjoy watching a film about cross-dressing and gender confusion. At the time of its release, some critics almost felt guilty for loving the movie.

Jack Lemmon and Tony Curtis star as Joe and Jerry (later Josephine and Daphne), Chicago musicians running away from the mob. They aren't mobsters themselves, but they witnessed a mob execution. In this wildest of the Wilders, the two don women's clothing, sign up with an all-female touring band and hit the road. Along the way, they befriend Sugar Kane, a ukulele-playing vocalist. Marilyn Monroe is immensely appealing as Sugar. It seems she has a fatal weakness for male saxophonists.

This romp, set in the Jazz Age, also stars George Raft as the mobster Spats Columbo. Joe E. Brown is an eccentric and lovable millionaire bachelor who falls deeply in love with the dowdy "Ms." Lemmon. Tony Curtis, madly in love with Sugar and hampered by his disguise, is at his absolute best. The film's very last line is a classic that has become part of our vernacular.

Some Like It Hot was Billy Wilder's fifteenth film. It was his second with Monroe, following the successful comedy *The Seven Year Itch. Some Like It Hot* was hugely popular when it was released and remains so as new generations of fans discover this treasure. Lemmon was nominated for Best Actor, but the film didn't win the Oscars it deserved.

EXTRAS

At long last, the appropriate DVD release of *Some Like It Hot* is available. The MGM/UA Special Edition is the one we've all been waiting for. First and foremost, the transfer is much better. It hasn't been totally restored, but it's of high quality. Sadly, a commentary wasn't done while Lemmon and Wilder were still both alive.

"A Nostalgic Look Back" is an interview with Curtis, who remembers the grand times they all had making the film. Older now, of course, he is a bit nostalgic. The personal poignancy of his memories adds to the intimacy of the interview feature.

"Memories from the Sweet Sues" is a new conversational interview with four of the women who played small roles as members of the band. They have a great deal to say about Monroe, her qualities as well as her personal problems. They exhibit a genuine sense of loyalty to the film

and to the cast, which makes it seem more like a family reunion than a DVD feature.

"The Interactive 3-D Hall of Memories" is a collage of
clips, photos, and behind-the-scenes glimpses.

The last feature is a collection of press materials from
the original release. You can enlarge the images by pointing
and clicking on the dots.

A Star Is Born

CAST: Judy Garland, James Mason, Charles Bickford, Jack Carson,
    Tommy Noonan, Amanda Blake, Lucy Marlow, Irving Bacon,
    Hazel Shermet
DIRECTOR: George Cukor
SCREENPLAY: based on the 1937 screenplays of Alan Campbell
    and Dorothy Parker
RELEASED: 1954 (181 minutes)
RATED: Not Rated

A Star Is Born is one of a handful of truly great 1950s movie
musicals. This film, Judy Garland's best, was in danger of
disappearing, but that tragedy was averted. This is director
George Cukor's remake of the 1937 film of the same title,
directed by William Wellman.

Garland returned to the screen triumphant in this look
at a woman's career on the rise while her man's is on the
slide. She hadn't been in a film for four years, but her voice
was in absolutely top shape. This is the movie where she let
it all out. The story is heartbreaking, one that mirrors
much of Garland's own life. She is a struggling cabaret
singer named Esther Blodgett, who finds a friend in an
actor whose star is fading. It's fading even faster than it
might because he takes comfort in booze. The actor in

question and Garland's costar was the great English actor James Mason, who gives one of his all-time best acting turns as an over-the-hill thespian who literally bumps into Garland while she is performing onstage.

The fabulous songs include "The Man That Got Away" and "Born in a Trunk," which are endearing Harold Arlen/George Gershwin tunes. *A Star Is Born* provides a perfect showcase for Garland's mighty voice and acting skills. It's also the definitive version of the story. It eclipses the earlier one and easily surpasses the 1976 version with Barbra Streisand and Kris Kristofferson. Garland's performance throughout justifies the legendary reputation the film richly deserved.

For some of us, this Garland film is enough. Even if she hadn't done anything else, her adult reputation was sealed with *A Star Is Born*. Cukor's direction is subtle and sensitive.

EXTRAS

It's so good to have the film rescued from the heap of rubble that it was assigned to, but we're greedy. There are a few extras that are worth watching. You can see three versions of "The Man That Got Away" as well as a deleted musical number.

The version now available includes "lost footage" that amounts to almost one half-hour. Garland was nominated for an Oscar for her performance. In fact, although she was in the hospital about to deliver a child, the cameras were all set up, assuming she might well win. The Oscar went instead to Grace Kelly in *The Country Girl*. Mason lost to Marlon Brando in *On the Waterfront*.

Features include original Hollywood premiere newsreel as well as thirty minutes from the actual premiere at the Pantages Theater. The party at the Coconut Grove looks more like home movies than anything else, but if you can't get enough of Garland, you'll appreciate this.

What matters is the excellent condition of this restored print and the miraculous fact that it exists at all.

Star Wars: Episode I—The Phantom Menace

CAST: Liam Neeson, Ewan McGregor, Natalie Portman, Jake Lloyd, Ahmed Best, Pernilla August, Frank Oz, Samuel L. Jackson, Ray Park, Ian McDiarmid.
DIRECTOR: George Lucas
SCREENWRITER: George Lucas
RELEASE: 1999 (133 minutes)
RATED: PG

George Lucas created such vivid worlds in *Star Wars* that we need only hear those Pavlovian words in order to salivate with anticipation. *Star Wars: Episode I—The Phantom Menace* continues his epic space opera. Lucas, the man behind Industrial Light and Magic and THX, once again has outdone himself with a visual masterpiece that imaginatively unfolds before us. Do not expect to be dazzled by masterfully acted scenes complete with intriguing dialogue interspersed with meaningful subtext. This is a feast for your eyes and imagination.

The enormous impact of the first trilogy cannot be disputed. Essentially, *Star Wars* is about the human condition, the eternal struggle for the completion of our past while grappling with an ever-expanding universe fraught with the forces of good versus evil. *The Phantom Menace* springs forward from where the original series emerged. It was met with some disappointment upon opening, yet it is still *Star Wars*. It can be enjoyed by all, audience and critics alike.

This DVD assuredly will become a collector's item. The sound effects and crystalline picture quality set the standard in 1999. In total, more than six hundred hours of footage was shot over a five-year period. Out of this material, Lucas derived the special features that accompany this DVD and make it worth the price.

What is different about this entry in the *Star Wars* saga? Let's start with the fact that *Episode I* is filled with an accomplished cast: Liam Neeson, Ewan McGregor, Samuel L. Jackson, and Natalie Portman. There is also a newcomer, Jake Lloyd, who takes on the role of the young Anakin Skywalker with gusto. They perform well individually and as part of the ensemble. Once again, Lucas transports us to multiple new worlds filled with creatures and civilizations that transcend the imagination.

In *Phantom Menace,* we encounter familiar themes of our own homogeneous civilizations on Earth e-created in magical and mythical themes leaving us truly astonished by the progress of digital computer animation. The integration between these digital landscapes, animated characters, and human actors is completely seamless. The creative minds at Industrial Light and Magic, Lucas's special effects company, seem to have no boundaries for imaginative creation in terms of exciting new worlds and their inhabitants. Everyone who saw the first *Star Wars* trilogy has been eagerly anticipating learning more about their favorite characters and the worlds from which they came. This will whet your appetite even further.

The "Podrace" is one of the highlights in *Episode I.* It is an audibly intricate and visually engaging action sequence. This specific scene exhibits the sheer genius of Lucas and his team. The race goes through canyons and caves with high-tech speed racers run by strange creatures with dirty tricks up their sleeves. The whole race was done with CGI and one little boy in front of the blue screen. Assuredly, you'll find many other unforgettable scenes to cling to throughout your numerous viewings. Since the original characters are so loved, this film wisely brings a little bit more background and story to them. There's history about where Obi-Wan came from, the Jedi traditions, and even Darth Vader insight. You even get some history on C3PO and R2D2. To see the master (Lucas) tell the story of our favorite characters from the beginning is perhaps the biggest draw of *Episode I—The Phantom Menace*.

EXTRAS

There's hours and hours of entertainment on the supplement disc. There are silent clips of the film, with poetry readings by the characters playing over the clips.

There are seven deleted scenes. Lucas and producer Rick McCallum comment on each scene and why it was cut. Either watch each scene, or you can watch the "Deleted Scenes Documentary," where you are given a bit more commentary.

There's an hour-long "making of" documentary entitled "The Beginning," which takes you all the way from the first day of writing the screenplay to the last day of filming. Here you'll see all the different creatures being created as well as all the costumes for Queen Amidala. There are interview clips of the cast with their thoughts about the film and their experiences during production. You'll go all over the world on set locations, from the Rolls-Royce factory in England to the deserts of Africa.

Even better is a documentary supplement of five short featurettes that go into more detail on various topics, from costume design to the recreation of Yoda and the fight scenes of the Jedi. There is also the Web documentary section, twelve mini-documentaries that were on the Web site before the release of the film. Although not too detailed (they didn't want to reveal all that much about the film before its release), they are still interesting to watch.

In the "Animatics" section, we get a little introduction to what animatics is and how it's used. Several scenes from the movie were created using animatics technology. You view them from the storyboards through the animatics to the final cut.

In a commentary feature on Disc One, Lucas, McCallum, and editor and sound producer Ben Burt, plus the visual effects team and animation supervisor, all contribute their takes on the production of the film. It's obvious that they were recorded separately, but the end result is fairly seamless. Lucas talks about how he likes to make his films tell the story visually, so that if you turned the sound off, you could still see a good film. The commentary gives a rather technical look from special effects to the storytelling. If you're feeling frustrated with keeping up with which one of the seven commentators is speaking a subtitle feature displays their names.

A DVD-ROM feature lets you get extra bonus material off the Web site.

As for eggs, the first one isn't really that exciting, but it's amusing. You can change the opening main menu sequence so that the backdrop is either on Tatooine, Naboo, or Coruscant on Disc One by hitting 2 for Tatooine, the audio button for Naboo, and 2 twice for Coruscant during the FBI warning when you first insert the disc into your player.

The next egg is the best. It's a bloopers reel, which also includes the DVD credits. This can be tricky depending on your player; there are several different ways to access this egg. On Disc One, go to options, highlight the THX logo, and hit 1138 on your remote. You can do this by selecting 11,3,8 or 10,1,3,8 or 10+,1,3,8 it all depends on your player. (Some of the older players won't let you do any of these.) The easiest way is just to jump to Title 3 directly. (You may have to look at the instructions for your DVD player to find out how to do this.)

There are two more eggs on the second disc in the deleted scenes segment. Once the deleted scene for the complete podrace sequence is on the screen, move the cursor to the Doc Menu icon and push right. This will highlight a small button. Hit enter, and you will be given a little bit more detail about the other creatures in the race. In the same menu, bring up the scene "podrace lap two," but don't enter it. While on the screen again, move the cursor as you did before to highlight the same button, and you will learn more about the race segment.

Star Wars: Episode II—Attack of the Clones

CAST: Ewan McGregor, Natalie Portman, Hayden Christensen, Samuel L. Jackson, Ian McDiarmid, Temuera Morrison
DIRECTOR: George Lucas
SCREENWRITER: George Lucas
RELEASED: 2002 (143 minutes)
RATED: PG

Episode II was filmed in a totally digital format. This digital image made it possible to enhance the already incredible special effects in the editing process. With amazing color, definition, and sharpness, you are transported into the surreal landscapes along with the characters. With hours of bonus features, *Attack of the Clones* should find its way into your DVD library.

Attack of the Clones begins with expanding turmoil and unrest in the galaxy. The Jedi Council is overwhelmed. The

Senate has the intention of assembling a standing army. This move is controversial. An attempt is made on Senator Amidala's life; Obi-Wan and his apprentice, Anakin Skywalker, have been assigned to protect her. Obi-Wan investigates the attempted murder, which leads him to a mysterious planet. Here we are introduced to young Boba Fett, who you may recall is the bounty hunter who captured Han Solo in *The Empire Strikes Back*. Obi-Wan finds out about the separatist group and the mysterious Count Dukoo, who turns out to be a former Jedi knight. In the meantime, Anakin has taken Padme back to Naboo.

There is much more dialogue than necessary; however, *Attack of the Clones* clearly outshines its predecessor, *Phantom Menace*. The storyline and excitement are more evident and developed—sometimes a bit too much, as in the newly forming romance between Padme and Anakin, which does not come across as all that believable. But it is still *Star Wars*, and George Lucas has created another enchanting space adventure with undertones of melancholy and unrest. View this episode as a necessary component for needed depth and setup to complete the next series piece in Lucas's opus, *Episode III*, which is scheduled tentatively for theatrical release in 2005.

EXTRAS

The second disc is filled with almost four hours of bonus material in the same format and design as *Episode I.*

There are two main documentaries. The first is "From Puppets to Pixels: Digital Characters in *Episode II.*" This tells us how the characters in the first movies were created using puppets. In this age of digital technology, computer graphics bring all these characters to life, including our favorite Yoda. An enormous amount of time went into re-creating the new Yoda image on computer. Close attention was paid to what the original puppet looked like while under the control of a puppeteer. The team re-created that feel from every wrinkle and lip movement to every hair on his head. You are also given background information for the CGI effects of many other scenes in the movie.

The second documentary, shorter than the first, is "State of the Art: The Previsualization of *Episode II.*" It's a more technical look at the film and how "pre-viz" helps in the early development of scenes to decide what kind of camera angles are needed and so forth. A step-by-step breakdown of certain scenes from the storyboards to the final cut is shown. Be sure to watch all the way through the credits of this documentary, because there are a few quite funny bloopers spliced in with them at the end.

You can watch the deleted scenes all individually with introductions or without, or play continuously with or without introductions. There are eight scenes. All are fun to watch. We suggest viewing with the introductions or commentaries, which enables you to understand not only what is going on, but the reasoning behind the cutting decision.

Three featurettes include "Story," where cast and crew discuss the main ideas behind Anakin Skywalker and his development into Darth Vader; "Love," which discusses the forbidden love story between Padme and Anakin; and "Action," which talks about how this movie really is an action film despite the love story and character development of Anakin Skywalker. Samuel L. Jackson talks about how people "get jacked in this movie," some of the action sequences, and the experiences of the cast filming them in front of the blue screen.

In "Dex's Kitchen," there are a few more behind-the-scenes sequences with Lucas and producer Rick McCallum. "Films Are Not Released; They Escape: Creating a Universe of Sound for *Episode II*" brings you into the making and developing of the sounds in the movie, from the seismic charges in the asteroid field to the growls and screams of different aliens. It's amazing to learn where the sounds come from. Who would believe that a regular household object like a plunger or the scream of a five-year-old could make up the incredible sounds of the universe with the alchemy of sound mixing?

"*Episode II* Visual Effects Breakdown Montage" is a before-and-after montage of ILM's visual effects wizardry, where you learn the differences in how special effects were created twenty years ago and how they are done today.

"R2D2: Beneath the Dome" describe R2D2 as one of the most difficult characters to work with. In the first episode, they had more problems than they can recall. Finally, they had to have two different special effects divisions come up with a robot that would function properly. In this segment are clips of the little guy in some of his greater moments. There's cast chat about him as well, and not what you might think.

In addition, there is a rather well-done commentary feature on Disc One, with the team at ILM, McCallum, and Lucas. It's one of the better and more entertaining of the commentaries.

With a DVD-ROM feature, you can access more bonus material off the Web site.

As on *Episode I*, there is a menu theme choice. Some DVDs will randomly choose a theme for you, giving you a different one each time. You can choose the theme you want by pushing the correct buttons during the FBI warning screen and PG rating screen. If you push "Audio" during the FBI screen, you will get the planet of Geonosis and the execution arena. During the rating screen, if you push "Audio," you will be shown the Coruscant theme and taken to the lower levels on the Naboo Royal crusier.

Just as on *Episode I,* there is a great blooper reel that also contains DVD credits. To access this one, go to the options menu on Disc One. Enter 1138 on your remote, just as you did for *Episode I.*

On Disc Two, you can see some funny college posters made by students using the *Star Wars* campaign. In "Dex's Kitchen," select the poster on the wall behind him, and you will be given a slide show of the student artwork.

The Sting

CAST: Paul Newman, Robert Redford, Robert Shaw, Charles
    Durning, Ray Walston, Eileen Brennan
DIRECTOR: George Roy Hill
SCREENWRITER: David S. Ward
RELEASED: 1973 (129 minutes)
RATED: PG

It was all so simple. With just the touch of a finger to the nose, one of the great swindles of all time was put together. If you didn't figure it out before the end, you were lucky; the movie is even better when you're surprised. This is one of those rare films where the less one says, the better, because you can really spoil somebody's party. So, assuming that there are more than a few of you who have either forgotten or never saw this award winner, we'll just give you a glimpse.

Paul Newman and Robert Redford play two slicksters. They are con men in the Chicago of the 1930s. They want to avenge their friend's death by putting the "sting" on big-time gangster Doyle Lonnegan (Robert Shaw). The wrap-up scene, as they successfully enact their swindle, is one of the most inventive schemes ever depicted on screen. Don't blink, however, or you might lose your place. It's wildly funny and terribly elaborate. Only the riverboat gamblers among us can follow ahead of the steps of these two.

Four years after George Roy Hill directed Newman and Redford in *Butch Cassidy and the Sundance Kid,* he returned with them, but to the scene of a new crime. This was an enormous box-office hit. It also won seven Oscars: Best Picture, Director, Screenplay, Editing, Costume Design, Art Direction, and Musical Score. By the time of this film, the Redford-Newman friendship was established; there's a fluid grace in the scenes between them. It doesn't get much better than this.

Scott Joplin's ragtime score, delightfully arranged by Marvin Hamlisch, gives the film its razzle. But it is Hill, Redford, and Newman who provide all the dazzle and much more.

EXTRAS

Nobody baked a cake for *The Sting*'s twenty-fifth birthday. Although there were plenty of rumors about a special edition, it never materialized. Perhaps one is coming for its thirtieth, but the quality of the transfer on the 1998 release is more than satisfactory. And every library should have *Butch and the Kid* with *The Sting.* It just wouldn't seem right any other way.

Think of this DVD as you think about your favorite restaurant where the food is sensational but the décor is plain. You know going in that it's just you and the food. Here it's just you and the film, but it's plenty satisfying, without dessert.

Sunset Boulevard

CAST: Gloria Swanson, William Holden, Erich Von Stroheim, Nancy
    Olson, Fred Clark, Lloyd Gough, Cecil B. DeMille, Buster
    Keaton, H. B. Warner, Anna Q. Nilsson
DIRECTOR: Billy Wilder
SCREENWRITERS: Billy Wilder, Charles Brackett, and D. M.
    Marshman, Jr.
RELEASED: 1950 (110 minutes)
RATED: Not rated

Gloria Swanson lives forever in the character of Norma
Desmond, the faded and crazed silent-film star of *Sunset
Boulevard*. Her enduring line, "I'm still big. It's the pictures
that got small," is recognized by just about anyone who has
even a passing interest in Hollywood's history. The pictures
have gotten bigger and brasher, violent and sexy, but this
one hasn't been diminished one iota during its more than
fifty-year life span.

Billy Wilder's take on Hollywood isn't sardonic, playful,
or lighthearted; this is a dark and unblinking look at what
Hollywood's culture can produce. *Sunset Boulevard* makes
Robert Altman's *The Player* look like the frolic it was intended to be. Wilder took out the scalpel and performed
the autopsy while the patient was still breathing.

Swanson has been described in many ways, but one at-
tribute that should be given to her is "sport." As in, how
terribly sporting of her to star in a film about a has-been,
when her own career had finished almost twenty-five years
before the release of *Sunset Boulevard*. How very game of
her to have Erich von Stroheim play her butler/ex-
husband/former director, when it was his miserably flawed
Queen Kelly that effectively ended her career. If you want an
example of art imitating life imitating art, look no further.

Either she was a very good sport, or she had a wickedly sophisticated sense of self-deprecating humor. Or, well, there is that other possibility, that she wanted a comeback, just like Norma D.

Norma Desmond lives in spooky, dusty grandeur in an old Hollywood mansion. She has a brilliant idea: she will be a star again by developing the story of Salomé into a major motion picture. But she can't write a screenplay. She's totally insane. It's the perfect opportunity then, as now, for the greedy, desperate, and struggling young screenwriter who seems to have lost his way with words. William Holden plays Joe Gillis, tailor-made for the job. He's dismissive of her at first but rather quickly warms to the notion of life without financial worry, even if it's with this strange woman in her house of horrors.

There's much about *Sunset Boulevard* that makes it a masterpiece. But it isn't because it is a subtle or understated indictment of the industry where Wilder's bread was always buttered. Author Ed Sikov says that the movie is about how very corrupt Hollywood can be. In one of the DVD features, he says of Holden's character, "He is willing to sleep with a has-been who is creepy and demented."

Swanson's performance was intentionally over the top and through the years has been imitated ruthlessly. What's interesting to ponder is just what Swanson was thinking when she was making the film. There's a certain cruelty to the script that gives one pause. When her old pals come to play cards with her, Gillis calls them the "Wax Works." The card-playing buddies were portrayed by the likes of Buster Keaton, H. B. Warner, and Anna Q. Nilsson. Maybe it just looks more vicious fifty years past the time. This is an old-style Hollywood motion picture we never tire of, so, Mr. DeMille, we're ready for our close-up of the special features.

EXTRAS

You'll want to purchase the "Collector's Edition" for the gossipy features as well as some excellent historical footage.

Sikov wrote the book *On Sunset Boulevard: The Life and Times of Billy Wilder,* and he is a wise choice for the commentary on the film. Equally informative and filled with interviews is "The Making of *Sunset Boulevard.*" There's a marvelous bit about a tea party in George Cukor's garden, where Cukor is credited with saying the role should go to Swanson. It's hard now to imagine anyone else playing Norma, but then there was that Broadway musical hit. Glenn Close talks about how it felt to play Norma Desmond onstage with Swanson in her head. Holden's part was written for Montgomery Clift, who declined it. At the time, Holden's early promising career was significantly stalled, and *Sunset Boulevard* was his comeback. It remains one of his finest film roles.

"Location Map" is diverting and great fun. Click on a location, and you'll see what was once there and what's there now.

"The Morgue Prologue" is not to be missed; we won't say more.

"Edith Head: The Paramount Years" appears on a few other deluxe Paramount DVD releases. It's a mini-documentary about an extraordinary woman who changed the way costume designers were seen. It was Head who helped establish the Oscar for costumes in 1948. The real reason she favored dark glasses is revealed. It's a telling testimony to the difficulty of being a professional woman in Hollywood who wasn't an actress. Distinguished designer Bob Mackie says of Head, "She wasn't the best designer in Hollywood, but she was the smartest."

Taxi Driver

CAST: Robert De Niro, Cybill Shepherd, Jodie Foster, Harvey Keitel,
   Peter Boyle, Leonard Harris, Albert Brooks
DIRECTOR: Martin Scorsese
SCREENWRITER: Paul Schrader
RELEASED: 1976 (114 minutes)
RATED: R

Taxi Driver's impact is hypnotic, grisly, and profoundly lasting. The film's nominal hero, Travis Bickle, lives in a netherworld between the past hell of Vietnam and the more mundane horrors of New York street life. He drives a cab, hangs out in Times Square dives, and lives in filthy isolation in his dismal apartment. He is ripe for explosion. Martin Scorsese gives us a nightmarish drama of personal shell-shock and urban paranoia with random bloodshed. It's a contemporary horror story with roots in Arthur Bremer's attempted assassination of George Wallace.

Travis (Robert De Niro) meets Betsy (Cybill Shepherd), who is a semi-friendly campaign worker, and Iris (Jodie Foster), who works the streets as a prostitute at only twelve years old. Their lives come together in a shocking eruption of violence. This put *Taxi Driver* into rating hell for a time, earning it the hated X.

Paul Schrader's screenplay isn't perfect. There are problems with focus and perspective. Although Scorsese's direction overall is superb, in places it is a bit heavy-handed. It's De Niro's performance, however, that is the reason you come back to *Taxi Driver*. Standing in front of his mirror, practicing his threatening and icy glare, he says sneeringly, "You talkin' to *me?*" His depiction of Travis Bickle has become one of the most enduring and scary images of post-Vietnam rage and isolation ever depicted on film.

EXTRAS

At last, a reward for the loyal followers of Scorsese's craft. It's Columbia TriStar's Special Edition that you're after.

The "making of" documentary is one of the best of its kind. It is more than one hour in length and includes Schrader with Scorsese as well as all the actors. Scorsese is a naturally gifted speaker, and he is much at ease discussing this seminal work. One only wishes that he would do this for all his films on DVD. There is still no audio commentary here, however, but the "making of" documentary is comprehensive enough that you don't feel at all cheated.

Storyboard fans will appreciate the comparisons from boards to shots. There's a picture gallery and the entire screenplay on your screen, not on your computer.

With this special edition, *Taxi Driver* receives much better treatment, and it's worthy of a purchase.

Terminator

CAST: Linda Hamilton, Arnold Schwarzenegger, Michael Biehn, Paul Winfield
DIRECTOR: James Cameron
SCREENWRITERS: James Cameron and Gale Ann Hurd
RELEASED: 1984 (108 minutes)
RATED: R

The cast and crew of *Terminator,* including director James Cameron and actor Arnold Schwarzenegger, went into production thinking it would be a sci-fi action film that might soon be forgotten. Little did they know it would launch their careers and become part of film history.

At that time, Schwarzenegger was a B actor. He had played leading roles in mediocre movies such as *Red Sonia* and *Conan the Barbarian*. His large frame and physique, along with his heavy accent, had made it impossible for him to grab more significant roles.

Cameron was just breaking into film direction, having previously worked as an art director. His first directing attempt was *Piranha 2: The Spawning*, a B horror flick. He never finished this project. He was fired for "artistic differences."

Schwarzenegger finally found a role that suited him. He was simply the perfect "Terminator T-800 model 101." Cameron, with help from the gifted producer Gale Anne Hurd, created a screenplay that was a big leap above a B-level script.

In the present day, we are introduced to Sarah Conner (Linda Hamilton), whose life is about to be turned upside down. A psychopath is systematically killing all the "Sarah Conners" in the phone book. So our Sarah Conner has been taken into protective custody at the police station. That won't stop Schwarzenegger, with his famous quote, "I'll be back." Luckily, a mysterious handsome stranger comes to rescue her: "Come with me if you want to live." At a time in the not so distant future, even more danger lies ahead for Sarah. Man has created machine, but machine has now destroyed man. Machines control the earth. A resistance force of humans are determined to destroy the machines and take back control. At the head of the resistance is Sarah Conner's future son, John Conner. The machines developed a time machine of sorts and have sent back their T-800 model 101. It's an indestructible robot concealed under live tissue, making him appear human. The mission is to "terminate" Sarah Conner so that John is never born. The resistance forces know of the plan and send back a soldier to protect her, Sergeant Kyle Reese (Michael Biehn).

Terminator is a cat-and-mouse game. Conner and Reese

are running from the machine that is systematically track-
ing them down. This action-packed thriller has you on the
edge of your seat from the beginning. Schwarzenegger will
surprise you; he *is* the Terminator. The entire cast delivers.

EXTRAS

This DVD is a double-sided disc. Side One is "dual layer"
and contains the movie, which looks better than ever.
Along with DVD-ROM features, scene selections, language
options, and the Dolby 5.1 sound, Side Two (which is single layer) contains all the bonus material.

There are two documentaries. *"The Terminator:* A Ret-
rospective" is about eighteen minutes long, with interviews
with Cameron and Schwarzenegger and behind-the-scenes
footage. "Other Voice" is a more recent documentary that
runs about an hour and has interviews with some of the
cast and crew, as well as cowriter and producer Hurd and
actor Biehn.

You are also treated to seven "terminated" scenes from
the movie, which you can view with or without commentary from Cameron. Some of these scenes, after watching
Terminator 2, probably should have been put back into the
film for the special edition because of their subtle foreshad-
owing of the second film.

"Still Galleries" on this DVD, along with the classic
production photos, publicity material, and special effects
stuff, also has artwork from Cameron and his original story
treatment.

Terminator 2: Judgment Day

CAST: Arnold Schwarzenegger, Linda Hamilton, Edward Furlong,
   Robert Patrick, Earl Boen, Joe Morton
DIRECTOR: James Cameron
SCREENWRITER: James Cameron
RELEASED: 1991 (135 minutes)
RATED: R

It's a difficult task to create a successful sequel to a huge
box-office hit. But the combined talents of James Cameron
and executive producer Gale Anne Hurd (who teamed together on the first film) once again were able to make an
exciting action thriller. This time around, the budget was
bigger, and the characters were stronger. *Terminator 2* has
glitzy special effects and a dramatic, cohesive story.

When we last saw Sarah Conner, she was pregnant with
her son, John. She was driving off into the desert but not
into the sunset. A storm was coming, and so was the rise of
the machines and the fall of mankind. Sarah has been
locked up in a mental institution for a "delusional disorder"
about the future. Dr. Peter Silberman (who in the first film
diagnosed Reese as being a paranoid schizophrenic) believes
Sarah has been traumatized by past events. He thinks she is
unable to distinguish fact from fiction. Her son, John, now
a rebellious street kid, lives with his foster parents, whom
he hates.

While he's hanging out at the mall with his friend
Miles, a cop comes looking for John. Because of some fairly
petty illegal activities, John makes a run for it, only to be
pursued by what seems to be an indestructible supercop.
Coming to save the day is the T-800 model 101, played, of
course, by Arnold Schwarzenegger. This time around, he's
the soldier sent back to protect John. Obviously not

human, the supercop is the new T-1000 model, made of liquid metal that can take any form. There's lots of action after they rescue Mom from the mental institution.

Terminator was more than just another action film because of its character development and plot. This time, there's even more. Sarah now is very physically toned, intense, and ready for war. John is a young kid who never had a father figure. While the T-800 is still a robot, he learns the importance of relationships. The dynamic among the three creates a new form of family. Sarah sees the T-800 as John's guardian angel and companion. John sees the T-800 as a new toy but also as a true friend.

As the story moves on, Sarah decides the only way to stop the rise of the machines is to eliminate the source of it all: Cyberdyne Systems.

Terminator 2 has fabulous special effects. The morphing of this liquid metal being who changes shape in an instant is startling. Did they stop the rise of the machines? (Apparently not, since *T3* has happened.)

EXTRAS

Visual effects and creative supervisor Van Ling oversaw the production of this "Ultimate Edition" DVD. He also produced the *Star Wars: Phantom Menace* DVD. His creative talents went into the production of a visually pleasing and feature-packed DVD. It was the first to bring us more than six hours of information on one disc! It's dual layered and dual sided. Some editions, however, have two discs instead of one; either way, the information is identical.

Side A, or Disc One, has two versions of the movie, the original release and the director's cut. There is a commentary feature as well, with twenty-six cast and crew participating. There's lots of technical insight from Ling and Cameron. Despite the enormous amount of information, all the interview clips work together very well. There is even a subtitle feature, which shows the names of everyone who speaks. Also on Side A are cast and crew filmographies and mini-bios.

Side B, or Disc Two, has three main sections: "Information Programs," "Visual Campaigns," and "Data Hub." In the "Information Programs," you are given two featurettes, "The Making of *Terminator 2: Judgment Day*" and *"T2: More Than Meets the Eye."* The "making of" documentary is thirty minutes long and interweaves behind-the-scenes footage with clips of the movie and interviews with cast and crew. You get an insightful look at the technical magic of *T2.* The second is a little shorter, focused on scenes that were cut from the film and the reasons for cutting them. A third selection, "Making of *T2* 3D: Breaking the Screen Barrier," is a short documentary about the making of the Universal Studios theme park ride.

"Visual Campaigns" has three U.S. theatrical trailers and five Japanese theatrical trailers.

The "Data Hub" section is where most of the information lies, subdivided into four sections, "Source Code," "Tactical Diagrams," "Interrogation Surveillance Archives," and "Data Core." "Source Code" has frame after frame of the orginal script that you can read from the screen, interesting especially for film students. "Tactical Diagrams" contains the storyboards for the film. "Interrogation Surveillance Archives" contains sixty different mini-featurettes on the making of the film from preproduction to the DVD. Finally, "Data Core" gives more supplemental features, including an article by Estelle Shay entitled "Battle across Three Dimensions" and the DVD-ROM feature.

This DVD should not be terminated. Packed with more bonus material than you can enjoy in one viewing, it delivers impeccable sound and picture plus hours of information for this box-office action hit.

Terms of Endearment

CAST: Shirley MacLaine, Debra Winger, Jack Nicholson, John Lithgow, Jeff Daniels, Danny DeVito, Betty King, Lisa Hart Carroll
DIRECTOR: James L. Brooks
SCREENWRITER: James L. Brooks (adapted from the novel by Larry McMurtry)
RELEASED: 1983 (132 minutes)
RATED: PG

This is an affecting, poignant tearjerker about a vain woman and her beloved daughter. It's one of the few of its genre that manages to pull out all the stops with such effectiveness. James L. Brooks milks the script for all the laughs and sobs it can bear, and beyond. However, the performances make the movie worth the weeping.

Shirley MacLaine and Jack Nicholson make up most of the movie, although Debra Winger is extraordinary as the dying daughter betrayed by life and her body. It's an all-star cast working with very high production values. These qualities and the seemingly eternal appeal of youthful death made this a smash hit at the time of its theatrical release. The film succeeds by taking its characters very seriously. Based on the novel by Larry McMurtry, the film utilizes his technique of having the characters whittle away at each other. The plot never risks the audience's intense emotional involvement. Winner of Academy Awards for Best Picture, Best Director, Best Actress (MacLaine beat fellow nominee Winger), and Best Supporting Actor (Nicholson).

EXTRAS

The only extra is a so-so audio commentary with Brooks and his co-producers. It's you and your Kleenex box. For many, *Terms of Endearment* stays on the very top of the preferred tearjerker list. If you're in need of filling that gap in your library, we say pick this one, because the acting and the story are excellent, endearing, and enduring.

Thelma and Louise

CAST: Susan Sarandon, Geena Davis, Harvey Keitel, Michael
    Madsen, Brad Pitt, Christopher McDonald
DIRECTOR: Ridley Scott
SCREENWRITER: Callie Khouri
RELEASED: 1991 (128 minutes)
RATED: R

Thelma and Louise rode out of town in Louise's vivid turquoise T-Bird, and nothing has ever been the same. At the time of its release, there was a great need to put this film into a category. It was *Bonnie and Clyde* but with two women. It was a road movie for chicks; it was *Butch Cassidy and the Sundance Kid* in modern times. The comparison obsession was relentless. This was a film that viewers had a great deal of trouble defining.

It's good to come to *Thelma and Louise* for the first time right now. It will always have its detractors and its loyal following, but the intense debate has died down. Finally, we are allowed to take this film on its own terms. *Thelma and Louise* is a unique look at what women might sometimes think they would like to do to men who act badly. (It's important to remember that Louise blows away a guy in a parking lot because he tried to rape Thelma.) After the shooting, they are on the run, and it's more than just self-defense against a would-be rapist.

Thelma was running away from a miserable marriage to a male version of a bimbo, played with stupefying annoyance by Christopher McDonald. Louise was running away from a life going nowhere; she worked as a waitress in a coffee shop that was more of a dive than a diner. Neither woman had any idea of what she ought to have done with her life or what actions she should take to fix her boredom, unhappiness, and lousy situation. In this regard, it's hardly a feminist classic, whatever that is supposed to mean. It's a fast-paced action film filled with more laughter than violence.

Harvey Keitel gives one of his most unforgettable performances as a detective who tries to bring them in before it's too late. He grows fond of them, and it's in the confusion of paternalistic roles as lawman and gentleman that the complexity of his character resides. If you've forgotten, they pick up a young and ridiculously handsome boy named J.D. (Brad Pitt) on the way. He teaches them how to hold up a store in a fairly elegant way. He also offers Thelma an even more important life-affirming experience.

You often can catch people in a little trivial quiz of your own. (This won't work for true movie buffs but does work for movie lovers of all kinds.) Ask the simple question: "Was the director of *Thelma and Louise* a man or a woman?" You'll frequently get the answer, "Well, a woman, of course." Wrong. The director was Ridley Scott, coming from *Alien* and *Blade Runner* on his way to *Hannibal, Gladiator,* and *Black Hawk Down.* If you're one of the people who answered "A woman, of course," in fact, you're not totally wrong. Screenwriter Callie Khouri would have liked to direct the film.

In the end, whatever category this film belongs to, the amazing screenplay, with its character development and dialogue, is what the film is all about. Geena Davis and Susan Sarandon are as well paired as any two could have been. They remain a joy to watch. Both were nominated for Best Actress. (The Oscar went to Jodie Foster because she survived the liver eater in *The Silence of the Lambs.*) It is true that, like Butch and the Kid, these female pals do leap from their disorderly and illegal experiences into the next sphere of reality rather than face justice.

Scott was nominated for Best Director but lost out to Jonathan Demme, also for *Silence.* Khouri took home the Oscar for Best Screenplay, and it's a good thing she did. Who knows, *Thelma and Louise* might have come back from the abyss and fired a few shots at the Academy.

EXTRAS
The MGM "Special Edition" is the third release of this film on DVD. There were previous editions in 1997 and 2000.

The special edition deserves the label, but by now we are all getting a trifle agitated about repeated releases of movies that should be done in a first-rate fashion from the beginning.

The Scott commentary has remained constant across all versions. He is the consummate professional, and his remarks are informative and expansive. He's totally comfortable in this new medium, and therefore his audio track is a pleasure. If you're unfamiliar with the scope and range of Scott's career, you'll particularly enjoy his autobiographical remarks.

The second audio track is with Sarandon, Davis, and Khouri. It's artistically a bit fragmented, but the women's strong appreciation for one another's work comes out clearly. In a humorous vein, Khouri comments on her reluctance to talk about the screenplay initially. You'll hear from her what a short time it took to write the script down. One suspects she was working on it inside her head for much longer than that.

"The Last Journey" is an hour-long documentary and is much better than most of the standard "making of" fare out on disc. It's loaded with details about how the film came to be and what Scott thought when he was approached. You'll also learn what Khouri was doing when she got this notion in her head. (Clue: it might be the reason the music track accompanying *Thelma and Louise* is so superior.)

There's a deleted scenes segment that isn't worth all that much, except for that yummy extra little bit of Pitt.

There's an alternative ending that's been hanging around from version to version, which isn't all it's cracked up to be. "Over the Edge" is nothing more than the end again, giving you the option of watching with storyboards. We are somewhat in the minority here, but we think the ending shot is as it should have been. You can view both choices and decide for yourself.

Unforgiven

CAST: Clint Eastwood, Gene Hackman, Morgan Freeman, Richard Harris, Jaimz Woolvett, Saul Rubinek, Frances Fisher, Anna Thompson
DIRECTOR: Clint Eastwood
SCREENWRITER: David Webb Peoples
RELEASED: 1992 (130 minutes)
RATED: R

In 1992, Clint Eastwood took away the Oscars for Directing and Best Picture. Gene Hackman won for Best Supporting Actor, Joel Cox for editing. Eastwood also was nominated for Best Actor. This is his story as much as it is the story of William Munny, the reformed gunslinger with a past that includes killing for the hell of it. With the love of a good woman, he faces down his sins to live honorably, albeit in the mud of a hog farm. After his beloved wife dies, things get mighty tough. With kids to raise and short on cash, hog farming isn't quite the avocation he thought it might be. Munny doesn't want to be wicked any longer, because he was cured of that and all other vices by his wife. But he doesn't want to fall on his face in the pig slop any longer, either.

By 1992, the American Western was a terminal patient already on life support. There were still Westerns being made, but the old format no longer satisfied audiences accustomed to the pyrotechnics of what the action end of the movie business could offer.

Although William Munny has hung up his weapons, in the opening shots you sense there's still one more fight in him. By this time, Eastwood was established as a world-recognized director and probably had forgiven those folks from his past who thought he wasn't all that much in the early days. His two mentors had died (Don Siegel and Sergio Leone); *Unforgiven* is dedicated to both of them. But Eastwood clearly had one more Western in him. What he gives us in *Unforgiven* is unforgettable. If someone was entitled to deliver the cinematic eulogy to the American Western, it should have been Eastwood; luckily, it was.

Schofield Kid (Jaimz Woolvett) appears as the moral dilemma in human form. There's a good bounty to be had in Big Whiskey (generic for any small Western town still run by a corrupt sheriff). The sheriff is Little Bill Daggett (Gene Hackman), who is capable of making a plea bargain for just about any sort of crime. William Munny has no intention of participating but is persuaded, perhaps because of the crime involved. We're never sure just why he decides.

What happens in Big Whiskey is a departure in plot for a Western, as indeed the entire film is a departure, as well as a critical examination of the Western as an art form. Cowboys upstairs in the saloon with the prostitutes is not a new story, but what happens to one of the women is a new kind of grisly. A whore named Delilah gives too much lip about a particular cowboy's personal equipment, so the cowpuncher in question cuts up her face. He doesn't stop there. But our anatomy lesson will. It's a slice-and-dice session. Nobody seems to care, especially Little Bill, the lawman, who settles it all with a trade for horses. But Strawberry Alice, Delilah's good friend, cares. So the women set up a thousand-dollar bounty fund from their savings.

The cinematography is dark and shaded. There's a sinister feeling to the town and to the moment in history it interprets. Little Bill is waiting for the bounty hunters and takes care of them as they come to town. Richard Harris, playing English Bob, is the first to get smacked around and thrown into the slammer. Morgan Freeman saddles up as well, playing Ned Logan. A major criticism of the film is that Freeman is used so little. Amidst the darkness and, by the way, not much violence, there is the critical subplot of what was happening to the West in the 1880s. English Bob, a famous gunman, lives off his reputation, no longer off the notches in his belt. He's accompanied by a writer, W. W. Beauchamp (Saul Rubinek), who makes his living by turning out penny thrillers about the "Old West."

In short, *Unforgiven* is the story of a moment in America's history. It's also a story of the life of the Hollywood Western. Primarily, it's testimony to Eastwood's no-nonsense talent and longevity.

If you missed *Unforgiven*, you'll be surprised by its staying power. If you saw it, you know what we mean. As for Eastwood, he's out of Westerns, but, fortunately, he's still with us. Eschewing the usual desire for cult popularity, Eastwood remains a classy and elegant artist. With or without the guns smoking, his talent still burns. He's unafraid to roll around with the pigs. He's willing to be beaten and lie in the gutter. He allows us to look and to see something quite important about the art of film, and ourselves.

EXTRAS

Be sure that what you've got is this version: *Unforgiven: 10th Anniversary Edition* (two discs).

Disc One has a full-length commentary by Eastwood's biographer and noted critic Richard Schickel. Schickel doesn't patronize the viewer. His remarks are involving and provide a good amount of new information. He is an obvious admirer of the film and of Eastwood's career and talks about the years it took Eastwood to come to this crossroad in his life. Schickel provides solid analysis of the development of the story and the characters.

There are a few other segments you can glance at on Disc One, but most of the action is on Disc Two. You should look at Eastwood's film clips before you pop in the second disc, however.

Disc Two is filled with documentaries and other unexpected surprises.

"All on Accounta Pullin' a Trigger" is narrated by Freeman and has clips, interviews, and chat. It's not long enough to be all that thought-provoking.

"Making *Unforgiven*" dates back to the time of the film's release, but it's likely you didn't see it. Hal Holbrook is the host of this one, and he takes a look at more than we usually get. There's the costume designer, a variety of crew members, and even the animal wrangler. What's good about this feature is the behind-the-scenes stuff, which is generous. There's a bit about Eastwood's career as well.

"Eastwood on Eastwood" is narrated by John Cusack and is a visual filmography. It's not every single movie he's ever been involved in, but it's a pretty big lens.

There's a treat at the end for true Eastwood fans, those who were with him from the beginning. It's an entire episode from the television series *Maverick* with James Garner. The 1959 "Duel at Sundown" showcases the young Eastwood in a supporting part.

As DVD extras go, we give this package a very high mark. Too often, the liner notes suggest great things, and you're let down. This isn't the case here. The features, plus the superior sound and picture quality, make this one a good bet for years to come.

Victor/Victoria

CAST: Julie Andrews, James Garner, Robert Preston, Lesley Ann Warren, Alex Karras, John Rhys-Davies
DIRECTOR: Blake Edwards
SCREENWRITER: Blake Edwards (based on *Viktor und Viktoria*, a film by Rheinhold Schuenzel and Hans Hoemburg)
RELEASED: 1982 (133 minutes)
RATED: Not rated

This sexual identity riddle should more than hold your attention. It's also a tribute to Julie Andrews by her husband, Blake Edwards. It was a gutsy film to make twenty years ago on several counts. While questions of sexual orientation were certainly in the open by the 1980s, there was still considerable wiggle room with regard to cross-dressing and other gender-bending. It's true that it's the same year Dustin Hoffman slammed into town as *Tootsie,* but *Tootsie* was a much simpler premise. Here the conceits are layered, providing a far more complicated plot rhythm. Think *Some Like It Hot* and *Tootsie* rolled together.

It was really Andrews's last big moment as the luminous star she is; her singing voice virtually was lost after this. She's a lovely stage presence, but it was always about that crystalline voice. You'll want this DVD because it is Andrews at her prime. James Garner is as wonderful as ever. Robert Preston is glorious. He deserved the Best Supporting Actor nomination, which he got, and the Oscar, which he did not.

Blake Edwards's broad comedy gets a lavish period production set in 1930s Paris. Although it's spiced up a bit with elaborate musical numbers, it's never as daring as the 1933 German film *Viktor und Viktoria* on which it was based. This revision takes gender confusion as its premise to tell the tale of a woman (Andrews) who masquerades as a female impersonator in order to win notoriety and fame on the cabaret circuit. It's a woman acting like a man acting like a woman.

Everything's fine until she discovers true love in the person of Garner as a visiting Chicago mobster. It's high and low farce all at once; you won't be bored. Besides Andrews and Garner, the zippy support of Preston, Lesley Ann Warren, and Alex Karras keeps the story a consistent diversion.

EXTRAS

The only actual extra is a joint audio commentary by Edwards and Andrews that we adore. In it, you'll learn the rather long literary history of this film, as well as other facts. It seems a pity that although it was nominated for many Oscars, it didn't win, except, of course, for the glorious Henry Mancini score. There's a small treasure hidden under the star on the main menu frame. It's a brief interview with Edwards about Andrews, "Blake on Julie."

Victor/Victoria is a funny film; it is more than it appears at first. Through the years, we've returned to it and each time taken away a little something new. Other films that seem to deliver so much satisfaction at the first viewing sometimes lose their appeal over time. This is just the opposite. It's an enduring story, and *Victor/Victoria* opened on Broadway years after its run as a movie.

Waiting for Guffman

CAST: Christopher Guest, Eugene Levy, Fred Willard, Catherine O'Hara, Parker Posey
DIRECTOR: Christopher Guest
SCREENWRITERS: Christopher Guest and Eugene Levy
RELEASED: 1996 (84 minutes)
RATED: R

It's the one-hundred-fiftieth anniversary of the founding of Blaine, Missouri. Enter Corky St. Clair (Christopher Guest). Corky is going to stage the musical *Red, White and Blaine.* Corky, almost a drag queen, claims to have a wife who never materializes, although his closets are filled with her clothes. Having seen the bright lights of New York but not even the underbelly of a flop on Broadway, he's moved to Blaine.

Blaine was settled mistakenly as part of the California coast, and it's been downhill ever since. A UFO landed, and a president received a wooden stool, making Blaine the stool capital of the country.

Guffman is delicious vaudeville at times. It isn't less

funny than *Best in Show,* but it is less sophisticated. Eugene Levy plays the town dentist, and Fred Willard is a travel agent who doesn't travel but did require a delicate surgical procedure.

Comedy abounds, and inevitably a few of the gags are labored. Who is Guffman? He's the man dreams are made of, the New York agent. Is *Red, White and Blaine* Broadway-bound? You'll see, but on the way to resolution, you'll have many laughs and sighs about the human condition.

EXTRAS

"Additional Scenes" are all worth watching. "Shirley Temple," number 12, is a hoot.

"Director's Commentary" is not a big payoff, optional viewing.

"Behind the Scenes" is quite rewarding, and you do find out the true location of Blaine.

The Way We Were

CAST: Robert Redford, Barbra Streisand, Viveca Lindfors, Bradford Dilman, Lois Chiles, Patrick O'Neal, Allyn Ann McLerie, Murray Hamilton, Herb Edelman
DIRECTOR: Sydney Pollack
SCREENWRITER: Arthur Laurents (adapted from his novel)
RELEASED: 1973 (118 minutes)
RATED: PG

This film is something between an "airplane movie" (see *You've Got Mail)* and a romantic classic. It's not Sydney Pollack's best work; it's hardly Robert Redford's. But somehow it stays on the list of favorites. In the end, despite its flaws, there's something about it that endures.

Perhaps because it was released during the political tumult of the 1970s, people often forget that the setting for *The Way We Were* is the 1930s through the 1950s. These decades took in everything from Hitler to Hollywood's blacklisting, and so does *The Way We Were*. The really important parts of the blacklisting story were ultimately left out of the script, which is too bad. (Pollack knows that story cold.)

Redford and Barbra Streisand have an incredible chemistry on the screen. Redford doesn't do all that much except look the part he was cast to play, a proper WASP, Hubbell Gardner. Streisand acts her heart out as Katie Morosky. You could say Streisand is playing herself as well, but she puts so much into her performance. Katie is a radical lefty Jewish girl who meets Gardner in college. They are certainly not meant for each other, but eventually, it looks as though the inevitable attempt to mix water and oil will be attempted. As the years after college unfold, they become a couple.

The movie follows their romance and relationship until its end. What breaks them apart is blacklisting, which did, in fact break apart many lives. It's the most honest part of the story. Unfortunately, it gets short shrift in the plot's development. There's plenty of political dialogue but too little about what really happened during this bleak period in American politics in general and the entertainment industry in particular. But then there is that Marvin Hamlisch score and the Marilyn and Alan Bergman lyrics, so one can be forgiving.

It's hard to beat the universal appeal of the ultimately ill-matched romance. You know you're being manipulated, but it's such a classy romance. The last scene remains one of the true weepers. If only Streisand hadn't reached out to touch those golden Redford locks, you might have been able to laugh it all off. But you can't.

Streisand was nominated for Best Actress but lost to Glenda Jackson in *A Touch of Class*, proving that winning the Oscar isn't everything, because it's this film that most people remember.

EXTRAS

What you get in the "Special Edition" is an excellent transfer. This is important for Redford fans in particular. Who wants to look at a fuzzy and grainy Redford?

You also get the following subtitles: German, French, Czech, Danish, Dutch, Finnish, Greek, Hebrew, Hungarian, Icelandic, Norwegian, Polish, Swedish, Turkish, Hindi, and Arabic. The proliferation of subtitle choices simply attests to the movie's global appeal. The notion of politically incompatible lovers is perhaps more timely now than ever before.

The audio commentary by Pollack has many lapses in it but is still worth a quick listen. Pollack seems determined to summarize the story for us instead of revealing what it was like to direct the film. Don't fret, because your frustration is quickly remedied by watching the real bonus of the features, "Looking Back," a full-length documentary about the making of the film.

"Looking Back" has much to offer. There are some terrific scenes deleted from the film that finally can be seen. You'll also hear writer Arthur Laurents; his remarks are a big help toward a fuller understanding of the film's origins. Hamlisch and the Bergmans talk about their music and a variety of struggles among Streisand, Pollack, and the musical trio. These may be just cinematic footnotes, but they are quite entertaining. Pollack is so much better on this documentary than on his audio that he is almost a different person. He is open, somewhat vulnerable, and often touching as he talks about his techniques. Streisand is less forthcoming than we anticipated. You won't find Redford anywhere on the commentaries, which is a shame.

For Streisand fans, we recommend *The Prince of Tides*, which is available on DVD as well. (It's a pity that her inventive *Yentl* is still not on disc.)

Prince of Tides is another look at the ill-matched couple. This time, it is the "way we are" instead of "were." It's based on Pat Conroy's novel of the same name. Streisand directed and played the lead. The book tells a powerful story of Southern family ties and family angst. The action develops around the suicide attempt of a Southern woman transplanted to New York. Melinda Dillon plays Savannah Wingo, who is being treated by a distinguished Manhattan psychiatrist, Susan Lowenstein (Streisand). Savannah's devoted brother, Tom, comes to New York to find out what's going on with his sister's health and meets with her doctor. The brother is Nick Nolte. Disregarding every professional standard, Lowenstein allows herself to become involved with Tom Wingo. They fall deeply in love. She's the shrink; they're both married. He lives in the South; she lives in New York. It's another doomed choice for our hero Barbra.

The cast is a good one and includes Blythe Danner, Kate Nelligan, Jeroen Krabbe (as Streisand's completely inappropriate husband), and Jason Gould (Streisand's son) as Streisand's son.

Here we have Nolte and Streisand as we had Redford and Streisand. This time, it's the reverse problem. Nolte delivers a towering performance, and Streisand is mediocre. However, her directing is sublime. If you're not familiar with Conroy's novels, they aren't the easiest to adapt to the screen. Streisand, armed with Conroy's screenplay in hand, did a first-class job.

Nolte received an Oscar nomination for Best Actor but lost to Anthony Hopkins in *The Silence of the Lambs*. The film itself was nominated for Best Picture but also lost out to *Lambs*. Streisand was not nominated for Best Director, which seemed unfair then, as it does now.

The extras on *Prince of Tides* are minimal. There's only a standard cast and crew profile setup and the ubiquitous trailers (including one for *The Way We Were*). There's a printed booklet in the case, however, which does provide some interesting remarks about the movie. If you want to see Streisand direction, you'll want this. But mostly, you want this for Nolte's portrayal of Tom Wingo. He surely would have won an Oscar had *Silence of the Lambs* been in a different year.

West Side Story

CAST: Natalie Wood, Richard Beymer, George Chakiris, Rita
    Moreno, Russ Tamblyn, Tucker Smith, David Winters, Tony
    Mordente, Simon Oakland, Ned Glass, Willliam Bramley, Eliot
    Feld, Bert Michaels, David Bean, Robert Banas
DIRECTORS: Robert Wise and Jerome Robbins
SCREENWRITER: Ernest Lehman (based on the play by Arthur
    Laurents)
RELEASED: 1961 (152 minutes)
RATED: Not rated

At the time of its release in 1961, *West Side Story* already had been a wildly successful Broadway musical. At first, there was some concern about how this remarkable urban musical ballet of the story of Romeo and Juliet would look on the screen. Would it still have its vitality, its edge of danger? Would the drama still hold?

Proving the fim's longevity as a great classic, MGM released its DVD collector's edition in April 2003. (Previous editions have been very disappointing.) Understanding the demand, the studio has given it full-star treatment.

For many of us, *West Side Story* was our own love affair. If you're a boomer who didn't grow up in the sophistication of Manhattan, count the weddings where you heard music from this hit sung at some interval in the ceremony. Often, those words, "One Hand, One Heart," could grip you in later life and make you giggle.

But we weren't about to giggle then. This was serious, edgy ballet drama, and parts of it were frightening. What was going to happen between the Jets and the Sharks? The bloodshed, which we are now so accustomed to seeing, was, in fact, a searing moment in the film.

Would *West Side Story* now just look like a relic from your grandmother's attic? Are we inured to violence and intergroup hatreds? Manhattan isn't the Manhattan of *West Side Story* for all the reasons we know too well. Mostly, we were afraid the movie would look precious and sentimental, maybe even goofy. All those folks dancing around and singing songs while police officers danced along? Would anyone still buy this?

Of course, we were very wrong. From the first dreamlike ballet sequence Jerome Robbins choreographed, all time slips away. You see *West Side Story* as if for the first time and, perhaps, as if in a dream. The Jets gang members dance the urban ballet sequence that opens the film. (The graffiti on a wall that states "Sharks Stink" serves as a decade clock.) It's slow and beautiful, and you get with the landmark film right away. *West Side Story* remains our Romeo and Juliet, just as the creators had hoped.

It's not what's happening with kids or urban areas now; it's what happens on that screen between these beautiful young actors that ignites the imagination. The love story of a girl from one ethnic group and a boy from another is the human story. The price to be paid for loving across these lines screams at us because it still happens.

Nothing about *West Side Story* ever seemed out of context; it remained, even in its most dramatic and violent scenes, an opera, a ballet, a musical, an eternal love story.

Stephen Sondheim was a young man when he wrote the lyrics to songs like "Maria," "Tonight," "A Place for Us," "America." They have stayed in our collective consciousness for more than forty years. Sondheim has gracefully taken us with him on his own life's adventure, giving us many subsequent theatrical joys. But this isn't to minimize the marvel of what he accomplished here.

West Side Story ends with almost the same twist as *Romeo and Juliet.* Only a slight alteration was needed to make you believe you were in 1950s New York and not in the middle of Shakespeare's manuscript. But all in all, it is the same story. Love doesn't conquer all when hate is busy working overtime. The kids hang out at a soda store owned by Doc, played by Ned Glass. He finally loses his patience and says to them, "You kids make this world lousy. When will you stop?" Last time we looked, adults were making the world lousy for kids. When will we stop? At least we have this masterpiece to use as a subtle teaching tool for our youngest preteens about what intolerance can do.

It's a rare feat to make a heartbreaking tragedy in a tough urban setting that still comes out as a piece of exquisite entertainment. You can thank Leonard Bernstein, Sondheim, and Robbins for that, along with the excellent help of director Robert Wise and a terrific cast. Natalie Wood shimmers off the screen, reminding us of the translucent and intense quality of her beauty; those who more or less grew up with her feel her loss here.

It's hard to know just where the place is that everyone can love and be loved. But as we hear the closing lines from that great song, we pray that Robbins and Bernstein have found it. They certainly belong in musical heaven for giving us *West Side Story*.

The movie swept the Oscars. It won Best Picture, won Best Direction, Best Supporting Actress (Rita Moreno), and Best Supporting Actor (George Chakiris). If you follow these tidbits, remember that Wood received an Oscar nomination for Best Actress, but it was for her work in *Splendor in the Grass*. No matter. Sophia Loren couldn't be beaten; she won for *Two Women*. However, *West Side Story* took away ten Oscars.

The Sharks and the Jets, the tough street gangs, aren't sinister any longer. Their differences seem minimal and their behavior (with the exception of the murders) almost benign. You feel that even policemen could deal with these kids. The world has continued at a pace far beyond the imaginations of Robbins, Sondheim, Bernstein, and author Laurents. And that sadly, is not for the better.

Maria is played by Wood; her Romeo, Tony, by Richard Beymer; Jets leader Riff by Russ Tamblyn; Anita by the unforgettable Rita Moreno; and Bernardo by George Chakiris. The supporting cast and the ensemble dancers and actors all made *West Side Story* perfect.

The dialogue is rusty, and maybe your younger friends will hoot in places, but they will sit very still for the unsurpassed dance routines, as well as for the ravishing Bernstein score. It is a very welcome trip down Memory Lane for many of the rest of us.

EXTRAS

The restored transfer in the deluxe DVD (Special Edition DVD Collector's Set, issued by MGM Home Entertainment) is dazzling. The kick is back in the kinetic musical. Watch yourself, or you'll be snapping your fingers and looking for a chain-link fence to vault. The energy of the film returns with the same force it had in the original theatrical release.

Bonus features include: "West Side Memories," which gives a behind-the-scenes look at the making of the film. We see the processes and difficulties that came about during filming; the choreography; the development of the music and lyrics; and the amount of exacting work that went into making each scene. We see the original storyboards for the film and the selection and development of the sets.

Marni Nixon ultimately gave voice to Wood's sweet rendition of "I Feel Pretty," but finally you can see the footage of Wood singing. "West Side Memories" is a new documentary, and runs an hour in length.

The storyboard-to-film comparison montage is done well. It's a continuous play of the storyboards cut with the final scene of the movie, while the musical score plays along. It runs about five minutes.

The goodies in the case include a souvenir scrapbook with an autograph of screenwriter Ernest Lehman, as well as other collectibles for the pack rat in all of us.

When Harry Met Sally

CAST: Billy Crystal, Meg Ryan, Carrie Fisher, Bruno Kirby, Steven Ford, Lisa Jane Persky, Michelle Nicastro, Estelle Reiner
DIRECTOR: Rob Reiner
SCREENWRITER: Nora Ephron
RELEASED: 1989 (95 minutes)
RATED: R

Would you own a movie for just one scene? Probably not, unless it's Meg Ryan and Billy Crystal in the deli scene.

When Harry Met Sally is a souvenir from the freshly postfeminist moment when everybody was confused. Being single wasn't what it was cracked up to be for some, but you weren't supposed to come right out and say it. Women were howling at jokes made at men's expense, all the while hoping to find Mr. Right or Mr. Right Now and shackle themselves inside an institution they were supposed to resent. The newspapers said that the chances of a woman over forty finding a husband were less than those for being attacked by a terrorist.

Nora Ephron was in many ways the comic voice of that time. It began with her excruciatingly funny and painful book *Heartburn,* based on the breakup of her own marriage. Ephron is always quotable. It's therefore annoying that this film has been compared so often to Woody Allen's films. Allen has made such an indelible imprint on moviegoers that the rights to Manhattan-based romantic comedies presumably are owned by him. Doesn't anybody out there get it? We're New Yorkers; we are all neurotics. Give Ephron a break.

Harry and Sally met in college and were casual pals, nothing more. They drove to Manhattan together when they graduated from the University of Chicago. They do well at annoying each other. She goes off to a career; he goes off to a career. They run into each other from time to time. Is this a movie or your basic Manhattan life? She has relationships and breakups. He has a marriage and an impending divorce. Finally, they decide they should be real friends. They won't have sex, of course, because then they couldn't be friends. It's back and forth and around the block; it is going to end with a wedding. Getting there is a joy.

It captures a moment many of us lived. Some of us got married, and some of us moved on to the next Harry or

Sally in our lives. Few of us were ever as witty as Ephron. We just thought we were. This movie is dialogue-driven, and what sparkling, acerbic talk it is. The deli scene where Sally fakes an orgasm holds up as one of the best side-splitters in movie history. By the way, the older female customer sitting at the table next to them, who quips "I'll have what she's having," is Rob Reiner's mother, Estelle Reiner, wife of Carl.

EXTRAS

We assume you're not such a spendthrift that you would buy a movie for just one scene rather than renting it overnight. So, if you've waited to satisfy your desires on this one, you're in good time. There is now a special edition that has supplements beyond Rob Reiner's labored commentary, the only feature available on the earlier releases. How could such a funny man and good director offer such boring commentary? Ephron needs to coach him.

The special edition has a "making of" documentary called "When Harry Met Sally." The reason the dialogue sounds so natural is that they took it from their friends' comments and stories about their own lives. Ephron and Reiner also talk about how they drew from their lives. Reiner is relaxed when paired with Ephron. They're obviously a good working team.

Reiner was a single man for ten years, and he was apparently in a fog for much of that time. Ephron is a close personal friend; they traded confidences. Then along came another pal, Andrew Scheinman, who had his own schtick (he co-produced the movie). Reiner began to see that single adults were experiencing similar growing pains on the road to new relationships. He saw Ephron, and he saw a movie. This documentary is one of the most interesting ones available on DVD. It's almost as much fun as the movie itself.

You'll learn that Meg Ryan came later to the group of buddies, but she added the essential element. Guess which one.

You'll need to take a pulse while watching or listening to the director's commentary. He needed more caffeine that day. There are some tasty morsels to be had if you've don't nod off. Which former U.S. president's son played one of Ryan's boyfriends? What was the original ending of the film? Who was the driving force behind certain editorial decisions? No, we won't tell you the answers. We had to listen to him, and so do you. It's a small tribute to pay to a director's first-rate job.

Afterward, reward yourself. There's a music video with a very young Harry Connick, Jr. (This is before he met Grace, in *Will and Grace . . .*)

X-Men

CAST: Hugh Jackman, Patrick Stewart, Ian McKellen, Famke
    Janssen, James Marsden, Halle Berry, Anna Paquin, Tyler Mane,
    Ray Park, Rebecca Romijn-Stamos, Bruce Davison
DIRECTOR: Bryan Singer
SCREENWRITERS: Bryan Singer and Tom DeSanto
RELEASED: 2000 (104 minutes)
RATED: PG-13

If you have not been a lifelong fan of the comic-book series *X-Men,* this movie may be harder for you to enjoy than for those who have been. *X-Men* first made their appearance in Marvel Comics in 1964 and sprang from the fertile minds of Stan Lee and Jack Kirby. One of the best comic-book series ever, its characters appear much more real than those in some of the other classic comics.

The *X-Men* are superheroes who fight against evil. They

are also characters who must deal with the same day-to-day problems that anyone who is different might face. As a result, this comic series was a huge success among teenagers, young adults, and anyone who felt the pain of being different, such as those who belong to racial and or religious minorities. *X-Men* is entertaining for anyone who appreciates a good comic-book series.

Here's a brief summary of the story of *X-Men*. Over several thousand years of evolution, human beings evolved. But the last evolutionary leap resulted in hundreds of mutations within the human race that produced beings possessing powers of unlimited possibility. These individuals are unaware of their unique abilities until puberty. It is at this time that their superpowers first present themselves and are usually out of control. (Think of the young rattlesnake that doesn't know how to control the amount of venom it uses.) The special creatures are feared and often hated by the rest of the population. But not all of them go into hiding. Two separate mutant groups organize themselves to help fight the oppression of the human race.

One group is led by Professor Charles Xavier (Patrick Stewart) or Professor X, who runs a school for gifted youngsters. Here the children learn how to develop and control their powers. He is assisted by the *X-Men:* former students Scott Summers (James Marsden), known as Cyclops because of the powerful and destructive rays that come from his eyes; Ororo Munroe (Halle Berry), known as Storm for her ability to control the weather; and Dr. Jean Grey (Famke Janssen), who has the ability of telekinesis. This group is politically active in fighting for the rights of mutants. Jean Grey is the spokesman for the group but doesn't reveal her powers.

The other group is led by an old friend of the professor, Erik Lehnsherr (Ian McKellen), known as Magneto for his abilities to control metal. A victim of the Holocaust, Magneto has come to hate the human race for its intolerance and is assisted by the Brotherhood of Mutants. There is Sabertooth (Tyler Mane), with an enormous prehistoric cat appearance and incredible strength; Toad (Ray Park), who has a very long, quick tongue and can leap large distances and spit venom; Mystique (Rebecca Romijn-Stamos), who can shift her shape into anyone or anything. Magneto plans to conquer and destroy the human race so that mutants can live freely and without prejudice.

In the meantime, one of the movie's best and most well-developed characters is introduced. Logan (Hugh Jackman), who is known as Wolverine (his appearance explains that one), has incredible regenerative powers to heal himself. His entire skeletal structure has a rare metal called adamantium fused to it, complete with retractable claws that come out of his hands. This feature was not a natural mutation; he was the victim of vile experimentation. He has no memory of how he became this way or what happened to him during the last fourteen years.

With a lower budget than was needed, this film had a hard time pulling it all together but succeeds overall. Unfortunately, many of the classic X-Men characters had to be left out, and Cyclops and Storm were not developed fully. With their fine acting talents, Stewart and McKellen brought an unexpected level of excellence to X-Men. However, the star of the film is Jackman. His portrayal of Wolverine is superb; his character is the most developed of all the X-Men.

It was difficult to make a movie that could appeal to lifelong fans as well as newcomers. The entire first half deals with the introduction of the storyline and all the characters and their powers. (This is terrific for those who have never heard of X-Men but can be annoying for those who know the story well.) After that, there wasn't as much time for the plot to develop appropriately within the time confines of the film. The result is a somewhat anticlimactic ending. However, the movie followed the original storyline of the *X-Men* well and gets high marks for making a workable cinematic compromise. Fans will be happy to know the film includes the love triangle of Jean Grey, her boyfriend Cyclops, and Wolverine, who truly loves her.

Here and there, Wolverine bantering with Cyclops provides a few bits of comic relief. If you know the comic books, the movie has several inside jokes. This is only the first film installment of *X-Men;* the sequel came out in 2003. With the plot and characters in place, the next movie will have more time and undoubtedly a bigger budget to create an *X-Men* story that will be sure to please all.

If this is all foreign to you but you're an action-comic fan, this is an easy way to become addicted to the *X-Men* saga. If you aren't satisfied with the ending, don't give up hope yet, because the next one may blow you away.

EXTRAS
There's impeccable sound quality as well as picture transfer, although the extras are somewhat lacking. There are some deleted scenes, but nothing close to the touted forty-five minutes director Bryan Singer cut from the film. There's an interview with Singer, but you have to keep pushing play to go from one segment to the next, as opposed to a continuous play function.

The menus are complicated and too busy. They can be frustrating to navigate. There are a few eggs on this DVD worth looking at, but nothing spectacular. One gives you sketches of two other *X-Men* characters that were not used in the film. Access the gallery art section, and highlight Wolverine's dotages. Another egg is accessible from the theatrical trailer page: highlight trailer A, don't press enter, and instead press the left button on your remote. This gives you a clip of *Spiderman* interacting with the *X-Men*. On the same option, if you highlight the rose in the background, you get a cameo clip of another Marvel comic.

The special edition DVD, however, is a different story. Released in February 2003, this two-disc set gives more than four hours of bonus features. Disc One gives the option to watch the movie in its original layout or with all the deleted scenes.

The presentation is still not pristine technically. As in the first release, you are given a cue during certain parts of the movie, and then you must hit enter on your remote to view the extra scene. If you choose, you can hear commentary from the director play while the bonus scene plays. After the scene plays, you are taken back to where you received the cue. The scenes themselves are highly enjoyable, but they would have been better made into their own special feature rather than attempting to fold them awkwardly into the movie. There is also a commentary feature on this disc that allows you to watch the movie with a behind-the-scenes feature. Again, you are given a cue to hit enter. It's all terribly cumbersome; it is also a highly ironic setup for a movie about critters with superhuman powers. Obviously, no *X-Men* were involved in the production of the discs.

There's good news on Disc Two, which is much better than the first, with menus that are easy to navigate. There are lots of scenes with written text, and some of it is hard to read. The text style, color, and font size could have been better chosen, but the material you get is worth the effort to see and read. You'll find a sneak preview of *X-Men 2* and a theatrical trailer. (There's a trailer for *Daredevil* as well.)

The "Evolution X" feature gives you a "making of" documentary that can be played all at once or by selecting

desired scenes from the index menu. There is also a huge
section on all the characters and cast, "The Uncanny Suspects." This section gives you Jackman's first screen test,
which is very funny. It also shows how they developed the
look of each character and how the film was cast. An art
gallery shows the original design ideas for the characters. A
special effects option gives a more intimate look at some of
the movie's biggest scenes. There's very interesting footage
about how the mutant powers of the characters were
brought to the screen. The final feature is "Reflection of the
X-Men," which follows the cast around to the film's world
premieres.

Y Tu Mamá También

CAST: Maribel Verdú, Gael Garcia Bernal, Diego Luna, Marta Aura,
   Diana Bracho, Emilio Echevarria, Griselle Audirac, Verónica
   Langer, Arturo Ríos, Ana López Mercado, Nathan Grinberg,
   María Aura, Andrés Almeida, Liboria Rodríguez, Juan Carlos
   Remolina
DIRECTOR: Alfonso Cuarón
SCREENWRITERS: Alfonso Cuarón and Carlos Cuarón
RELEASED: 2001 (105 minutes)
RATED: R *(cut)*, not rated *(uncut)*

Introduce yourself to two young men, Tenoch and Julio,
who have been friends since childhood. The film is set in
contemporary Mexico. Tenoch comes from an upper-class
family; Julio's family struggles in the working class. As the
film begins, the boys have just graduated from high school
and are saying goodbye to their girlfriends, who are on
their way to Italy for the summer. With the girlfriends
away, the boys are determined to fill their summer with pot

smoking, drinking, and the eternal quest for sex, even if it mostly means masturbation. At a cousin's wedding, we meet the film's third, but crucial, character, Luisa Cortes. She's the wife of one of Tenoch's many cousins and is from Spain.

She is beautiful, worldly, elegant, and also about ten years older than they are. The boys are instantly attracted to her. The hilarious scene at the wedding where they try to impress her as they fumble around is a classic. While her cool demeanor keeps them from being too forward, they are most anxious to be in her company. She inquires about things to do and see in Mexico, especially the beaches. The boys tell her about an enchanted beach that they have decided to go to over the weekend, which they call Heaven's Mouth. They describe it to her in great detail; it's a secluded beach, with white sands and clear waters. Of course, they have no idea what they are talking about but invite her anyway. She doesn't understand it is a fantasy, but as she has no intention of going away with them, it doesn't seem to matter at that point.

Her husband is away, and one evening she receives a phone call from him. He's been drinking, and he begins to cry over the phone and to confess his infidelity. After his confession and her heartbreak, she suddenly feels a sense of liberation and decides to go on the excursion with the boys. They are caught completely off-guard by her phone call. But ever eager to please, and with their hormones raging, the boys pick her up and set off on an adventure. (First there is a very complex negotiation to obtain an automobile. It's incredibly amusing, and we won't spoil it for you.)

They have no idea where they are going. They have no idea what they are going to do with this older woman they both have a crush on. But they proceed as if they haven't a care in the world. Prior to the trip, there's another howling scene with maps and advice. This journey to a beach that doesn't exist with a gorgeous woman who has been betrayed by her husband sets the movie's mood and tempo. This is a road trip movie the likes of which you won't see again soon.

During their trip, we view the Mexican countryside. A haunting off-camera narration tells of the political problems and poverty of Mexico, as well as throwing in some surreal asides. The cinematography is outstanding. We are also given a bit of insight into the thoughts of the characters as they drive together.

The main story is the relationship that forms between the two boys and Luisa. Her demeanor has changed considerably since their first encounter. She is funny, witty, and not at all as she had been around her uptight, pompous husband. She quizzes the boys relentlessly about their activities, their girlfriends, and their sex lives. Some sexual tension starts to build, because she is very explicit about her questions and wants lots of details.

Luisa starts to tell them things she thinks they need to know in order to be men and real lovers. They are all very candid and comfortable with one another. They make jokes about everything from masturbation to farting. And while it's obvious the boys are clueless, you accept and love them as Luisa does. It doesn't sound that appealing on paper, but there is a sensuality and a sexuality that pervade this film. It's an exceedingly erotic film that constantly surprises.

This is one of those rare movies that ends up being far more than you expected; it's not just entertaining but filled with vitality. The ending catches you up, and we won't even whisper a sentence about that.

It's a movie that delivers important messages about love and life, but it is so intertwined with the humor and sex of the story that it never bogs down. *Y Tu Mamá También* doesn't get in its own way, as is the case with so many other films that have attempted a similar theme. This one's not trying to prove anything or make a point, and because of that, it does both superbly. Another welcome thing about *También* is its open and refreshing view of sex. The comfort with which the three experience and discover one another is filled with acceptance of faults and joy at the marvels of human individuality.

EXTRAS

The special features are simple and great. There is a short, sexy, comedic film by the director's brother and cowriter, Carlos Cuarón, that is wonderful and absolutely required watching. There are three deleted scenes. A commentary feature lets you watch the film while listening to the commentary of Gael Garcia Bernal, who plays Julio, Diego Luna, who plays Tenoch, and director Alfonso Cuarón. (Unless you can understand Spanish fairly decently, you won't get much from this feature. But if you do, it's hilarious. The boys and the director tear apart the whole film, making jokes about everyone and everything.)

There is also a "making of" feature that's extremely well done. It contains footage of the filming. It appears they all had as much fun making the film as the characters had on their voyage of self-discovery.

You've Got Mail

CAST: Tom Hanks, Meg Ryan, Greg Kinnear, Parker Posey, Jean
    Stapleton
DIRECTOR: Nora Ephron
SCREENWRITER: Nora Ephron (adapted from the play *Parfumerie*
    by Miklos Laszlo)
RELEASED: 1998 (120 minutes)
RATED: PG

It's Friday night, and it's been one of those weeks. Nothing disastrous has happened in your life, but nothing has worked out quite right, either. You're drained from attending to a million pesky details that never seem to end. You've had several meetings canceled, postponed, or rearranged. You're tired; your family and friends are annoying you. Or (perish the thought) you might be annoying them.

It's time for comfort food. It's a macaroni-and-cheese kind of night, quick to fix but so satisfying. You want to watch something on DVD, but you don't know what. You certainly don't want to be scared or challenged. You don't want to have to follow difficult storylines. More than anything, you want everything in the movie to work out perfectly. No, you want everything in the movie to work out exquisitely. It would be good to laugh a little, maybe cry just a tear or two. It would be awfully nice if there were a dog in it, or a cat.

We call this genre "airplane movies." You're stuck on a long flight; you're overtired and don't really want to work. Or in the rush to get to the airport, you realize you've forgotten the book you were halfway through. You're not tired enough to snooze, and you surely don't want to talk to the person sitting next to you. You retreat into the airplane's movie. (Usually, the airplane movie offering is a great deal more comforting and reassuring than the food they serve you on flights these days.)

So what do you need on your home DVD library shelf for a night like this? *You've Got Mail.*

We actually saw this film for the first time on some endless flight and found it entertaining and strictly "movie lite." But when we saw that the DVD version had a few interesting feature gimmicks, we gave it another try. It's so frothy it evaporates as fast the foam on your overpriced cappuccino. But it holds its own very nicely in its featherweight division. The story and the characters grow on you.

Nora Ephron couldn't lose with this one. She put together an A team of actors, all of whom obviously delighted in their roles. She had the charming 1940 film, *The Shop Around the Corner* (with James Stewart and Margaret Sullavan) as a foundation for the story (based on the Miklos Laszlo play). Meg Ryan's character is Kathleen Kennedy, who owns a small and beloved children's bookstore, which her mother (now deceased) founded. Tom Hanks plays Joe Fox, a young bookstore chain tycoon, who is the grandson of an even bigger tycoon. His family corporation is going to open up a mega-bookstore right around the corner from hers. It's the inevitable death knell for her business. The two meet and hate each other; actually, she loathes him.

She seeks advice and comfort at home, online. There she's known as *shopgirl*. Soon they become friends through a chat room. She confides all her business problems to him, and he returns her e-mail messages with excellent suggestions. Just as in *The Shop Around the Corner,* each has no idea who the other is. But that doesn't last long in this rendition.

He figures it out before she does. The only truly scary part of this movie is Parker Posey, who plays Joe Fox's nasty-tempered girlfriend, Patricia. (She is reprising her role in *Best in Show,* but she's given far fewer laugh lines here. We're meant to despise her.) Kathleen's boyfriend isn't just a standard-issue egotist; he's also politically incorrect. We know his fate.

It's going to end just the way movies like this were made to end. You'll be happy. They'll be happy. She will forgive him even though her bookstore will close (like all the other independent bookstores). You'll be happy if you're in the right mood. You'll have your macaroni and cheese piping hot from the microwave. (It's best to stir once and put it back again for a minute.) There is, of course, a dog, a great big sloppy, love-me-love-me dog that belongs to Joe. Did we mention an adorable pair of little kids?

Ephron is capable of far more than this. *You've Got Mail* works well within its limitations. Our only complaint is that Ephron is overly fascinated with her ability to write snappy lines. The dialogue is too predictable, which makes the two lead characters more like cardboard cutouts of the perfect West Side couple than real people. But do you really care?

No, you don't. You've got your comfort food. You've got your comfort movie. You've got Hanks and Ryan, who are actually together on screen for more than five minutes this time. You've got some lovingly photographed street and shop scenes in Manhattan. You're happy. That is the point of comfort food. It always works.

Ephron's earlier film with Hanks and Ryan, *Sleepless in Seattle,* is also an airplane movie. We think *Sleepless* is probably the movie they play in first class, though, because there is a bit more meat to the story.

You don't need to have shelves and shelves of airplane movies in your DVD library. You need just a few that sparkle for what they are. Those few can sustain you through a cold winter, a bad cold, a bad hair day, or just when you're feeling generally crummy.

EXTRAS

The extras are appropriate to the movie. Think of an old-fashioned cupcake with gobs of butter cream frosting on top. That's what these extras are. Nothing demanding, just the dessert course.

This time, we started with something other than the audio commentary when viewing the features, and it was a welcome change. The "HBO First Look" with Ephron is great. We liked the tour of New York's Upper West Side. This is well done and highly entertaining. Ephron takes you through her neighborhood in a rather special way. Ephron and producer Lauren Shuler-Donner are on the full-length audio commentary. If you have a DVD-ROM feature in your PC, there are any number of goofy but amusing things to see and do. We especially liked the scene comparisons with *The Shop around the Corner* and its sister, the musical *In the Good Old Summertime.* (While the disc is still in your DVD player, however, do watch the original vintage trailers for those classics.) If you don't have DVD-ROM capacity or want to stay on the screen, some of this can be found in the HBO documentary. Hidden brief interviews are located on the scene selection menu. Try 57, 58, 59, and 60.

There's also access to chat rooms with the DVD-ROM capability. We didn't activate that special feature. After all, we're married. But if you're single, you might try it. Perhaps your Meg or Tom is out there in cyberspace waiting for your message.

Zelig

CAST: Woody Allen, Mia Farrow
DIRECTOR: Woody Allen
SCREENWRITER: Woody Allen
RELEASED: 1983 (79 minutes)
RATED: PG

Z is for *Zelig*, who appeared everywhere but really was nowhere.

Welcome to Woody Allen's rendition of a mockumentary using historical footage as well as interviews with living stars and famous people. It's audacious and witty. Basically a sendup of the newsreel format, with an underlying theme about the twentieth century's need to be famous, in the Warhol sense, if only for fifteen minutes.

Allen is Leonard Zelig, an ultra-conformist whose fame is achieved for being able to adapt physically and mentally to any situation by changing his appearance. The cinematic cleverness is what provides the laughter. There's Zelig with Chaplin, Babe Ruth, and Hitler, too. Remember that the always innovative Allen startled us by meeting deceased celebrities long before Robert Zemeckis did the same thing in the sappy *Forrest Gump*, where Tom Hanks was shaking hands with President Kennedy. Our timid pal also is seen with the pope at the Vatican and at a glamorous garden party hosted by writer F. Scott Fitzgerald.

It's not Allen's best film, but it's his most inventive and unusual visually. It's comic and sad all at once. Mia Farrow plays Dr. Eudora Fletcher, who tries to cure him but falls in love with him.

EXTRAS

As usual with Woody Allen films, you get very little besides the film itself. All you get here is the theatrical trailer. Unless you want to invest in the entire Allen collection, which is boxed in volumes (three sets by now), you can buy each separately. It's entertaining, an Allen entry that fills out our suggested Allen choices. Besides, where else can you hear Nobel Prize–winning novelist Saul Bellow say, "He was, of course, very amusing, but at the same time touched a nerve in people, perhaps in a way in which they prefer not to be touched."

Hot Dogs and Ice Cream Cones:
The Best DVDs for Kids

Remember when a hot dog could turn a regular day into a routine one? Or when the whole world could be made good again by just one ice cream cone with the right sprinkles on the top of it?

Movies do that for children, and for adults too. Although we have attempted to give you a guide for building a varied adult DVD library, there are a number of films for the younger viewer in the book. These include: *Billy Elliot; E.T.; Harry Potter; Lord of the Rings; The Secret of Roan Inish; Shrek; Singin' in the Rain; The Sound Of Music;* and *Star Wars.* Here are a few more DVD's we recommend highly for the younger audience. They are: *Babe; Fly Away Home; Kolya; Lady and the Tramp; The Lion King; Monsters, Inc.; Snow White and the Seven Dwarfs; Stuart Little; Toy Story;* and *The Wizard of Oz.*

Babe

CAST: (Voices): Christine Cavanaugh, Miriam Margolyes, Danny Mann, Hugo Weaving, Miriam Flynn, Russie Taylor, Evelyn Krape, Michael Edward-Stevens, Charles Bartlett, Paul Livingston, Roscoe Lee Brown

(Live): James Cromwell, Magda Szubansk, Zoe Burton, Paul Goddard

DIRECTOR: Chris Noonan

SCREENWRITERS: George Miller and Chris Noonan (from the novel by Dick King-Smith)

RELEASED: 1995 (89 minutes)

RATED: G

Everyone thinks the grass is always greener in the other pasture. But who could have known a pig would think so, too? Babe is a pig raised by a friendly border collie. The dog decides this little piglet, who somehow didn't end up at the market, should be one of her puppies. Whatever Babe's original destination, she has a natural ability to herd. She really wants to herd and not end up as a sandwich at a farm picnic lunch. She goes far with a gentle word and a loving set of human and animal relatives. *Babe* was a box-office sensation for good reason. It won the Oscar for Best Visual Effects. What is the message of *Babe?* Strive high; be kind; never give up. Sounds like a good motto for all of us. (Subtitles are available in Spanish.)

Fly Away Home

CAST: Jeff Daniels, Anna Paquin, Dana Delany, Terry Kinney, Holter Graham, Jeremy Ratchford, Deborah Verginella, Michael J. Reynolds, David Hemblen, Nora Ballard, Serena Paton, Christi Hill, Carmen Lishman
DIRECTOR: Carroll Ballard
SCREENWRITER: Robert Rodat (from the book by Bill Lishman)
RELEASED: 1996 (110 minutes)
RATED: PG

No, you should not let your children fly a small plane from the North to the South so that their pet geese won't die in the winter's cold. But you should let them see this film. Treat it as pure fantasy; it might help you later on with family arguments. It's a bit on the sentimental side, but it's beautiful visually. You get Anna Paquin and Jeff Daniels together as father and daughter. It's a wonderful tale about a father who might not be quite glued down all the way. His daughter has a spirit of adventure and love of animals. Yes, birds do count as animals.

The extras are wonderful. They consist of two documentary features adults will find compelling. We particularly liked "The Ultra Geese," the documentary behind the movie. Director Carroll Ballard and cinematographer Caleb Deschanel provide an enjoyable audio commentary. There's quite an amusing tale or two about stars Paquin and Daniels.

Kolya

CAST: Zdenek Sverak, Andrei Chalimon, Lubuse Safrankova,
Ondrej Vetchy, Stella Zazvorkova, Irinia Livanova, Lilya Malkina
DIRECTOR: Jan Sverak
SCREENWRITER: Zdenek Sverak
RELEASED: 1996 (105 minutes)
RATED: PG-13

This film works for children about age ten and up. It's an old theme but is given new life in this unique Czech drama-comedy about a grumpy man who falls in love with a five-year-old who happens into his life. We've never seen this somewhat overused plot dealt with in such a believable way. It's not a weeper, it's the real deal. For older children (twelve to fourteen), it's also a look at life under the Soviet occupation of Czechoslovakia. The main character, Franta Louka, is a concert musician, a cellist, and a bit of a lady's man. How Kolya comes into his life and changes it is a pleasure from its first frame to its uplifting last. The movie won the Oscar for Best Foreign Film.

Miramax has provided few supplements, but they are high-quality ones. The behind-the-scenes segment is the best. There are cast interviews and comments by director Jan Sverak. They fill out the story of *Kolya*'s making very nicely.

Lady and the Tramp

CAST: (Voices) Peggy Lee, Barbara Luddy, Larry Roberts, Bill
    Thompson, Bill Baucom, Stan Freberg, Verna Felton, Alan
    Reed, George Givot, Dal McKennon, Lee Millar
DIRECTORS: Clyde Geronimi and Wilfred Jackson
SCREENWRITERS: Ward Greene and Erdman Penner
RELEASED: 1955 (75 minutes)
RATED: G

After all the techno-wizardry of contemporary children's
films, take a trip back in time with *Lady and the Tramp*.
You'll be surprised. This 1955 classic Disney animation still
delights. If you're lucky, you can pack a room with three
generations of fans.

It's class warfare among the canines. Lady is a purebred
cocker spaniel, raised to expect only the best. That is, until
her human parents are rude enough to have a child. Then
there is the arrival of cats. (Not cats too!) Lady takes it on
the lam and finds love in an unexpected place. The love interest is Tramp, a feisty fellow who knows the world. You'll
love this for the voice of Peggy Lee as a variety of characters
and for her "Siamese Cat Song." Cinemascope was used in
the original feature, and it was the first time for a Disney
animation. It works well in its DVD transfer.

There's a very expensive Disney collection of animated
children's movies. If you're looking to stock up quickly on
children's classics, you might consider it if your budget per-
mits. It includes *Lady, Pinocchio, 101 Dalmatians, Hercules,
The Mermaid, The Lion King,* and *The Jungle Book.*

The Lion King

CAST: (Voices) Jonathan Taylor Thomas, Matthew Broderick, James
    Earl Jones, Jeremy Irons, Moira Kelly, Niketa Calame, Ernie
    Sabella, Nathan Lane, Robert Guillaume, Rowan Atkinson, Zoe
    Leader, Madge Sinclair, Whoopi Goldberg, Cheech Marin
DIRECTORS: Roger Allers and Rob Minkoff
SCREENWRITERS: Irene Meechi and Jonathan Roberts
RELEASED: 1994 (89 minutes)
RATED: G

Once upon a time in the late twentieth century there was a
terrific film called *The Lion King*. This was before the hype
turned it into a multinational franchise and before the
wildly popular stage version. The movie still stands as a
good fable for children, although there's some upsetting animal violence that isn't appropriate for anyone younger
than about six.

What *The Lion King* did for meerkats alone is quite remarkable. There's hardly a child around who doesn't know
about the meerkat now, thanks to this film and the voice of
Nathan Lane. As we came out of the theater at the time of
its release, one of our favorite child critics asked, "What is
the lesson from this film?" Well, we wondered what *she*
thought it was and asked. She replied, "I think it's that the
boy animals get to play the good parts, and the girl animals
don't." Nonetheless, it's a must for your library. Avoid the
"Read Along DVD," which is more of a marketing gimmick than anything else, unless your children won't stop
bugging you for it. We say hold on—there's always an enhanced and more expensive version just around the corner
in Disney Jungle Land.

Monsters, Inc.

CAST: (Voices) John Goodman, Billy Crystal, Mary Gibbs, Steve Buscemi, James Coburn, Jennifer Tilly, Bob Peterson, John Ratzenberger, Frank Oz, Bonnie Hunt, Steven Susskind, Jeff Pidgeon
DIRECTORS: Peter Docter and David Silverman
SCREENWRITER: Robert L. Baird (from a story by Jill Culton)
RELEASED: 2001 (92 minutes)
RATED: G

Monsters, Inc. is not as irresistible as *Shrek* but still an excellent choice for the matinee set.

Most of us know the Randy Newman song from the film, "If I Didn't Have You," which won the Oscar for Best Song.

Monsters, Inc. is part of a new revolution in animated films made with the assistance of computers. We found the characters in *Shrek* far more appealing, but *Monsters, Inc.* has a wide and varied following. Monsters and thoughts thereof scare children, but these fuzzy and weird little guys are afraid of kids.

You'll want the 2002 Collector's Edition, a two-disc deal. It's not as glorious as the *Shrek* boxed set, but this a winner, too. Highlights of Disc One include an audio commentary by the director and producers. It's interesting for the trials and tribulations of the animation process. A delightful "Nemo" teaser is also on the first disc.

Disc Two is the gateway to an evening of family fun. You can choose one of two doors, "Mike" or "Boo." There are features and shorts galore. Don't miss any of it. Especially be sure to see "For the Birds," "Monster Flies," and "Design Door."

Snow White and the Seven Dwarfs

CAST: (Voices) Roy Atwell, Stuart Buchanan, Adriana Caselotti,
Eddie Collins, Pinto Colvig, Billy Gilbert, Otis Harlan, Lucille La
Verne, James MacDonald, Scotty Mattraw, Moroni Olsen, Harry
Stockwell (all uncredited)
CREATOR: Walt Disney
SCREENWRITERS: Ted Sears and Richard Creedon
RELEASED: 1937 (83 minutes)
RATED: G

Who is the fairest of them all? This picture, in point of fact.
Often a cult favorite for adults, it's the classic tale for children of all ages. In 1939, Walt Disney received an honorary Oscar (and seven tiny ones) for *Snow White*. He was honored for creating a miracle in animation innovation, and so it remains sixty-five years later. You'll want to purchase the special edition. The 2001 release has a commentary by Disney himself.

Everything has changed since Disney stunned the world with this technique, but in many ways nothing has changed. The basics were all put together with this film. Everybody we know has a favorite dwarf; ours are Bashful and Sleepy. The extras are incredible if you purchase the Platinum Edition.

We especially like the animated short "Goddess of Spring" (1934), the "Heigh-Ho" singalong, and "Dopey's Wild Mine Ride Game." You'll get Barbra Streisand singing "Some Day My Prince Will Come."

Of course, you'll want to watch the documentary "Still the Fariest of Them All," a "making of" segment. Also worth your time is "Abandoned Concepts, Restoration, and Deleted Scenes."

We leave you to deal with the many underlying themes

of *Snow White* and whether we really want little girls to wait for princes to awaken them from slumber. Don't worry; it's really about the seven little guys.

Stuart Little

CAST: Michael J. Fox (voice), Geena Davis, Hugh Laurie, Jonathan Lipnicki, Nathan Lane (voice), Chazz Palminteri (voice), Steven Zahn (voice), Jim Doughan, David Alan Grier (voice), Bruno Kirby (voice), Jennifer Tilly (voice)
DIRECTOR: Rob Minkoff
SCREENWRITER: M. Night Shyamalan (from the book by E. B. White)
RELEASED: 1999 (84 minutes)
RATED: PG

Stuart Little is based on the unforgettable children's book by E. B. White. White wrote like an angel for both adults and children. It's hard for any film to compete with the majesty of his language and his gift for character description. Even with the voice of Michael J. Fox, Stuart Little the film mouse isn't as captivating as Stuart Little the book mouse. However, this is a terrific DVD for children, and the story of a family with a mouse for a child is a contemporary fairy tale that's hard to criticize. Nathan Lane makes a convincing mean cat, Snow Bell. We found a number of flaws with the film, but our appropriate-age screeners found it just sublime.

It's packed with extras. (You also can buy the set *Stuart I* and *Stuart II.*) The extra features include games for children. For adults, there's commentary by director Rob Minkoff and another by animator Henry Anderson and John Dykstra, the "bells and whistles" man. And there's

Michael J. Fox reading the story, for those nights when you're too lazy for that bedtime chore.

Toy Story

CAST: (Voices) Tom Hanks, Tim Allen, Don Rickles, Jim Varney, Wallace Shawn, John Ratzenberger, Annie Potts, John Morris, Erik Von Detten
DIRECTOR: John Lasseter
SCREENWRITERS: John Lasseter and Andrew Stanton
RELEASED: 1995, 1999 (81 minutes, 92 minutes)
RATED: G

Unless you enjoy being corrected by a second grader, we're here to say there isn't a movie called "The Ultimate Toy Box." The movies *Toy Story I and II* are boxed in a deluxe set called *"The Ultimate Toy Box."* It won't surprise children to learn that toys are real, have feelings and desires, and sometimes have to fight for their rights. For the rest of us, it might be instructive. Adults enjoy these films for the famous names who give voice to the animated toy characters. Children love these films because they capture the reality in which they live with their toys in an uncanny and convincing way. Don't just slip these into your player and disappear; watch them with children. You might be surprised at how you feel at the end.

The deluxe toy box contains some of the best and most extensive supplemental material out there. As in *Shrek,* there is plenty here for the adult mind to contemplate as well. We liked the outtakes as well as the audio commentaries about the creative dilemmas involved in this animated fantasy.

The Wizard of Oz

CAST: Judy Garland, Frank Morgan, Ray Bolger, Bert Lahr, Jack
    Haley, Billie Burke, Margaret Hamilton, Charley Grapewin, Pat
    Walshe, Clara Blandeick, the Singer Midgets
DIRECTORS: Victor Fleming and Richard Thorpe
SCREENWRITERS: Noel Langley, Florence Ryerson, and Allan
    Woolf (from the novel by L. Frank Baum)
RELEASED: 1939 (100 minutes)
RATED: G

One forgets that, first and foremost, children deserve a special claim on *The Wizard of Oz*. It's become so much a part
of our vocabulary and our sensibility that we need to step
back from it and watch as a child sees it for the first time.

It is then that you will know just where "somewhere
over the rainbow" really is. It is in the hearts and eyes of
children. It is also in the soul of anyone willing to believe in
Dorothy, her red shoes, Toto, and the need to be transported to a different reality.

The DVD has perfect sound, color, and clarity. Angela
Lansbury hosted a documentary in 1990 that is part of the
extras. There are a few deleted scenes and some fascinating
historical material. Be sure to watch the clips from the
1933 Oscars and the odd excerpts from the previous attempts at the film (1914, 1925, 1933). Actually, the features are quite good, but it's the movie that matters.
Remember, it's all about that yellow brick road.

Index of Actors

Index of Directors